George Thorpe
and
The Berkeley Company
A Gloucestershire Enterprise
in
Virginia

Norborne Berkeley, Lord Botetourt (*Courtesy of His Grace the Duke of Beaufort and the* Gazette – *photograph Mr. D. Ireland*)

George Thorpe
and
The Berkeley Company
A Gloucestershire Enterprise
in
Virginia

Eric Gethyn-Jones

ALAN SUTTON
1982

Alan Sutton Publishing Limited
17a Brunswick Road
Gloucester

First published 1982

Typesetting and origination by
Alan Sutton Publishing Limited.
Photoset Plantin 10/12.
Printed in Great Britain
by Page Bros (Norwich) Limited.

Foreword

It seems altogether appropriate that Canon J.E. Gethyn-Jones has written this splendidly researched and interesting volume so full of meaning to Virginians and all Americans, as well as our British friends, who wish to know more about our early beginnings in America and the spirit of those who came here to launch a new beginning in a new world. It was a time of adventure and romance filled with excitement and hope.

On the North side of the James River, between Jamestown and Richmond, is Berkeley Hundred, one of the early private 'colonies' in Virginia. Some thirty-five of our English forebears led by Captain John Woodleefe sailed from Bristol, England, on the ship *Margaret* and arrived in Virginia on 4 December 1619 after a voyage of almost two and one half months.

A day of Thanksgiving was celebrated when they came ashore at Berkeley Hundred for they were 'all in safety and perfect health.' Among the first three main groups of Berkeley colonists were men of substance and learning, fully equipped to conduct their affairs in England and Virginia, much like the Virginia Company that preceded them to Jamestown.

Berkeley has been a working plantation in Virginia since 1619, and a handsome brick manor house was built there early in the Eighteenth Century. Here was born Benjamin Harrison, V, a signer of the Declaration of Independence and a post Revolutionary Governor of Virginia, and his son, William Henry Harrison, the ninth President of the United States. Today, while privately owned, Berkeley has been magnificently restored and is open to the public as one of America's distinguished historic shrines.

Here also is re-enacted each year the Virginia Thanksgiving Festival to commemorate the first regularly scheduled Thanksgiving service on American soil.

May I express for all who read these pages our sincere gratitude to the author for this scholarly and historical work.

Mills E. Godwin, Jr.
2 March 1981

Contents

Illustrations

Maps

Acknowledgments

The research into the life and work of George Thorpe, and the formation and activities of the Berkeley Company, has been a protracted process, beginning in 1968. After my retirement in November 1976 the tempo increased considerably. During the eleven years past I have received courtesy, help and guidance from many people, societies and organizations.

Locally, Mr. I.E. Gray, one-time Gloucester County Archivist, and his successor, Mr. B.S. Smith, and their colleagues too, must be mentioned. The members of the Gloucester County and City Libraries, and those at Bristol University have given great help. I am also very grateful to the following Libraries and bodies: the Bodleian and Rhodes Libraries at Oxford, the the Public Record Office, the British Library, the Westminster City and Lambeth Palace Libraries, the Society of Genealogists (London), the Public Information Office at the House of Commons, the History of Parliament Trust (University of London), the City of Portsmouth Records Office and Trinity College, Oxford.

In America in 1974, 1977 and 1978 great courtesy and help were extended by the Library of Congress (Washington, D.C.), New York Public Library, the University of Virginia (Charlottesville), the Virginia State Library and the Virginia Historical Society (Richmond), the Swem Library at the College of William and Mary, the Institute of Early American History and Culture and the Colonial Williamsburg Foundation Research Archives – all in Williamsburg, the Jamestown Foundation, the Berkeley Plantation, and Governors Mills E. Godwin and John Dalton and their staff at the Capitol, Richmond. To Governor Godwin I am especially indebted for so graciously consenting to write the Foreword.

While I am exceedingly grateful to a large number of individuals I feel that special mention must be made of the following in America: Dr. Edmund Berkeley and Dr. George Reece of the University of Virginia, Dr. John Neville, Editor of the Virginia Colonial Records Project and Mr. Prentice Price, both at the State Library (Richmond), Dr. Henry Grunder (Rare Books) and Miss Margaret Cook (Manuscripts) at the College of William and

Mary, Dr. Thad Tate, Director of the Institute of Early American History and Culture, Dr. Edward Riley, lately Director of Research for Colonial Williamsburg, and Dr. Noel Hume, Director of Excavations at Wolstenholm (Carter's Grove), all at Williamsburg; Dr. Philip Barbour (then visiting the College of William and Mary), Mr. Parke Rouse, Director of the Jamestown Foundation, Mr. Malcolm Jamieson, (Berkeley Plantation), Dr. Maija Cole (Yale Center of Parliamentary History), and Dr. Frederick Fausz (St. Mary's College of Maryland). In England, in addition to Mr. Irvine Gray and Mr. Brian Smith, I wish to offer my sincere thanks to Dr. Harry Porter (Cambridge), the Revd. Dr. John Platt and Dr. Nicholas Mann (Pembroke College, Oxford) and also the Master and Fellows of Pembroke for their generous research grant which enabled me to be in the United States for five weeks in 1978. My greatest thanks, however, must be reserved for Dr. Joan Thirsk (St. Hilda's College, Oxford) for her constant guidance and supervision, and for her shrewd criticism and kindly encouragement at all stages of this project. I am, of course, fully responsible for the views, interpretations and suppositions put forward, and also for the errors which may remain.

I wish to acknowledge sincere gratitude to the following for permission to quote, in some cases extensively, from certain original documents or unpublished works in their possession or care:

1. Berkeley Castle Muniments, Thorpe wills, 'In favour of "The Trustee of the will of the 8th Earl of Berkeley, deceased."'
2. Dr. F.J. Fausz, Ph.D. Dissertation and Article in *Cavalcade*.
3. Gloucester City and County Library, Smyth of Nibley Papers.
4. The Master and Fellows of Magdalene College, Cambridge, Thorpe's letters in the Ferrar Papers.
5. New York Public Library, Smyth of Nibley Papers, Manuscripts and Archives Division, the New York Public Library, Astor, Lenox and Tilden Foundations.
6. Yale University, MS. E 327, Kenneth Spencer Research Library, transcript, the property of Dr. Maija J. Cole.
7. Dr. H.C. Porter, extracts from the will of Revd. Alexander Whitaker in *The Inconstant Savage: England and the North American Indians, 1500-1600*.
8. The Colonial Williamsburg Foundation, negatives of five Smyth of Nibley Papers, the property of New York Public Library – see above.
9. Finally I am most grateful to my son, Mr. David J. Gethyn-Jones, for the dust-cover illustration and for drawing the map of the Berkeley area on p. 21.

Abbreviations

Brown I	Alexander Brown, *The Genesis of the United States*
Brown II	Alexander Brown, *The First Republic in America*
Campbell	Charles Campbell, *The History of the Colony and Ancient Dominion of Virginia*
Craven I	Wesley F. Craven, *The Southern Colonies in the Seventeenth Century*
BGAS	*Bristol and Gloucestershire Archaeological Society Transactions*
Kingsbury I-IV	Susan Kingsbury, *The Records of the Virginia Company of London* (4 vols.)
NYPLB	*The New York Public Library Bulletin*
Smyth I	John Smyth, *The Smyth of Nibley Papers* in the New York Public Library
Smyth II	John Smyth, *The Smyth of Nibley Papers* in the Gloucester Public Library
Smyth III	John Smyth, *Smyth's Lives of the Berkeley* (vols. 1-2) and *The Berkeley Hundred* (vol. 3).
Smyth IV	John Smyth, Smyth's *Gloucestershire Men and Armour*
Stith	William Stith, *The History of the First Discovery and Settlement of Virginia*
VCH	*Victoria County History*, followed by the name of the county
VMHB	*Virginia Magazine of History and Biography*
WMQ	*William and Mary Quarterly Bulletin*

Where Kingsbury or in Kingsbury follows Ferrar Papers, Manchester Papers, Smyth Papers I, II, III, IV etc., it will be understood that Dr. Susan Kingsbury has transcribed and printed, usually in full, the cited document from the respective collection.

Bemiss, op.cit., will always refer to his important work – *The Three Charters of the Virginia Company of London, With Seven Related Documents; 1606-1621.*

Date: dating will follow the modern form, i.e., January to December.

Spelling: in most instances quotations from early manuscript and publications have been modernized, but punctuation has not been altered. Names, *usually*, are in their present forms.

Introduction

Soon after coming to Berkeley in 1967 I read Smyth's *Lives of the Berkeleys* and *The History of the Hundred of Berkeley*. Thus I learned that a George Thorpe had sailed to Virginia in 1620 and there had died. Furthermore the Editor of those works referred to a large collection of Smyth papers now in New York Public Library. Curiosity was aroused, but no English book of reference contained mention of Thorpe and Virginia in the 1620s. It was fortunate that Dr. Susan Kingsbury's *Records of the Virginia Company of London* (four volumes) was one of the first American publications which came to my notice. Suddenly, metaphorically, 'the sky lit up', and from those records and others quoted by Dr. Kingsbury, it became apparent that here was a story of a Gloucestershire enterprise, ignored for three and a half centuries in this country, which deserved to be researched and told. This now seems strange, because much of the material was here in our own country in such depositories as the British Library and the Public Record Office.

As a busy parish priest I had little spare time beyond the summer holidays for serious research, and in any case *Trevisa of Berkeley* had become a project. Consequently I filed all references to Thorpe or the Berkeley Company and wrote a number of short articles on different aspects of this local 'venture'.

The first real break came in June 1974, when I was invited to Virginia to give what they termed the 'Key-note' address at the Virginia Thanksgiving Festival to be held at Berkeley Plantation in November. The trip began in the northern areas and then moved south to Richmond, Williamsburg and Berkeley. The programme included receptions, press conferences, T.V. and Radio appearances and talks to various bodies. The principal subject for those engagements was the Berkeley Connection, with particular reference to the Berkeley Plantation Thanksgiving Service ordered in 1619 to be kept in perpetuity. That tour was strenuous, but enjoyable, and I shall always be deeply indebted to those who hosted and managed me, the late Mrs. Robert Duncan (Alexandria), Mr. John T. Hanna (Richmond) and Mr. Malcolm Jamieson (Berkeley Plantation). In addition I owe a great deal to the friendly patronage of His Excellency Mills E. Godwin, Governor of Virginia. While at

Richmond I was able to visit the State Library and the Swem Library at Williamsburg, and met scholars working in the seventeenth-century settlement period. Two days were spent at Berkeley Plantation under the guidance of 'Mac'. Here was an enthusiast who had literally saved the plantation from almost certain extinction, and was imbued with a vision of distinction for its future. This was the moment of final decision. Mac's enthusiasm was infectious, and though I did not agree with all his claims and interpretations the point of no return had been reached. The history of George Thorpe and the Berkeley Company must be researched carefully and made known in Britain, and more fully appreciated in Virginia and in the United States generally. This decision was made easier by reason of the fact that *The Dymock School of Sculpture* was already in the hands of the publisher, while the *Trevisa of Berkeley* manuscript was almost finished. In 1975 two Presidential addresses on the Berkeley Company and Plantation were prepared for 1976.

Retirement in November 1976 enabled more time to be devoted to this new subject, and a 'retirement holiday' in 1977 was spent by my wife and myself on a Greyhound tour of ten southern States and ended with two weeks at Richmond and Williamsburg. During that time a visit was made to the University of Virginia at Charlottesville. Despite several T.V. engagements considerable time was spent in the principal libraries.

Early in 1978 Pembroke College, Oxford, offered a generous research grant which enabled me to spend five weeks at the Library of Congress, Washington, D.C., the University of Virginia, the State Library, Richmond and in Williamsburg (The College of William and Mary and the Colonial Williamsburg Foundation.)

This essay then is the result of research undertaken both in this country and in the United States. It attempts to record the achievements of a group of mainly Gloucestershire men and women drawn principally from the Berkeley Vale, the Cotswold Edge and the Hayles area, who in true pioneer spirit set out to establish a new 'Berkeley Town and Hundred' in Virginia in 1619. Their foundation still stands as a memorial to their endeavour and courage, and I hope that this story will help to gain for them some little of the local and national recognition they so richly deserve. I feel that Governor Mills E. Godwin, when in 1977 he wrote 'I wish to thank you as Governor of Virginia and for the people of the Commonwealth for your fine work in helping to document the first official Thanksgiving in the new world at Berkeley Plantation.', was really saying that the people of Virginia were pleased that a little more light was being thrown on a party of settlers who so early in America's history gave so much, in most instances their very lives, to ensure the establishment of a colony which became the great American nation. To those intrepid pioneers, with George Thorpe, their great religious leader as one of the five sponsors, I dedicate this work.

The publication of this work has been assisted by a generous subvention from the Bristol and Gloucestershire Archaeological Society. This is gratefully acknowledged.

1

Berkeley, Wanswell Court and the Thorpes

'George Thorpe, a leading member of the Berkeley Hundred [Virginia] . . . is one of those shadowy figures that move across the early pages of American history about whom we would like to know more than has been discovered.'[1] So wrote Professor W.F. Craven (Princeton) in 1949. This work is an attempt to satisfy, to some degree, that demand. The investigation will be concerned primarily with the life of George Thorpe (1576-1622) of Wanswell Court, Berkeley, Gloucestershire, the establishment of the Berkeley Company, which settled in Virginia, and in which Thorpe was much involved, and its final elimination. Thorpe's obvious humanitarian, religious, and, indeed, missionary feelings, while in Virginia will be considered. These appear to have been in line with those same ideals which were stated or implied in the original colonization charters granted to the Virginia Company. The same basic instructions were also contained in many orders and directions issued by that London Company[2] to the individual Presidents of the Council and Governors of Virginia, and indeed to the settlers in general, up until the Indian massacre of 1622. In a modified form they were maintained during the following two years, at the end of which period the London Company's charter was revoked, and Virginia became a Crown Colony.

When I embarked on this investigation, a careful study of many published works and more than thirty unpublished theses and dissertations, both in this country and America, established that the field for this study was virtually virginal. But there existed also a number of primary original sources of importance and reliability which could help to throw some light upon Thorpe, the Berkeley Company, and their colonial activities. Amongst these were the records of the Virginia Company of London, and the Ferrar and Manchester Papers. But by far the most valuable were those of John Smyth of Nibley.[3]

The majority of the personnel of the Berkeley Company, whether sponsors, adventurers, tenants at halves or indentured servants, were like Thorpe, born and bred in Gloucestershire, while many of them were natives of the Berkeley Vale, the Cotswold Edge, or the Winchcombe area, during the last quarter of the sixteenth century or the first two decades of the seventeenth. Thus it is not surprising that much of the material upon which our scanty knowledge of these men – and some women too – and their enterprise in Virginia is based upon the writings and collections of one man, namely John Smyth of North Nibley, who was the steward of the Berkeley Hundred in Gloucestershire and self-appointed historian of the Berkeley family. He came to live at Nibley in 1596 and died there in 1641. In addition he was one of the four original sponsors of the Berkeley Company, formed in 1618-19 to found the new 'Town and Hundred of Berkeley' on the banks of the James river in Virginia. Smyth, clearly, was the secretarial member of the quartet of adventurers, and by virtue of that position, and also because of the nature of his normal occupation, and his intimate knowledge of the whole area, he was well acquainted with the names and backgrounds of many of the members of the Berkeley contingent who sailed for the Company's grant during the years 1619-22.

Just how deeply John Smyth was involved in the life of the Berkeley Vale of Gloucestershire can be judged by a fuller account of his early life and family origins.

John Smyth, the son of Thomas Smyth of de Hoby in Leicestershire, was born in 1567. He was educated first at the Free School in Derby. In 1584 he entered the Berkeley menage at Callowden near Coventry as companion-attendant of Thomas, the son and heir of Henry, Lord Berkeley. Smyth had with him as a fellow companion-attendant young William Ligon of Madresfield Court in Worcestershire. These three shared the same tutor, Edward Cowper of Trinity College, Oxford, prior to entering Magdalen College, Oxford, in February 1589. In 1592 he became a student at the Middle Temple before returning to the service of the Berkeleys in 1596 as Steward of the Berkeley Castle family; in the following year he was appointed Steward of the 'Hundred and Liberty of Berkeley', an office he held for many years. The admissions book of the Middle Temple records that Smyth was called to the Bar in 1605.[4]

Smyth married, as far as is known, twice. His first wife, Grace, whom he married at Nibley on 5 October 1597, was the daughter and heir of William and Alice Thomas, and the widow of John Drew of Nibley, and 'A well dowered lady'. She was buried at Nibley on 11 November 1609. Smyth's second wife, whom he married on 9 January 1610, was Mary, the eldest daughter of John Browning of Coaley. They had five sons and four daughters.

It is generally supposed that Smyth had no children by his first wife, a view supported by the genealogical table printed at the beginning of volume one of Smyth's *Lives of the Berkeleys*.[5] There is, however, in a letter of Thorpe to

Smyth, written from Virginia in December 1620, a reference to two sons (not named) of Smyth who clearly were much older than Smyth's two eldest sons by his second wife, John who was born on 8 September (and baptized on the 12th) 1611, and Thomas who was baptized on 27 December 1613. This puzzling statement will be examined later.

Smyth died 25 February 1641, and was buried at Nibley on the 27th. He left a number of important manuscripts, some of which were lodged in Berkeley Castle, while others remained at Nibley House. The Smyth family continued to reside at Nibley until the second half of the eighteenth century, when Nicholas Smyth and his wife, Anna Maria, née Leighton, moved to Condover Hall in Shropshire, which had been devised to Anna Maria by her grandmother's will of 1750. Condover Hall came in 1864 to Reginald Cholmondeley, the heir general and representative of John Smyth, the one-time Berkeley Steward and one of the sponsors of the Berkeley Company in 1619.

In the 1880s the Condover Library was dispersed, but fortunately three groups of Smyth's manuscripts in that collection have been preserved as complete units, and constitute with Smyth's *Lives of the Berkeleys* and his *History of the Hundred of Berkeley*, one of the most important assemblages of primary source material for this study.[6]

Berkeley, from whence came the principal figure of the Berkeley Company, is situated in the extensive lowlands where the Vale broadens out, and where much of the land is less than one hundred feet above sea level. It is a large parish made up of the medieval borough and the three tithings of Alkington, Hamfallow and Hinton. These latter contain a number of hamlets of varied sizes, e.g., Bevington, Breadstone, Clapton, Halmore, Newport, Purton and Wanswell. The town itself is sited on a knoll rising some fifty or sixty feet above the surrounding water meadows. The economy of the parish, indeed of most of Berkeley Vale, has from time immemorial been based largely upon agriculture in varied forms. Leland wrote, 'The Town of Berkeley is no great thing, but it stands well, and in a very good soil.' He added that 'clothinge' had been of importance in the past, relying no doubt upon the Cotswold fleeces[7] and the mills of the Berkeley Avon. The decline in the wool industry in the sixteenth and seventeenth centuries had considerable repercussions in the small towns and villages along the Cotswold Edge, and down into the Vale.

It is clear from Smyth's *Lives of the Berkeleys* that by the seventeenth century the Berkeley pattern of land ownership, as described by John Marshall in the following century, was largely in force. He wrote 'The Earl of Berkeley,[8] whose principal residence is situated near the centre of the vale, is the owner of a considerable share of it. Lord Ducie has an estate in it. There are other off estates, and a considerable yeomanry, considering the advantage of the situation, this vale contains few principal residences.'[9] Marshall stated that the farms of any size were sparse, though the tendency was for these to become larger, thereby 'increasing the number of poor.'[10] Grassland predominated, with the emphasis upon dairying,[11] but he added that most of the Vale appeared 'to have been formerly under the plough.'[12].

The tithing of Hamfallow contains the hamlet of Wanswell which lies about a mile and a quarter north of Berkeley's town centre. It is mentioned in a deed of the time of Henry II when certain lands there were held by a Walter Fitz Alwin. In the time of Henry III the estate was farmed by Henry de Wanswell whose widow, Isabella, married Philip de Leicester, who in 1256 obtained a licence from the convent of St. Augustine's, Bristol, to build a chapel at his manor house. In 1270 the property was sold for one hundred marks by Henry de Wanswell, the son of the above Henry, to Robert de Stone, who also purchased from Henry lands in Stone and Woodford for 112 marks. The site of the latter's manor house, Old Court, at Stone can still be seen, but there are no structural remains visible above ground. Robert was succeeded by his son Thomas, who acquired further lands in Wanswell and elsewhere from Thomas II, Lord Berkeley.

On the death of Thomas in 1316 the Stone properties passed to his elder daughter, while the Wanswell estate – including the rented portions – was inherited by the younger daughter, Alice, who married John Saniger whose lands adjoined the Wanswell estate.[13]

John Saniger, the grandson of John and Alice, inherited the Wanswell estate and married Isabel a daughter of John de Albiniaco or Daubeney, Lord of Kingsholme, now part of the city of Gloucester, through whom came further considerable properties. Their grandson, yet another John Saniger, died without issue in 1402 when his two sisters inherited. Elizabeth died without issue and the whole of the estate came to Isabel, who married John Thorpe, a burgess of Bristol, in 1402. Thus Wanswell came into Thorpe hands.

The burgess stock, grafted on to the strong rural tradition of the sinister side of the partnership, which itself had been improving its monetary and social standing by matrimonial alliances, consolidated the position, and by the sixteenth and seventeenth centuries the family was contracting marital unions with some of the leading families in the Vale and the Dean Forest.

To the lands in Wanswell held by the Thorpes of the Berkeleys was reserved a military service not precisely defined, but which tradition suggests to have been a type of 'Castle Guard' that represented the duty in times of

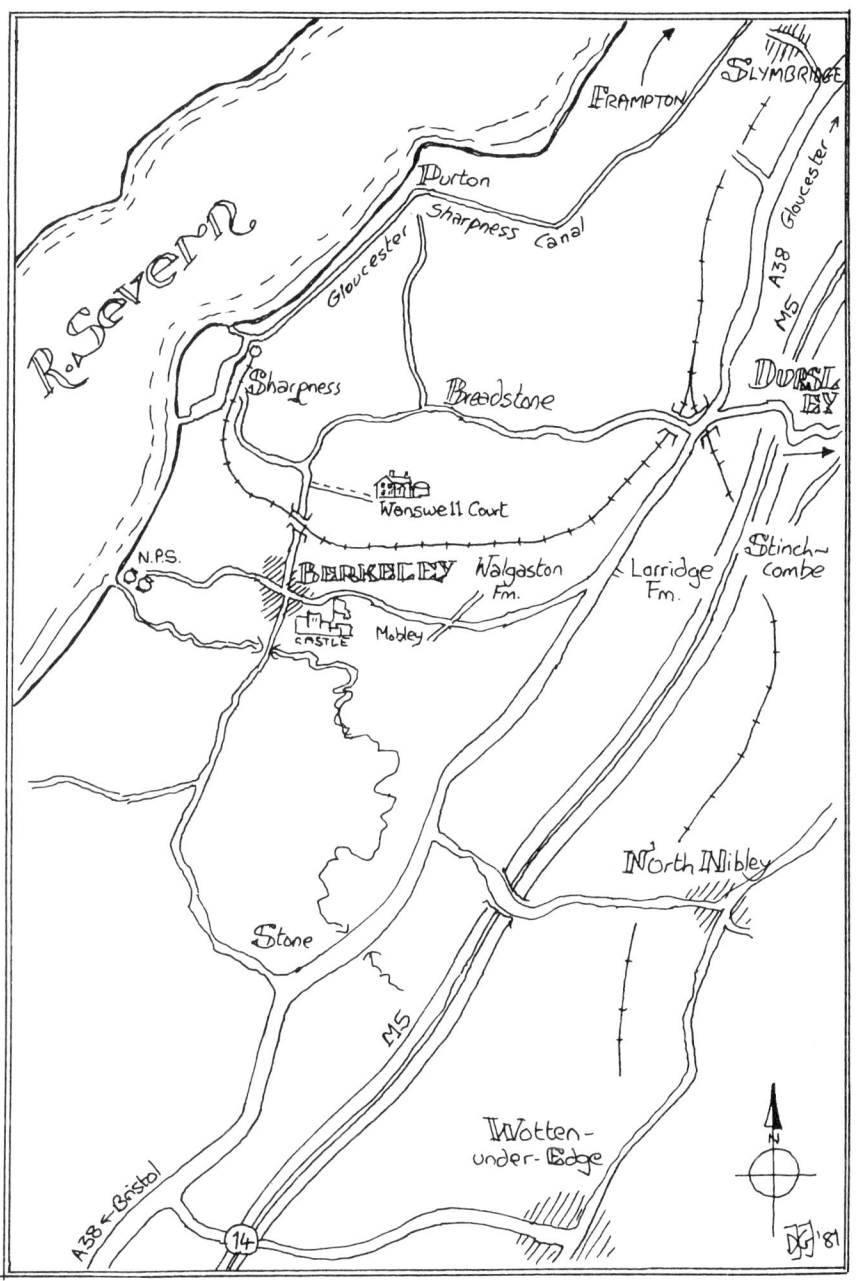

Scale approx. 1": 3 miles — 1:150,000

Berkeley and Wanswell area

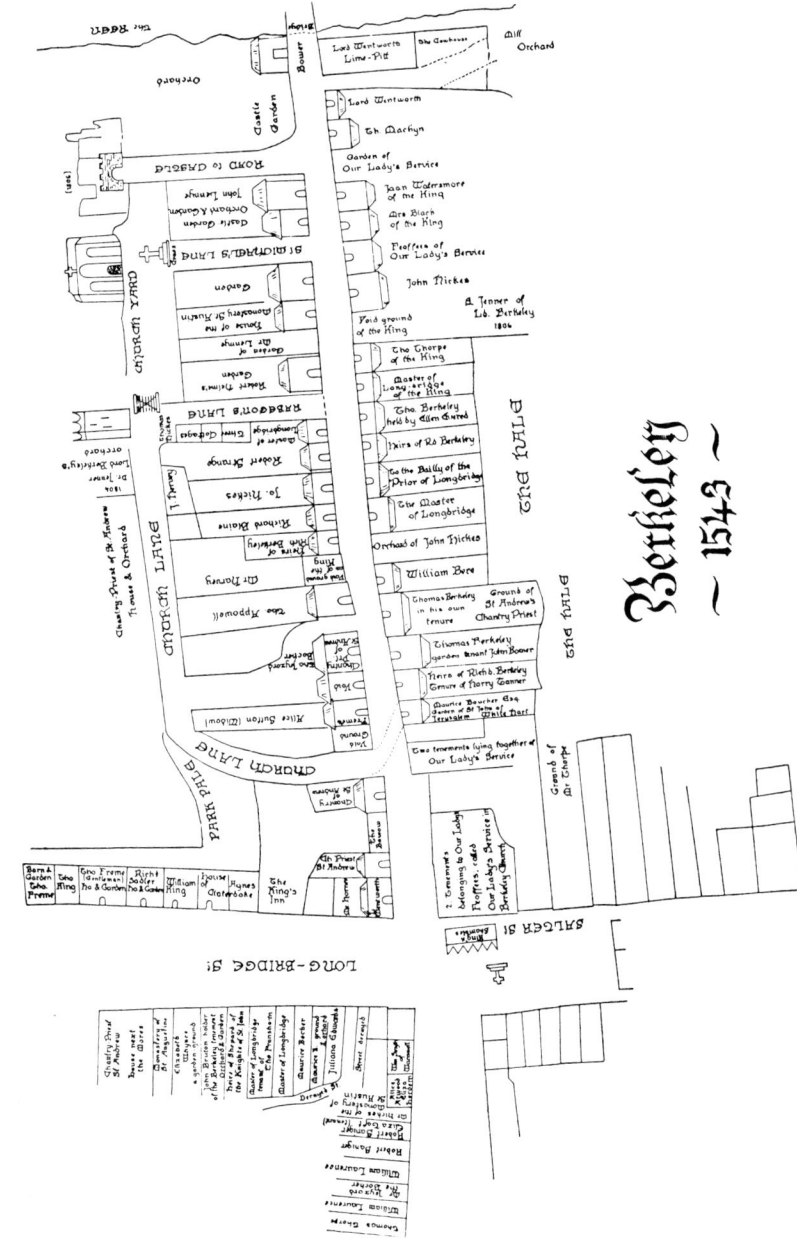

Berkeley ~ 1543 ~

need of garrisoning a tower in Berkeley Castle still styled 'Thorpe's Tower'. This explanation was put forward by the Berkeley steward, J.H. Cooke.[14] Because of the extreme difficulty of obtaining access to the records in the Berkeley muniments room, heavy reliance has had to be placed upon the published Smyth manuscripts, Jeayes' *Charters and Muniments in Berkeley Castle* (which deals with only a portion of the contents of the muniments room) and the fortunately numerous wrirings of two stewards whose interests in the family and estates were considerable, namely James H. Cooke and James Peters, and the latter's son, Francis, who acted as a temporary steward during the last war.

This first John Thorpe of Wanswell Court, by marrying a lady possessing property both in Berkeley and Kingsholme, Gloucester, set the family pattern for the acquisition of land. His son, John the Younger, considerably extended his estate in 1456 by the purchase of lands in Lorrange, Walgaston and Halmer, properties or farms which marched with his Wanswell estate to the north-east and south-east. These acquisitions included the 'ancient messuage' of Wikeselm with 55 acres. John II married twice. His first wife, Isobel (surname not known), died childless. By his second wife, Margaret Toite, John had several children, only two of whom are of concern, Richard and Margery. Number 611 of the select charters amongst the muniments in Berkeley Castle is a grant from James, Lord Berkeley, to Thomas Berkeley, Esquire, his son, of 'a messuage etc in Clopton' (Clapton) - probably Willis Elm, within the Berkeley manor. The deed is dated 1464, and the witnesses were Walter (Devereux), Lord Ferrers, Sir John Barre, Maurice Berkeley of Beverstone, Maurice Denys and John Thorpe.[15] Perhaps Thorpe is there as a principal land owner within the manor, with, maybe, holdings marching with the Clapton estate. To John is attributed the pulling down of the manor house and chapel built by Philip Leicester, and the erection of the older eastern half of the present house, with its well preserved hall and parlour. Wanswell Court had become, possibly, after the castle, the most imposing private residence within this large parish, clearly indicating the rising fortunes and social standing of the Thorpe family.

John II died in 1469, and was succeeded by his son, Richard, who married Margaret Loffe of Monmouth. This lady brought with her 'a fair inheritance there and in the villages adjoining.' The marriage of Richard's sister, Margery, to William Davis of Dursley, however, diminished the Wanswell estate, for she took with her as part of her dowry the Wikeselm property, which was, and is, an attractive holding. Smyth, writing nearly two centuries later, perhaps with some feeling because his daughter, Ursula, had married William, son and heir of George Thorpe, said it was 'severed from the Capital messuage of Wanswell Court.' To Richard and his heirs were reserved a 'pound of comin and a heriot after every decease for ever.'[16] Smyth also recorded that on 6 July 1494 'an award was made which settled peace between Richard Thorpe of Wanswell, Esq, on the one part, and William Reme alias Freme[17] then a Justice of the Peace on the other part, whereby the controverted tenement in the High Street in Berkeley was awarded to the said Richard Thorpe and his heirs, where yet it is with William Thorpe esq.'[18]

Richard died in 1514 and was succeeded by his son Thomas I, who was Receiver to Maurice VI, Lord Berkeley. He had, in 1512, as a member of Lord Berkeley's contingent, served with the British Army, commanded by the Marquis of Dorset, in Spain.[19] Thomas married twice. By his first wife, Alice Dastin, he had a son, Thomas II. His second wife, known only by the name Joan, had no children.

Thomas II was still a minor when his father died in 1525, and was 'thereby in ward' to King Henry for his lands at Kingsholme, Gloucester. Thorpe fortunes had been gradually ascending. They had increased their estates and, judging from the 1464 grant, were beginning to associate with leading local families.

Before his death Thomas Thorpe held, besides his Wanswell Court estates, and those in Monmouthshire and Kingsholme, properties within the town of Berkeley itself. This may be seen on a copy of a sixteenth century plan of part of the borough drawn by St. Clair Baddeley, the Gloucestershire historian.[20] Two of those Thorpe holdings were dwellings, while the third is merely described as 'land', but, as it was close to the centre or market square, and seemed to have had access thereto, it must have represented a desirable enclosure. The smaller of the two domestic tenancies was in the unnamed Marybrook Street, while the house in High Street, here also nameless, appears to have been one of greater size and importance, if the graphical representation on the plan has any significance. As this dwelling was held by Thorpe 'of the King', that assumption may well be correct.

It was Thomas II who made the final break-through into the inner circle of the county gentry by his marriage to Margaret the daughter of William Throckmorton of Tortworth, head of a prominent Gloucestershire family. Their son, Nicholas, born in 1537, was but five when his father died in 1542, and in consequence he, like his father before him, became a ward of the king for the Kingsholme Estate.[21]

Nicholas Thorpe's academic training is uncertain, but it seems possible that his teenage education was received in the City of London. It is unfortunate that, until about the last quarter of the sixteenth century, the admissions book of Gray's Inn records only the names of the new students

Wanswell Court, Berkeley – the home of George Thorpe

Wanswell Court. The Hall roof (*Courtesy of Mr. D. Ireland*)

Berkeley Castle and Church by J. Kip. Note the separate tower of the church.

and the date of their registration. Consequently one can only speculate on the entry 'Nicholas Thorpe' in the year 1554, and a bracketed note which gives 1555. This could be Nicholas of Wanswell, and I believe may well be, for the following reasons: (1) The date 'fits' well; (2) George, his eldest son, was later also educated in two of the Inns; (3) I can only trace one other Nicholas Thorpe in the large number of Thorpes recorded in the admissions books of the Middle Temple, Inner Temple, Gray's Inn, Lincoln's Inn and amongst the alumni of Oxford and Cambridge. This second Nicholas, of Surrey, Gent, matriculated from New College, Oxford, on 15 November 1588, aged thirteen. There is no Nicholas in the registers of St. Martin in the Fields, London between 1567 and 1619 during which there were twenty-five Thorpe entries, representing at least three possibly related families, one of whom was the Wanswell branch. Nicholas of Wanswell, however, had a son, Nicholas, who was baptized in Berkeley Church on 8 April 1577, and figures in his father's will of 1600. A burial entry of 9 November 1617, 'Nicholas Thorpe, Gent' probably refers to him.

Nicholas senior continued to advance the family's fortunes and raise its social standing by marrying in 7 Eliz. (1565) Mary, the daughter of Christopher Wilkes alias Mason and niece of Sir John Mason, a Councillor of State. Mary's dowry included the manor of Charelton *(sic)* in Middlesex. Smyth stated that they had issue George and others. A complete picture of the family cannot be built up, since the sixteenth century Bishop's Transcripts for the parish of Berkeley are only extant for 1571 (beginning in July) to 1578 and 1596-9, and the Berkeley Church registers for that period are also very imperfect and much fragmented.[22] Nevertheless, by the examination of both series of manuscripts a fairly full picture of the family may be obtained after their first four years of marriage.

1569	September	Baptism of '..han (Joan?) daughter of Ni...s Th(o)rpe
1571	7 August	Burial of Elizabeth Thorpe
1573	31 July	Baptism of John Thorpe
1573	9 August	Burial of John Thorpe
1576	1 January	Baptism of George, son of Nicholas Thorpe, Esq.
1577	April	Baptism of Nicholas, son of Nicholas Thorpe, Esq.
1581	April	Baptism of Agnis, daughter of Nicholas Thorpe, Esq.

In view of the fact that the two entries relating to John almost follow one another and that infant mortality was high, and observing that no title, e.g., Mr., Gent., etc., is attached to the name, one can suggest that John died aged ten days. As the Thorpes were then people of some standing, it is probably that Elizabeth, who also has no title, was a child or very young person. Thus it would seem that Nicholas and Mary had at least five children between 1566 and 1578, with the possibility of other children (who probably died young if my reading of the will of Nicholas is correct) in or about '67, '68, '70 or '72.

On the death of Mary (date not known) Nicholas married Anne (née Hill), the widow of William Lawrence, Gent., of Canonbury, Berkeley, who until his death in June 1578, had been Steward to Henry, Lord Berkeley. Smyth said that Nicholas and Anne had issue, but gave no names. The problem of the identification of the above children and others mentioned in the will of Nicholas will be discussed briefly at the end of this chapter.

By a deed of 1571 the Earl of Dorset conveyed the considerable manor of Canonbury to Nicholas Thorpe Esq., William Lawrence, Gent., and five other persons,[23] who agreed amongst themselves as to their respective portions and the divisions of the annual tenth – a royal levy of 47s. 5d. Lawrence appeared to have obtained the largest section, as it was laid down that the Crown dues would be paid 'at the house of . . . Lawrence in Berkeley called Can[on]bury.'[24] Nicholas further increased his estate in 1572 by the purchase of 'divers lands and tenements' called Butlers. This property was made up of 80 acres of meadow and pasture and five acres of wood, while the house included the 'ancient messuage of Oldlands Place', which Thomas Butler, the father of Ann Butler who sold the estate to Thorpe, had bought from John Oldland.[25]

To the western side of the medieval manor house of Wanswell is a Tudor extension which, it is said, was added either by Nicholas or George. Circumstances and architectural style, suggest that the credit for this addition to the building should go to George and not his father.

The will of Nicholas Thorpe, senior, dated 24 February 1600, and proved at the Prerogative Court of Canterbury 5 June 1600, is in the muniments room at Berkeley Castle.[26] The dates of death and burial are not known. The will begins with the usual paragraph bequeathing the soul, and is followed by interesting entries, some of which are today obscure because of the lack of identifying detail, while others are suggestive and may help to explain certain of the heir's actions soon after his father's death.

Anne, the wife of Nicholas, was to have accommodation for life at Wanswell Court, and, on condition that she claimed no dowry and released all title to lands and tenements, she was to retain all plate and other goods which she brought with her. Furthermore she was to receive an annuity of

£30, and was to share with sons William and John an estate, which George, the heir, must create, made up of Great Read Croft, Little Redd Croft and Redd Croft Meadow. Their tenure was to be for seventy years at a rent of 4s. p.a. Son Nicholas was to receive £300, sons William and John £200 each, and son-in-law, Richard Lawrence, £100, subject to Richard and his heirs not bringing a suit against George.

These bequests are followed by the statement that wife Anne, 'and her son Lawrence' must accept the conditions laid down, or all dispositions to her, William, John and Richard would be void. All this suggests that sons, William and John, were the issue of Nicholas and Anne, and that Richard Lawrence was the son of Anne by her first husband, William Lawrence. Furthermore it indicated that Richard had married a daughter of Nicholas by his first wife, Mary. This could have been Joan (?) baptised in September 1569, or else Agnis, baptized in April 1581, or some other daughter whose baptismal entry has been lost.[27] It would appear most likely that Joan was Richard's wife, for (1) Nicholas was baptized in April 1577, (2) William Lawrence died in June 1578, (3) Agnis was baptized in April, 1581, and so could well have been the daughter of Nicholas and Anne.

George and his heirs lawfully begotten were to receive all lands and tenements. If George had no issue the above would go to Nicholas and his lawfully begotten heirs, and likewise remainder to William or John or to the rightful heirs of the said Nicholas. The residue of the estate also went to George, who was the sole executor.

The outside bequests were few. The poor of Berkeley, Saniger, Halmer and Wanswell were to receive £3, while the two daughters of John Frier, Anne and Mary, were each to receive a cow. The overseers of the will were Sir Henry Winston Kt. and Joseph Baineham.

NOTES

1. W.F. Craven, *The Southern Colonies in the Seventeenth Century, 1607-1689*, Louisiana State University Press, 1949, p. 143.

2. Probably the most concise work on these documents is: S.M. Bemiss, *The Three Charters of the Virginia Company of London with seven related documents; 1606-1621*, No.4 of the Jamestown 350th Anniversary Historical Booklets, University of Virginia, Charlottesville, 1957. The original charter of 1606 envisaged two companies, one based on London and the other on certain south-western ports such as Bristol and Plymouth. In effect the latter failed to develop, and the London Company absorbed many of its sponsors and its Virginian interests.

3. e.g., *Smyth of Nibley Papers* (New York Public Library), *Ferrar Papers* (Magdalene College Library, Cambridge), *Manchester Papers* (Public Records Office), *Wyatt Papers* (British Library), and the *Records of the Virginia Company of London* (Library of Congress, Washington, D.C.).

4. The office of steward of a manor was a judicial one for which legal knowledge and training was required.

5. Sir John Maclean, who edited this work, said of the table (vol.1, p.vi) that it was 'compiled chiefly, from the records in the College of Arms, courteously furnished by Stephen I Tucker, Esq. *(Somerset Herald).'*

6. i. *The Smyth of Nibley Papers* in the New York Public Library. Sold by Quaritch of Piccadilly (Cat.: No. 87) in 1888.
ii. *The Smyth of Nibley Papers* in Gloucester County Library. Presented to them in 1921 by Alderman Edwin Lea.
iii. *Gloucestershire Men and Armour*. Acquired by Lord Sherborne, and published in 1902.

7. Thomas V, Lord Berkeley, 1523-32, of whom Smyth wrote that he might be termed 'Thomas the Sheepmaster', was reputed to have sheared annually more than 5,000 sheep at Beverstone.

8. George II, Lord Berkeley, 1658-98, was created an earl by King Charles II, in 1679.

9. John Marshall, *The Rural Economy of Gloucestershire . . .*, London, 1796, 2 vols. Vol. II, p. 89. A facsimile reprint by Alan Sutton Publishing Limited, Gloucester, 1979.

10. Ibid., p. 90. Marshall added (p. 92) that 'The Farmeries are very simple and, in general, very mean.' This comment should be borne in mind when Thorpe's home, Wanswell Court, in Berkeley, is considered.

11. Ibid., pp. 94-137. Cheese was a major item in the local economy, selling at £30 a ton. Marshall stressed the superior quality of the local product, pointing out that 'What, in the kingdom at large, is termed GLOUCESTER CHEESE; particularly DOUBLE

GLOUCESTER; is in Gloucestershire, called 'DOUBLE BERKELEY'. One of my late parishioners, Mr. Hubert Spratt, of Hamfields Farm Berkeley, R.I.P., 1972, once remarked that he had made about 1,200 lb. of cheese per week 'until I lost my slave labour'. That was until his three daughters got married! Thus, with frequent mention of cheese and cheese markets at Berkeley in early publications and records, it would appear that cheese has been a principal export for centuries and up until some twenty to thirty years ago.

Marshall stated that the Gloucestershire breed of cattle was one of the two most popular in the county in his day. Comparing his description of these cattle with those transported to Virginia in the early seventeenth century, at the time of the Berkeley Company's foundation of their plantation (1619), it is clear that the Gloucestershire breed was represented in the colony at that early date.

12. Ibid., p. 93.

13. The Sanigers, in the early days, were often called Swanhunger. Their family home, Saniger Farm, is still so named. There were Sanigers living in Berkeley as late as the nineteenth century.

14. The only documentary evidence of this Castle guard tenure appears to be a Court Roll for the manor of Ham, holden on the 16th May, in 42 Eliz. (A.D. 1600) when the Homage presented the death of Nicholas Thorpe, who died seized of the manor of Wanswell 'holden by the sixteenth part of a knight's fee, the yearly rent of £4 8s. 8d., and by keeping one tower in the Castle of Berkeley called Thorpe's Tower.'
    J.H. Cooke, 'Wanswell Court and its occupants for seven centuries', *BGAS*, vol. VI, pt.2, 1881-2, p. 314.

15. Jeayes, op.cit., p.188.

16. Smyth III, vol.3, pp. 382-3. It is interesting to record from the evidence of the Berkeley Church registers, that Thorpes were living at Wikeselm in the last half of the seventeenth century.

17. Freme's monumental brass is sited just south of the high altar in Berkeley Church. He held his property of the Berkeleys by an annual payment of twenty horseshoes and their nails.

18. William, was, of course, the son of George Thorpe and son in law of John Smyth.

19. J.H. Cooke, op. cit., p. 315.

20. Copies of the brochure containing this plan are known only in the County Library, Gloucester, and in the White Lion Antiques, High Street, Berkeley, but a few yards from the site of the Thorpe house, whose owners have reproduced copies of the plan. The brochure is titled the *Price of a Tudor Marquisate*, but has no date. St. Clair Baddeley in his introduction wrote 'The barely readable decayed original plan came into the hands of an American in London who after long delay kindly permitted the transcription, together with a few insertions obviously made by a later hand . . . possibly by Shrapnal.' The insertions referred to relate to the Jenner family.

In August 1979 I was shown a number of sheets, or fragments of sheets of paper, on which were sketched areas of Berkeley Town. Because several of those items depicted parts of the High Street and contained the above mentioned references to Jenner property, and in view of the obvious age of the paper and the nature of the hand, I suspect that those sheets were Shrapnell's first draft of a possible copy of the original 'ancient' map of the town illustrated in St. Clair Baddeley's brochure. Shrapnell was a close friend of Dr. Edward Jenner. It is interesting also to note that in the two sketches of the town square, the Thorpe 'ground' of Baddeley's illustration has a definite façade facing the square, indicating, presumably, that a substantial house was built on the property. I have used the spelling Shrapnell because he signed his name thus, and it is the form found in registers of Berkeley Church. William Fisher Shrapnell, F.S.A., was a 'Surgeon' in Berkeley, but Jeayes wrote that he was 'sometime Steward of Berkeley'. He died in 1817. Another of the above sketches extends Longbridge Street (now Canonbury Street) beyond the details on St. Clair Baddeley's plan, and would appear to indicate that part, at least, of Longbridge Priory lay to the south of the road.

It will be observed that the map identifies a number of properties which then belonged to various religious foundations.

21. Smyth III, vol. 3, p. 376.

22. The first two Berkeley registers for 1558 to 1654 were only returned to me in 1975 from the Castle, where they had been since the Berkeley inheritance case was heard before the House of Lords in 1810. The earlier one was in very bad condition, fragmented and many other entries completely indecipherable.

23. This is Smyth's account – Smyth III, vol 3, p. 144. Jeayes says (p.221) of Selected Charter 746, that the 'confirmation and declaration of uses . . conveyed to Nicholas Thorpe the Manor of Canonbury . . .', and mentioned no others.

24. This house, 'modernized' in Georgian times, is the house in which we have lived since retirement in 1976.

25. Smyth op.cit., pp. 222 and 384.

26. I am greatly indebted to 'The Trustee of the will of the 8th Earl of Berkeley, deceased', for permission to reproduce the details of the Thorpe will. I am also grateful to Mr Brian Smith, the County and Castle Archivist, for transcribing the will, never before published, which will be found in greater detail in appendix 4.

27. In the Gloucester Diocesan Records, Box B4/Q15 80.1, is an account of trouble between a Richard Lawrence, of Berkeley, and Joan his wife. The document is dated 'c.1630-40', and refers to an incident of 'about . . . seven years last past'. Might this be the Richard of this study? If so, it would suggest that his wife, who was a daughter of Nicholas Thorpe, was George's eldest known sister. A Mr. Chester (JP), a name which figures later in this work, is also mentioned.

2

George Thorpe – The Central Figure

George Thorpe's educational background, excepting only the occasional allusion to him as a learned man, is never mentioned in the brief references to him in letters, records of the Virginia Company of London, the Smyth of Nibley papers, or similar sources. It is clear, however, that the adjective 'learned' must have had a substantial foundation in fact.

Thorpe's early schooling probably took place locally. The most likely centres were Bristol, Cirencester or Gloucester, where four well established schools are known to have existed during the last quarter of the sixteenth century. Unfortunately no nominal rolls of pupils at those schools at the appropriate period are known to have survived, and as Thorpe does not appear amongst the records of the alumni of Oxford or Cambridge, there is no 'lead-back' via the individual college admissions books.

Three of those schools have associated with them names which have a familiar ring when the records of the Virginia Company of London are examined. These are:

1. Cirencester Grammar School.
2. Bristol Grammar School.
3. The Crypt Grammar School, Gloucester. [1]
4. The remaining school, the King's or Cathedral School in Gloucester, appeared to have had no connection with Virginia. The lists of the Oxford *alumni*, however, contain the registration of a George Thorpe, who entered Trinity College in 1659. The entry gives no further details. The College admissions book, however, is specific. It reads: 'Georgius Thorpe ex agro Gloustrensi, et villa Wanswell in parochia Berkley, patre ijus generoso, in Schola Gloustrensi a M^{ro} Russel postremo instructus, Annorum circiter 18 admissus est. Comminsalis Oct 1. 1659 Sub tutrlu M^{ri} Willis.' Here was the son of William, the eldest son and heir of our subject George, of Wanswell and Virginia. The Master Russel was the master of the King's School, Gloucester, who died in 1659. [2] It is possible that George Thorpe, senior, may have received his primary education at that school.

Thorpe's later education has never been referred to by any authority, contemporary or of more recent date. Thus my search had to start *ab initio*. Oxford and Cambridge provided only negative evidence, and yet Thorpe was held to be a learned man. A review of Thorpe's activities in Virginia revealed an acquaintance with, indeed a working knowledge of, the legal system and of the text books required to enable the laws of England – by which it had been laid down that the colony should be governed[3] – to be interpreted and administered. The selection of Thorpe by the Virginia Company Court to assist the Colonial Governor, Sir George Yeardley, in the investigation relating to the complaint by Lady Delaware of maladministration of her late husband's affairs and estates in Virginia, and also in to the case against Captain Argall, recently Lieutenant Governor, have been dealt with elsewhere,[4] and so has Thorpe's own reference to examining witnesses 'commonly until midnight'.[5] These appointments appear to demonstrate that Thorpe's legal knowledge was appreciable.[6] Furthermore, his statement relating to the shortage of legal text books, and his request for specified works of reference to make good that deficiency in the colony,[7] strengthen the above assumption. Accordingly the records of the Inns of Court in London were examined. These honourable bodies are today four in number – Gray's Inn, Inner Temple, Lincoln's Inn and Middle Temple. Certain others once existed, some of which were subsequently absorbed by the 'big four'.

Sir John Fortescue in his *De Laudibus Legum Angliae* (1468) explained that the Inns of Court were basically 'schools where young Englishmen were taught singing and dancing and all the accomplishments and commendable qualities requisite for English gentlemen,'[8] and that their main function and objective was to 'inculcate into their young students ideals of public service, breadth of vision and a national outlook.'[9] Sir Lyndon Macassey, in his commemorative booklet continued that 'In those days the narrow scholastic life of the Universities sowed no such seed in the hearts and minds of the young Englishman who was studying at them. From their beginning the Inns of Court discharged their great mission to the national benefit until down to the close of the seventeenth century, and it was not till then that legal studies began seriously to be adopted as their paramount responsibility.'[10]

Thus with the known close association of the Middle Temple, through many of its members,[11] with Virginia and later with the developing new American nation, a relationship still close and personal, their admissions book seemed the obvious starting point. There in fact was the entry for George Thorpe. The entry reads:

20 Feb. 1598 George Thorpe. Gent. Late of Staple Inn, son and heir of Nicholas Thorpe of Wanswell, Gloucestershire, Esq.

Other admissions relating to members and relations of the founders of the Berkeley Company also appear:

> 1593 Thomas Dale, son and heir of Matthew Dale Esq. apprentice of the Law and fellow of Middle Temple, Grundisburgh, Suffolk, Gent.
> 1594 John Smyth, late of Clements Inn, Gent, son and heir of Thomas Smyth, late of Hoby, Leics, Gent.
> 1617 Maurice Berkeley, son and heir of Richard Berkeley of Stoke Gifford.

Entries of Tracys, Throckmortons, Roes and of the Scudamores of Herefordshire also appear – families which were all related to George Thorpe by marriage.

The above statement that Thorpe had previously been a member of Staple Inn initiated an unsuccessful search for the admissions book and other records of the former Inn. [12]

All that can be said with certainty today is that Thorpe received the latter part of his educational training in the more liberal atmosphere of the Inns of Court, and that while there he probably accepted the traditions of those honourable and erudite societies, absorbing both the tuition suitable for a gentleman's son, which in his case obviously included some measure at least of familiarity with the law, its background requirements and administration. Whether or not that sense of dedication and service to God, his nation, and mankind in general, which was the hallmark of his life in Virginia, can be attributed directly to the traditions and teachings at Staple Inn and the Middle Temple is debatable. Rather I believe that Thorpe was not then motivated by those latter influences, but that they lay latent and unperceived until awakened years later by a sequence of events in which Sir Thomas Dale [13] – of whom more anon – played a major role.

In October 1598, presumably while Thorpe was still on the books of the Middle Temple, George bought a 'close of pasture containing about 7 acres, near Berkeley Town, called Boddicraft alias Berricraft', [14] from John Clutterbooke of Hinton 'and of Jane his wife, or her inheritance'. A stronger interest in landed estate developed almost immediately after, with the death of his father.

The death of Nicholas, senior, in 1600 must have caused considerable problems for George, the heir. He was twenty four years of age, well connected and may still have been at the Middle Temple. His future would now need to be reconsidered. As heir to the Wanswell Court estate he had a responsibility to himself and all members of the family, whether of the full blood or half. There was, also, the matter of the substantial financial bequests to his brother Nicholas, the brothers (or more likely half brothers) William and John, and finally brother-in-law, Richard. His step-mother had been bequeathed accommodation at the Court and was to receive an annuity of £30. He also had to create an estate for her and for William and John.

These hard facts would present quite a challenge, and could well, unless the situation was taken firmly in hand, be the cause of real trouble. His step-mother, Anne, probably had with her her young sons William and John, and Agnis too would be at the Court, while Anne's son, Richard, by her first marriage, and her daughter in law who was also her step-daughter, were probably living in the Lawrence family home, Canonbury House. If he, George, did not return home, Nicholas junior could be isolated, and an attempt at expropriation would be a distinct possibility. This situation may well have been in the mind of Nicholas senior, when into his will, made a short time before his death, he included the clause that the bequests to what could be called the 'Lawrence' party, were conditional upon Richard and his heirs bringing no suit against George, and all conditions being followed by wife Anne 'and her son Lawrence', otherwise all dispositions to wife Anne, sons William and John and son-in-law Richard were 'to be void'.

It may well have seemed to George that it was essential for him to return home at once and take over complete control, thereby establishing his seigniorage. He probably deemed it desirable to set up, at least temporarily, a separate establishment for himself. This could best be achieved by marriage with the daughter of some influential family. Finally, an extension to the Court would confirm for the future the separateness of the two households, and would help ensure the authority and 'protection' of a new wife. These varied problems may well have been the reasons behind certain of George's decisions and actions during the next two or three years.

The first obvious move made by George was to marry Margaret, the daughter of Sir Thomas Porter (lately of Llanthony near Gloucester), at St. Martin in the Fields on 11 July 1600, thus adding considerably to his list of important relations, even though it was merely by marriage. His new brothers-in-law included, Margaret's brother, Sir Arthur Porter, Sir John Danvers, Sir Gabriel Pyle, Sir Richard Walsh and the Denis family. These matrimonial relationships of George may help to explain his later appointments and his ultimate involvement in the Virginia Company of London.

The marriages of George's grandfather and father, Thomas and Nicholas, had brought the Thorpes into a genealogical relationship with several families of considerable standing in the West of England, families who were not unknown in the city and at court. An examination of the genealogical tables in the appendices demonstrates how narrow was the circle within which so often families such as the Berkeleys, Throckmortons, Roes, Denises and Scudamores married. This appears to be especially true of the heirs and the elder children.

Like the equine stud there were the excursions in search of new blood, but time and time again they returned to the old, principal blood lines.

George's mother was a niece of Sir John Mason, a Councillor of State. George's father was a cousin by marriage of Henry Berkeley (son of Sir Richard Berkeley), whose mother in law was a daughter of William Horwood, the late Attorney General. Likewise he was a blood cousin of Sir Thomas Throckmorton, whose wife was the eldest daughter of Sir Richard Berkeley, and cousin also of Anne Throckmorton (sister of Sir Thomas) who married Sir John Tracy, the father of William Tracy. Thus he was 'uncle' in varying degrees to three of his sons's future partners in the Berkeley Plantation enterprise, i.e., Sir William Throckmorton, Richard Berkeley, whose wife was a sister of Sir Thomas Roe, and William Tracy. Within the 'family' at one or more removes, were several other important personalities of the time, e.g., the Scudamores, Baskervilles, Bainhams, Sambrookes and Sir Edward Coke, who in his day had been Lord Chief Justice. Furthermore the brother of 'cousin' Mary, Sir Thomas Roe, even at that period was an up-and-coming young man with a good 'London' background, e.g., his grandfather had been Lord Mayor in 1568, and his uncle Sheriff in 1597 and Lord Mayor in 1608. This then was the network of kin in which George stood; it gave a fine start to any able and aspiring young country gentleman, especially one who was a son and heir.

In the following year, 1601, George sold the estate of Bellamies in Nibley, and two years later parted with some other properties in outlying areas. This may well have resulted from having to find ready cash to enable him to honour his father's bequests to the three other sons and son-in-law, Richard. Another reason may have been the fact that his step-mother, Anne, had been granted accommodation in Wanswell Court by the will of her husband, Nicholas. There were thus, now, three family units with possible claims for 'house-room' in the Court, (1) George (who had inherited the property) and his newly wedded wife, (2) Mrs. Anne Thorpe, (3) possibly Nicholas with or without a wife. The Court, as such, was not large enough for two, let alone three, 'wifely domains,' especially when one was the wife of the heir, and the other a dowager who had had an undisputed reign for ten or twelve years. The substantial addition to the Court could well, architecturally, have been built about that period; thus providing accommodation for at least two families, in more or less separate establishments. Such a building programme would take considerable time as well as money, thus presenting a further problem, that of residence while the alterations were being carried out.

The obvious solution, and the one which Thorpe probably decided upon, was for him and his wife to set up a temporary home in some nearby estate house. This would give Thorpe's bride a completely free hand and spare her firstly possible interference from Mistress Anne, who, if the will of Nicholas is indicative, may have been of a forceful nature, and secondly the inconvenience which would be inevitable with a major building programme. A suggestion as to the identification of such a house will shortly be made.

Amongst the select charters in Berkeley Castle is one dated at Westminster, 21 February, 45. Eliz.[15] (1603). It is a 'Grant from the Crown to George Thorpe, Richard Webbe, and John Mathieu and their heirs in perpetuity of the Manor of Canonbury, Co. Glouc. at an annual rent of forty-seven shillings and fivepence.' This is a revised copy of the Letters Patent issued to George's father and six others some years earlier. Smyth said that during the intervening years there had been exchange or sale of portions, and that as a result of 'inequality or other mistakes' and 'in consideration of £188. 9s. 8d.' new Letters Patent were obtained from the Queen.[16]

Select Roll no. 54 in Berkeley Castle is 'The joint accompt of Anthony Huntley,[17] Gent, and John Machin, general woodwards, purvayers and overseers of buildings and husbandry' of Henry, Lord Berkeley, for the period 1 May 1604 to 4 July 1607. Amongst the entries of considerable interest to rural economists is one relating to George Thorpe's Severn fisheries – probably between Sharpness and Halmer.

It reads: 'Paid for the charges in dressing and barrelling of li great Sturgeons in Wine, Perry, Vinegar, Vessels, and other necessary, whereof the one was taken in the "put" of Thomas Hurne of Greenstreet and the other in the "puts"[18] of George Thorpe, Esquire, in the tenure of Robert Smyth in the River of Severn within the hundred of Berkeley, £5. 15d.'[19] These royal fish are still occasionally caught at Berkeley, but the practice of sending them to the Royal Household has ceased.[20]

In 1605/6 came Thorpe's first known court appointment, that of Gentleman Pensioner.[21] The list of these officers during the reign of James I are contained in rolls 36-41, Box I, P.R.O., E.407. George Thorpe is not mentioned in roll 36, which covers 1603/4, but his name appears in the following MS. (roll 37 – 1605/6), and he is still listed in no. 41 (1614), which is the last extant roll of the reign.

The Gentleman Pensioner's obligations involved duties of a personal or domestic nature on behalf of the sovereign or royal household for stated periods, combined with service of a military nature should occasion demand. Thus during the tours of duty Thorpe would be required to reside in London. Remembering that he remained a Pensioner up until, and including, 1614, it is probable that Thorpe possessed a Town House from 1605, or soon after. It would be reasonable to assume that this non-lucrative but sought-after post came Thorpe's way through the influence of one or more of his well-placed friends and relations. That Thorpe did not reside permanently in London, however, is clear from the next chronologically dated document relevant to him. Furthermore his position regarding the Wanswell estate and his family obligations could not be ignored, but would require some measure of personal attention and supervision.

In August 1608, Henry, Lord Berkeley, Lord Lieutenant of Gloucestershire, reviewed 'All Able and Sufficient Men in Body fit for His Majesty's Service in the Wars, within the County of Gloucester'. This catalogue constitutes John Smyth's MSS. nos. 14-16.[22] These were edited and published, with the permission of the owner, Lord Sherborne, in 1902, under the title of '*Men and Armour for Gloucestershire* in 1608.'[23] This brief biographical survey has rendered possible the probable identification of certain members of the various parties sent out between 1619 and 1622 to settle and staff the Berkeley plantation in Virginia. Of particular importance for this study is the fact that it throws some light upon George Thorpe and his local residence and social standing during the middle years of the first decade of the seventeenth century.

On the evidence of this document it appears probable that Thorpe did not bring his bride to live at Wanswell Court where his stepmother and the younger members of the family would have been living. In that return it is recorded that Thorpe, who incidentally 'hath one musket and a caliver furn[ished]', was then living in Halmer – today known as Halmore, a hamlet within the ecclesiastical parish of Berkeley, and at its centre as the crow flies, less than half a mile away from Wanswell Court. Two, perhaps three, houses in or near Halmore suggest themselves as possible sites for Thorpe's 'bridal' home. Firstly there is Acton Hall (630 yards from Wanswell Court), not itself an old house, but one with older foundations, or Halmore Farm (800 yards), both of which are in the middle of Halmore. A third possibility is Priors Wood, a substantial farmhouse which although not actually situated in Halmore could well be classified as such. Yet another possibility is that Thorpe may have rented Oldlands Place, still, at that time, in the ownership of the Oldland family. Parcels of land once attached to that estate had been bought by Nicholas Thorpe from Anne Butler in 14. Eliz., along with the Butler lands.[24] Oldlands Farm today is only about 400 yards, as the crow flies, from Wanswell Court. It is not, however, the original Oldlands Place, the site of which is not known, and which could possibly have been the predecessor of Acton Hall.

The entries in *Men and Armour* for Halmer bring out two other interesting points relating to Thorpe. Firstly, he is designated 'Esquire', a title which was not often in earlier documents given to his father who usually received the appellation 'Gent', although he was termed Esquire in his will. Secondly, it shows that George had seven servants who were fit for military service, out of forty-one such able bodied men in Halmer. The significance of these two statements concerning his rank of Esquire, and the employment of seven male servants of military age and fitness can only be fully appreciated when a detailed analysis is made of the military potential of the Berkeley Vale and Cotswold Edge. It must be emphasised that Smyth, the compiler of this survey, was discriminatory to the point of fastidiousness in his social nomenclature both in this work and in the Smyth of Nibley Papers, which form so important a background to this research.

In the *Men and Armour* returns of the twenty towns, villages and hamlets tabulated below, it will be seen that Thorpe's position as an Esquire and one employing seven personal servants places him in a category apart. Of the approximately 1380 physically fit men within the area, Thorpe is one of only two to whom Smyth gives the rank of Esquire. Twenty-six Gents are recorded, one of whom is Smyth himself, and amongst the twenty-five others so designated are several who made the hopeful voyage to Virginia in either 1619 or 1620. Even amongst the named lords of manors, the majority of whom were not included in the list of potential soldiers, it is worth noticing that, of those below the rank of Knight, only two out of four received the title Esquire.

The second point to be observed is that nearly 160 personal servants are recorded. In most cases this means a single servant to a particular master. There are, however, a number of instances where persons, including gentlemen, yeomen, husbandmen and some of the more prominent tradespeople, e.g., clothiers and weavers, are recorded as employing two or very occasionally three servants within the military category. Thorpe with his seven servants heads the employers' list. Lady Berkeley, living at Bradley in the parish of Wotton, comes second with five such employees. Thorpe's position as head of the family, his matrimonial alliances and his royal appointment probably explain the unusual size of his personal household.

Further reference to the following table will be made when the Gloucestershire background of the Berkeley Company is examined.

In 1609 George Thorpe took lease of a part of what were, and are, termed 'The New Grounds' along the Frampton/Slimbridge Severn shore, for a term of fifty-one years, an agreement which involved him and others in intermittent litigation almost until he sailed for Virginia in 1620. The cause of the trouble was the Severn in which his forebears had held fishing rights for generations.[25] To understand even partially, the root of the disputes one has to appreciate

Borough / Town / Village / Hamlet	Numbers in Men and Armour	Esquire	Gent	Yeoman	Servant	Husbandman	Labourer	Clothier	Weaver	Broad Weaver	Dyer	Fuller	Mercer	Tucker	Baker	Butcher	Carpenter/Joiner	Cooper	Glover	Innkeeper	Mason	Miller	Saddler	Shepherd	Shoemaker	Smith	S U B	Taylor	Tanner	Trained Soldier	Clothmaker
Berkeley Bor:	100	-	3	11	17	4	10	-	9	-		3	1	3	2	4		1	1		1	2	-		7	6	8	7	5	8	
Alkington	107	-	1	10	5	10	12	2	36	-		7				1	1			3						2	13	2		9	1
Bevington	19	-	1	6	1	3	4		1																	1	4	1			
Breadstone	11	-	1	-	1	1	4		-							1	1										2			1	
Clapton	17	-	-	6	4	6	1		-																	3	1			3	
Halmer	41	1	-	2	11	3	13		7													2				1	1	1		2	
Ham & Hamfallow	26	-	-	7	4		5		1						2	4						1				1	2	1			
Hinton	46	-	-	-	6	25	6		5																		8	2		1	
Pedington	16	-	-	4	3	1	4		-								2										3	-			
Sanyger	8	-	-	1	1	4		2																			1	-			
Stone	35	-	2	-	3	-	6	1	7			2		1			1	1				1				1	5	2			
Wanswell	25	-	1	1	2	7	5		2							2	2					1					3	-			
Total for Berkeley Ecc	451	1	9	48	58	64	70	3	70	-	-	9	3	1	4	6	15	3	1	4	-	6	2	-	7	12	53	17	5	24	1
Cromhall	60	-	-	-	4	13	8	5	20				1					1			1						1	5	3		5	
Cromhall Abbots	20	-	-	-	3	7		1	5								1					1					4				1
Cam	123	-	3	3	21	27		6	-	40		15				1	2										13	1	1	2	
Hill	40	-	-	2	3	11	13		-		1					1	2										6	1		2	
Cowley (Coaley)	116	-	1		9	42		2	-	35		6					4	2				1				2	13	4		14	
Stinchcombe	63	-	1	3	8	8		11	33			-		2													8		1	7	
Slimbridge & Hurst	121	-	1	9	14	12	11		35			4		2			2	2		1		1			5	2	17	5		2	
Huntingford	3	-	-		1	-			-			-		2																	
Synwell	71	-	1	2	7	3	9	2	26			3					1	2				1			3	3	3	2	1		
Wotton Bor:	151	-	3	3	2	2	4	15	32	-	-		6	4	-	1	5	2	-	2	1	-	4	-	-	2	19	14	-	11	-
Woodmancote	59	-	-	1	1	2		-	24		4		-		10	-	-				-	-	2	4	1	1	1	5	2	2	-
Dursley	104	-	-	1	19		-	13	26	-		10	2	-	-	2	1	-	3	-	4	-	-	-	-	7	2	9	2	8	-
Uley	57	1	-	3	1	3	6	3	11	19	1		-	-	-		1	-				-			2	-	-	-	5	8	-
Owlpen	17	-	-	-	-	2	-	13		-	1									-				2	-		1	-	3	-	
Combe	39	-	-	-	4	12	-	-	1	14			-				1					1			1		2	1	1	-	
Wortley	50	-	-	-	4	9	2	3	12	-	-	8	-	-	-	-	3	-	-	-	1	-	-	1	4	2	-	12	-		
N. Nibley	132	-	1	4	4	14	9	6	58	-		15	-	-	2	7	-	-	2	-	-	2	-	-	2	-	14	3	-	11	-
	1226	1	11	31	105	165	64	68	296	109	5	69	6	16	1	14	27	2	7	2	12	15	-	1	27	14	122	38	3	77	1
Berkeley Ecc	451	1	9	48	58	64	70	3	70	-	-	9	3	1	4	6	15	3	1	4	-	6	2	-	7	12	53	17	5	24	1
Total	1677	2	20	79	163	229	134	71	366	109	5	78	9	17	5	20	42	5	8	6	12	21	2	1	34	26	175	55	8	101	2
Winchcombe	163	.	-	-	-	13	36	6	4	-		4	-	4	10	5	3	9	-	1?	-	-	5	6	5	-	15	2	4	-	
Todington	30	-	1	-	12	3	7	-	1	-	-												2	-	1		-	-	-	-	-
Hayles	10	1	1	-	4	2	-	-																			-	-	-	-	-
Farmcote	12	-	-	-	10	2																					-	-	-	-	-
Greet	10	-	-	-	3	2	2	-	-														1	-			-	-	-	-	-
Gretton	33	-	-	-	-	14	11	-	-																	1	2	2	-	7	-
	248	1	2	-	29	36	56	6	5	-	-	4	-	4	10	5	3	9	-	?	-	-	8	6	7	2	17	2	11	-	

the peculiarities of that river, especially in the above parishes and at Awre on the other side of the Severn. From time immemorial the Severn in that area has periodically changed its deep channel from the Forest of Dean side to the opposite bank. This has resulted in the erosion of the banks on the one side and the building up of new land on the other. Saxton's map of Gloucestershire shows that in 1577 Slimbridge (and Frampton also) had gained perhaps 200 acres of fresh land at the expense of Awre. This soil, an amalgam of the liquified Slimbridge lias and the powdered red sandstone and red marl from the Forest side, was extremely fertile. Attempts (not very successful) had been made in past centuries to secure the retention of the newly deposited land, but it was not until the beginning of the seventeenth century that the Berkeley Estate, of which Slimbridge was a part, took a firm hand. Understandably the Foresters were indignant, for if the project was successful they lost, for ever perhaps, 200 acres of rich soil. The area newly gained was termed the warth, and that which lay between the sea wall and the river – nearly a mile wide in that area – was called the dumbles, the limits of which were constantly changing.[26] All this resulted in a long period of litigation, a costly exercise for all concerned.

Smyth filled nearly sixteen folios of his MS. – eighteen pages of volume 3 – with his description of the protracted troubles and the final case. Three short extracts must suffice for those early ten years and the final suit of 1637.[27]

1. (p. 330) There were 'concerning grounds new gained from and left by the river Severn, called the new warth and the new gotten grounds, for common pasture claimed thereon by the inhabitants of Slimbridge and Frampton, divers great and tedious suits from 7. Jacobi for 10 years after in the Courts of Kings Bench, Common Please, Chancery, Court of Wards, and Starchamber, have multiplied; wherein the Lord Berkeley's two farmers, Arnold Oldisworth and George Thorpe Esquires, were sometimes plaintiffs and sometimes defendants'.

2. (p. 337) 'Exchequer suit brought in the name of the King by Sir John Banks his Majesty's Attorney General, and prosecuted by Sir Sackville Crow Baronet and others . . . before the said Sir Sackville Crow, Sir Bainham Throckmorton[28] Baronets and Francis Smyth, (who made themselves Commissioners, taken out also and solicited by themselves,) . . .'

3. (p. 346) 'This Trial falling so suddenly and unexpectedly of, prevented me from delivering an Invective speech, which with some bitterness I had determined to have spoken in Court at the end of my Evidence, before the Jury against Sir Sackville Crow especially'. On page 345 Smyth records that 'By one Decree in Chancery in 9. Jacobi; and by 4. decrees in the Court of Wards, in 12, 13, 15, et 16, Jacobi R., whereby the possession of the grounds in question (amongst others) was established for Oldisworth and Thorpe,[29] under whom, three of the now defendants do claim.'

These legal wrangles cost money, and are said to have caused Oldisworth debts of around £4,000. They also cost Thorpe heavily, and were one of the two main reasons for the sale of much of his estate before he left England in 1620. His share in the financing of the Berkeley Company, was, of course, the other.

George Thorpe's wife, Margaret, née Porter, was buried at Berkeley church 10 March 1610, possibly in a family pew.[30] There appear to have been no children of that marriage, unless either or both of the following children who were baptized and buried at St. Martin in the Fields, London, the church in which George and Margaret were married 11 July 1600, were their offspring:

1. John Thorpe, baptized 28 January 1602, and buried March 1602
2. Richard Thorpe, baptized 6 October 1603, and buried 2 March 1614.

On 21 February 1611 George Thorpe, Esquire, married Margaret Harris of the city of Bristol, Generosa, (daughter of the late David Harris, gentleman, a citizen of that city and possibly a member of the Tanners' Guild) at St. Pancras Church, Soper Lane, London, by licence.[31] The children of this union are dealt with in some detail in chapter 3.[32]

Thorpe is frequently referred to as a Member of Parliament in contemporary and later records. Details, however, relating to his election to Parliament and his activities in the House are sparse.

His name appears in the massive 1878 *Return of Members of Parliament* in the corrigenda and appendix. The entry – under Southampton (County) reads:

'John Griffith
George Thorpe Esq.   Portsmouth Borough'

but there is no indication that Thorpe was resident in the borough and, like so many burgesses, may well not have been.[33]

The details of Thorpe's contributions to parliamentary debates must, of necessity, be based mainly upon the *Journal of the House of Commons*. There are several contemporary, though brief, parliamentary diaries which throw a little light on some of the 1614 debates, and occasionally amplify, or clarify, certain passages.[34]

Thorpe's parliamentary experience was short lived in that the 1614 Parliament, known as the 'Addled Parliament', to which he was elected, opened on 5 April 1614, and ended its brief life on 7 June. This was the second Parliament in the reign of King James I. The first was summoned on 19 March 1604, and continued in office until 9 February 1611. He was denied the opportunity of further experience and service in the national legislative body because the third Parliament of the reign was not convened until 30 January 1621, by which time Thorpe had been in Virginia for seven months, where he was already a member of the Governor's Council of the colony.

Thorpe's recorded contributions to the debates in the House are few. On 5 May 'An Act against the vain and wasteful Consumption of gold and silver, in gilding or silvering within this Kingdom' came up for its second reading. This was followed by the second reading of 'An Act concerning Apparel'. These, after brief discussions were referred to committees. The principal subject that day for debate concerned the 'King's Business'. The House was opposed to any imposition, or claim for the imposition, by the Sovereign, of taxes or levies upon 'commodities' without the consent of Parliament – 'the King had claimed it in open Parliament', it was stated.[35] Sir Thomas Smyth maintained that 'the King cannot impose without Parliament', and that from the time of the Danes and Saxons to that of Edward I this had been the accepted practice. From then on, in times of war, there had been occasional peremptory royal impositions. Mr Christopher Brooke later strongly supported the bill, and moved 'to consider the bill, and pass it, as it should be amended.' He then proposed that the Lords might be informed, and that, if necessary, a conference with them should be held. Mr Thorpe then rose and said 'That he intended the same Motion. – Addeth, that a Petition to his Majesty, if the Lords and we confer, that he should be pleased to be present. – Thinketh a Satisfaction to the King, from both Houses of Parliament, the best that may be.' MS.E 327 shortens and simplifies Thorpe's contribution to the debate thus – 'Mr Thorpe agreed with him [Mr Brooke] and wished if it might be, the King might be moved to be present to hear the arguing of it.[36]

On the 16 May the House began with several short debates, one of which was to have been on the Virginia Company. Mr. Brooke, however, moved that 'the Virginia Business may be Tomorrow, Seven of the Clock.' Later the House desired legal advice, and so 'The Sergeant sent with his Mace' for 'learned Counsel'. Later in the debate 'Mr. Thorpe moveth, that, if any man can speak anything for the King's Right of imposing without Parliament, they shall do so.' MS.E 327 states that 'Mr. Thorpe moved that if any of the House could maintain the question for the King he should speak.'[37]

On the following day, 17 May, after brief discussions on various subjects, the 'Virginia Business' was debated. It was 'Ordered, My Lord of Southampton, My Lord Sheffield. etc. shall come in, to hear the Treaty of the Virginia Business'. A short history of the background to, and the establishment of, the colony followed. Conflicting opinions were expressed, e.g. (1) now was the time for consolidation; (2) the question of Conquest was raised, and the example of Spanish methods in the 'Indies' and of Don John D'aquyla in Ireland were cited; (3) the 'Conquest' of Virginia was just; (4) 'Our usage of the Indies merciful and respective'; (5) our conduct 'might prove to a war'.

This debate has been included here because of opinions which will shortly be expressed. MS.E 327 gives a clearer and somewhat longer account of this debate. Thorpe is not mentioned in the minutes of the Commons Journals for the 17th, but MS.E 327 records that 'Mr Thorpe preferred a bill against all tenants for committing of waste.'[38]

On 1 June one of the main debates centres around the second reading of 'An act against new Buildings, dividing of Houses, receiving of Inmates, and severing of Fields, in or near about the Cities of London and Westminster.' This bill had been rejected by the last Parliament. Mr. Alford moved 'to have the Bill committed; for else there will be such Increase of Poor, as will draw Infection etc. – Moveth, it may be considered'. Later in the debate Mr. Thorpe also moved 'to commit it.' The House finally decided that a committee should be set up to meet 'his Majesty's Privy Council . . . This Day Sevennight, in the Chequer Court.' MS.E 327 does not mention Thorpe's contribution. In the Journal the list of that committee is given and it includes 'Mr. Thorpe . . . Sir Maw[rice] Berkeley . . . Mr. Rich. Berkeley.' Thus ended Thorpe's parliamentary career.

Reflecting on Thorpe's brief contributions to the debates in the House, one is astonished that he appears not to have spoken when Virginia policies were debated.[39] He had already invested in the Virginia Company of London, and within a short while became involved in further colonial projects, i.e. the Bermudas 1615, the East India Company (£300) 1618, Smyth's Hundred in Virginia 1618. Bearing in mind Thorpe's apparent silence when the conquest of Virginia, the treatment of the natives and the possibility of an Anglo-Indian war were debated in the House, one is inclined to suggest that his deep feelings towards the Indians, as seen in 1620-2, was something which developed later.[40]

Thorpe was involved in two other appointments at this time, which must here briefly be mentioned.

Probably the first of these was that of membership of the King's Council for Virginia. The details are contained in the Kimbolton MS. No. 288.[41] This document records 'The names of such as have been chosen to be of his Majesty's Council for Virginia since the date of the Patent' (12 March 1612). Then follow twenty-five names which, judging by arrangement of social gradations, appear to be grouped into three periods. Thorpe is listed in the first group of nine, which Brown[42] believed represented the years 1613-16, while the second represented 1617-18, and the third 1619.

The date of the remaining appointment is also not known. This was the office of Gentleman of the King's Privy Chamber, a desirable but not very lucrative position, for which his membership of the Gentlemen Pensioners had, undoubtedly, been a stepping-stone. This 'promotion' must have taken place after 1614.

These two appointments do not fall strictly within the limits of this chapter, but have been introduced here so that a complete catalogue of Thorpe's appointments here in England may be recorded. Thorpe's official appointments thus run as follows:

1. Gentlemen Pensioner (1604/5)
2. Member of the Virginia Company of London (by March 1612)
3. Member of Parliament (1614)
4. Member of the King's Council for Virginia
5. Gentleman of the King's Privy Chamber

There is no real evidence as to which of the last two appointments came first, but I suspect that the above is the probable order.

This is a record of which any commoner might be pleased. It will be seen later that in Virginia also Thorpe established a reputation and status which earned for him the praise and respect of his peers.

NOTES

1. *VCH*, Gloucestershire, vol. II, p. 388ff., 355ff. and 344ff. Of these the Crypt had as its master in 1551-2 (and until perhaps 1553-4) a Nicholas Oldysworth. Later, in the seventeenth century a family of Oldisworth occupied Bradley House in Wotton-under-Edge parish. Arnold of that family was the son of Edward Oldisworth and Tacy his wife, who was the daughter of Sir Thomas Porter. Her niece, Margaret Porter, was George Thorpe's first wife. Of further relevance is the fact that Arnold bought a portion of Thorpe's interests in the Berkeley Company in 1620, and later sailed with William Tracy's party to Virginia, where he died at a date not known.

2. David Robertson, *The King's School, Gloucester*, Phillimore, Chichester, 1974, pp. 52-56.

3. Royal Charter no. I, 1606, See S.M. Bemiss, op.cit, p. 5.

4. See chapter 6.

5. Smyth I, 30, Letter from Thorpe to Smyth, dated 19 December 1620.

6. It must be pointed out, however, that Smyth (Smyth III, 3, p. 330) commenting on 'divers great and tedious sutes' in which both he, Thorpe, and Arnold Oldisworth had been involved, wrote that the others had not 'at that time (*c.* 1604-10) . . . as much legal knowledge . . . Though otherwise prudent men . . .' It should be remembered, however, that Smyth was a lawyer who had been called to the Bar, and he may well have been contemptuous of those whose legal training fell short of his, and secondly that Smyth certainly in his later additions to the *History of the Manor of Berkeley* is critical, indeed derogatory at times, in his remarks about Thorpe, an attitude engendered, it may well be, by personal jealousy. This possibility is discussed below.

7. Ferrar Papers no. 1023. Letter to Sir Edwin Sandys. See chapter 7.

8. Cited in Sir Lyndon Macassey (Master of the Middle Temple), *Middle Templars' Associations with America*, Private Printing Office of the Times Publishing Company, 1957, p. 8.

9. Ibid.

10. Ibid.

11. Sir Francis Drake, Adrian Gilbert, Sir Walter Raleigh, Sir John Popham and Sir Edwin Sandys were all members of the Middle Temple. *Register of Admissions to the Honourable Society of the Middle Temple*, Vol 1, Temple Bar, 1949, *Sub nomine.*

12. e.g., Gray's Inn which absorbed Staple Inn, The Prudential Assurance Society which occupy the surviving Staple Inn buildings, P.R.O., H.M.C., and the Guild Hall Library.

13. Perhaps he who was admitted to the Middle Temple in 1593.

14. Smyth III, vol. 3, p. 214. This shows what a short distance the town of Berkeley then extended northward of the square – possibly not more than 200 yards. The small building estates of Lower and Upper Berrycroft, Canon Park, Hill Crest and The Leys, *c.* 1920-76, a total of more than 100 houses, probably represent this seven-acre close.

15. Jeayes, op.cit., Charter no. 838, p. 243.

16. Smyth III, vol. 3, p. 145.

17. Perhaps the son or grandson of Elizabeth, sister of Margaret Thorpe (neé Throckmorton), grandmother of George Thorpe. See genealogical tables in the appendices.

18. Two types of fishing weirs have been used on the tidal areas of the Severn for centuries. The one is made up of several hundred open-ended elongated and narrowing basketwork traps, termed putchers. These units, of about six feet in length, are set in banks of two to seven units high. They are principally salmon traps and have to be removed during the closed season. The second type of weir is made up of a single line of much larger basketwork traps called putts. They are basically the same shape, but measure from six to seven feet across the mouth, and are made in three sections which fit together. The last and narrowest of these is woven closely so that it will hold eels, and, it is said, even shrimps. The putt is too heavy and cumbersome to remove at the end of the season, and is, instead, rendered incapable of taking salmon. Both the putcher and the putt are still in use locally.

19. Jeayes, op.cit. p. 282.

20. The last one was taken up, personally, by car by the late Captain H.J. Baldwin, agent to the estate, on 3 July 1953. He described the occasion thus: 'I telephoned to Lady Berkeley's solicitors reporting the "catch" and pointed out that it was customary on the Berkeley Castle estate for the Lord of the Manor to offer a royal fish such as a sturgeon to the reigning monarch. Information from Lady Berkeley came back to me at 10.30 that morning confirming that she had offered the sturgeon to Her Majesty who had graciously accepted it. Also I was requested to accompany the sturgeon to London and personally hand it over to the Comptroller of the Household at Buckingham Palace. This, I arranged, would take place at 3.30 p.m in the afternoon . . . this particular sturgeon was seven feet long and weighed 150 lbs.' Yet unpublished account by Captain H.J. Baldwin – MS. held by his widow, Mrs. A. Baldwin, in Berkeley.

21. The 'King's Chamber', controlled by the Lord Chamberlain, had two divisions, the Outer and the Privy Chamber, each with its own personnel. The outer chamber represented the areas of the place where the Sovereign could be seen by all who had the entrée to the court The establishment for this department included fifty Gentlemen Pensioners, with their own Captain, Lieutenant, Standard Bearer and Clerk of this Chaque. The Privy Chamber was the area to which the king retired for privacy. There only the highly privileged had access.

22. These MSS. were probably purchased when the Cholmondeley collection at Condover Hall was broken up (see chapter 1 above).

23. This work contains much of interest relating to these potential soldiers, who are recorded by hamlet or parish, and are divided into three broad age groups, i.e., (1) 'that man to be about Twenty', (2) 'about forty', (3) 'between fifty and threescore'. Their stature and physique are indicated by the type of weapon they are considered capable of bearing, i.e., '(p) Showeth the man to be of the tallest stature fit to make a pikeman, (m) . . . of the middle stature fit to make a musketier, (ca) . . . of a lower stature fit to serve with a Caliver, (tr) . . . a trained soldier', and '(sub) a subsidy man'. Frequently too their social standing, e.g., husbandman, yeoman, gent or esquire, is made clear, while the occupations of most men are given, e.g., labourer, tanner, servant to . . ., or weaver etc.

24. Smyth III, vol. 3, pp. 222, 384.

25. Smyth III, vol 3, p. 345.
(a) 'By a fine at common law levied by John Thorpe in 2.H.4. of two Rocks and fishing places in the Severn . . .' (b) 'By an Action of waft in 18.H.6 brought by John Thrope against Ecton for 3 fishing places or rocks.' In a Severn bailiff's manual – no date, but prior to 1916 when Lord Fitzhardinge died, (lent to me by the late Mr. Maurice Haines, one of the last of the retired 'professional' fishermen on the river) certain fishing rocks are mentioned as belongong to Lord Fitzhardinge along with an account of the places where the following fishing instruments were sited. There were at Bottwell Rock 200 putchers; at Bull Rock 300 putchers, 24 putts, 150 yards of hedges and 3 stop nets; at Haywards Rock (rented by the above Mr. Maurice Haines, 1918-54) 300 putchers, 300 yards of hedges and 20 putts, and at Venus Rock 800 putchers. Today the castle estate owns all the Severn fishing rights in Berkeley. The above rocks are the only 'fishing' rocks in the parish. Consequently it must be assumed that Thorpe's fishing 'rocks' wcrc thrcc of the above.

26. When I first shot geese and duck at Frampton in the late 1940s, the main deep channel lay under the Frampton/Slimbridge bank. Suddenly some years later it moved over to the Awre shore. This has resulted in the loss of many acres of grazing land for the Berkeley and Clifford (Frampton) estates.

27, In addition to Smyth, see F. Peter, *The Frontier of a Barony – The New Grounds at Slimbridge in Gloucestershire.*

28. Son of Sir William Throckmorton of the Berkeley Company.

29. A Thorpe farming account for that area in 1626 is as follows:

53 sheep sold	£21 4s. 0d.	less	Tithe	£3 0s. 0d.
23 lambs sold	£ 5 15s. 0d.		Wages	£3 0s. 0d.
Received for				
Tack	£72 3s. 10d.		Thistle cutting	4s. 0d.
			Ditching	2s. 4d.
Total	£99 2s. 10d.		Total	£6 6s. 4d.

Profit £92 16s. 6d.
Quoted by Francis Peter, a Land Surveyor, whose father, James Peter, was agent to the Berkeley Estate (1872-1919). Mr. F. Peter naturally, had access to the records in the Muniments Room at the Castle. He himself deputized as temporary agent to the estate

when Captain Baldwin, T.D., was away on active service, 1939-45. His book, from which the above accounts were taken (p. 23), was published in 1948. See footnote 27 for title.

30. Appendix 7. Perhaps Margaret I was buried in the family pew, as was Margaret II.

31. Margaret's mother was Anne, the sister of Sir John Bennett, Kt., of the City of London, and Thomas Bennett, citizen and merchant of London. See appendix 5.

32. pp. 53-4.

33. Mr. W.N. Yates, Portsmouth Records Officer, said that the records of the parliamentary elections in Portsmouth have only survived, and that fragmentarily, from 1660. He also stated that Thorpe appeared 'in a list of burgesses in 1617 (Election book, 1598-1638, our reference C.E. 1/4)'

34. e.g., i. 'A Parliamentary Diary for 1614.' This is contained in W. Notestein's 'Commons Debates, 1621' vol. VIII, pp. 628-56.
ii. 'A summary of what was done in the Parliament begun the 5 April, 1614, gathered by Sir John Holles . . .', printed by the Historical Manuscripts Commission – Portland Manuscripts, IX, pp. 132-9.
iii. In addition the Carnegie Institution of Washington D.C. published in 1924 volume I of their *Proceedings and Debates of the British Parliaments respecting North America*, edited by L.F. Stock.
iv. However, the most important of these, from the point of view of this study, is that designated MS. E327 in the Kenneth Spencer Research Library. This has been transcribed by Dr. Maija J. Cole of the Yale Center for Parliamentary History. Dr. Cole most generously furnished me with copies of the pages of her transcription on which Thorpe's contributions are recorded. The accounts of Thorpe's part in the debates in the Commons' Journal and those in MS. E327 can thus be compared.

35. C.J., vol. I, p. 472

36. Ibid. p. 473; and Cole, op.cit., p. 21.

37. Cole p. 58.

38. Ibid., p. 61.

39. Dr. Coles transcription of MS.E.327 establishes that Thorpe was present in the House on 17 May.

40. It may well be argued that Thorpe did speak on the issue of Virginia, but that neither the recorder of the Commons Journal nor any of the known private diarists, made mention of his speech. I do not incline to this view, believing that had Thorpe in 1614 possessed strong feelings on the subject, his contribution to the debate would have been such that it would have found inclusion in some record.

41. The Duke of Manchester's records.

42. Brown I, pp. 796-7.

3

The Hidden Years 1614-18

1. FRESH ORIENTATION

The period 1616-19 seems to mark a turning point in Thorpe's life. Sparse though the evidence is, it must be considered with some care. It will involve an exploration of circumstantial evidence, in an attempt to explain the apparent metamorphosis which Thorpe underwent in those three years 1616-19. Until 1614, at least, all the surviving indications portray Thorpe as a man who was typical of his time and background, a man who was climbing the social ladder, and was concerned with financial affairs and the acquisition or retention of worldly possessions, with its natural corollary, the maintenance of a household commensurate with his position. The catalogue of his progress, bearing in mind that he came of an untitled though well connected family, is impressive – educated at Staple Inn and the Middle Temple, Gentleman Pensioner, Gentleman of the King's Privy Chamber, Member of the Virginia Company of London, Member of Parliament, and finally Member of His Majesty's Council for Virginia. These appointments, judged by most standards, represent a considerable achievement.

The near certainty that he possessed a London house and his known sizeable establishment in Berkeley – over and above the Wanswell Court estate – and his involvement in repeated legislation relating to the New Grounds at Slimbridge, appear to indicate an aspiring country gentleman, ambitious of participation in court and the commercial affairs of the city. As far as may be seen in the brief references to his career in London and Berkeley, he had little, or no obvious, concern for humanitarian or religious matters.

On 29 June 1615, King James granted to a group of 117 adventurers, including George Thorpe, 'a charter of incorporation, by the name of the Governor and Company of the City of London for the Plantation of the Somers Islands, with the sole government and power to make laws, conformable to the Laws of England . . .' (Brown I, pp. 770-1, citing the *Colonial Entry Book*, vol. 17, pp. 1-46). These islands are better known today as the

Bermudas. The adventurers named included, along with Thorpe, Henry, Earl of Southampton, William, Earl of Pembroke, Lucy, Countess of Bedford, Sir Thomas Smith, Sir Edwin Sandys, Sir Samuel Sandys, Richard Martin, George Berkeley, Nicholas Ferrar, William Felgate and Ralph Hamor – all men who had already played a part in the development of the Virginia Company, or who would figure in its future history until its demise in 1624. Here then is Thorpe's second involvement in colonization, a purely financial venture.

Early in 1616, Sir Thomas Dale, a relative by marriage of Thorpe, after five years in Virginia, latterly as Deputy Governor, embarked for England and landed at Plymouth on 12 June. He brought with him John Rolfe and his wife, Pocahontas, in addition to ten or twelve other Indians of both sexes and varied ages. It is clear when the several contemporary and later accounts of Dale's arrival are put together that his coming with a large Indian contingent caused a considerable stir, and made a deep impression upon some of his contemporaries.

1.   Stith in his eighteenth-century *History of Virginia* briefly recorded that Dale arrived at Plymouth on 12 June, bringing with him 'Pocahontas, and Mr. Rolfe her husband; and carrying with them several young Indians of both sexes . . .'

2.   Alexander Brown (Brown I, p. 782) stated that Dale 'brought a very interesting party of people, including our old friend Molina,[1] Pocahontas, Rolfe and others; he started with Lymbry[2] also, but had him executed on the way.'

3.   Brown (Ibid. p. 789) also quoted extracts from two letters written shortly after Dale's arrival. (i) In the first,[3] Lord Carew informed Sir Thomas Roe, yet another relation of Thorpe, that Dale 'hath brought divers men and women of that country [Virginia] to be educated here, and one Rolfe, who married a daughter of Pohatan (that barbarous prince) called Pocahuntas, hath brought his wife with him . . .'; (ii) in the second quotation, in a letter from John Chamberlain to Sir Dudley Carleton, it is stated that Sir Thomas Dale arrived from Virginia and brought with him some ten or twelve old and young of that country, 'among whom the most remarkable person is Pocahuntas.'

4.   E.D. Neill, in his *History of the Virginia Company of London*,[4] pp. 96-7 added the fact that 'among those who came with Pocahontas as a counsellor was Tamocomo, who had married her sister.'

5.   Charles Campbell also mentioned 'some ten or twelve old and young of that country',[5] acknowledging the source of his information as *The Court and Times of James the First*, vol. 1, p. 415, but on page 119 Campbell told more of the history and purpose of Tamocomo's visit, whom he calls 'Tomocomo'. He was the 'husband of Matachanna, one of Powhatan's daughters, being a prince, and esteemed a wise and knowing one among his people, Powhatan . . . had sent him out to England, in company of Pocahontas to number the people there, and to bring back to him an account of that country.'

Thus it is clear that the Indian party of about a dozen included three groups of people. Firstly, there was Pocahontas on what, judging from her reception, might be termed a 'state visit', to help popularize Virginia, and, so it was hoped, to encourage interest and investment in, and emigration to, the colony. Secondly, came Tamocomo, who, though he could not seriously be termed a spy, was at least entrusted with the task of preparing for the mighty chief of his homeland, a report on the country of England and upon the white people who had invaded his territory and were establishing what promised to be a permanent and expanding settlement. Finally, there were the other Indians, of whom as least some were brought over to be educated, and, though this was not specifically stated, were to be led towards conversion to christianity and membership of the Church of England. Possibly the idea behind this educational scheme was that they would then return to their own people as missionaries. This policy was openly declared on other occasions when similar projects were mooted.[6] Some information on the subsequent movements of these three groups has survived. Pocahontas died in the following year just before her scheduled return to Virginia, and was buried at Gravesend.[7] Tamocomo returned safely to his native land, and presumably made his report, which may well have increased the Indian's anxiety at the constant encroachment of their territory by the white settlers. Of those to be educated, perhaps ten or so, insights can be gained into the activities of three of young females of that party from the surviving court books of the Virginia Company, and also from Captain John Smith's *General History*, from which sources the following quotations are taken.

The first of these entries, dated 11 May 1620, relates to one of the girls who had contracted tuberculosis. The minutes record that

'The Court, taking notice from Sir William Throckmorton that one of the maids which Sir Thomas Dale brought from Virginia, a native of that country, who some times dwelt a servant with a mercer in Cheapside, is now very weak of a consumption, at Mr Gouge's in the Black Friers who hath great pains to comfort her both in soul and body, whereupon for her recovery the Company are agreed to be at the charge of xx^S a week for two months, if it please God she be not before the expiration thereof restored to health or die in the mean season for the administring of Physic and Cordials for her health and that the first payment begin this day sevennight because Mr. Threr [Treasurer] for this year reported his Accompts were shut up,'[8]

Then was added the following information demonstrating the generosity of a Gloucestershire figure:

'Sir Wm. Throgmorton out of his private purse for the same purpose hath promised to give XL^S: all of which money is ordered to be paid to Mr Gouge through the good affiance the Company hath of his Careful managing thereof.'[9]

The reference to the welfare of the girl's soul suggests that she had been educated, and that religious instruction had been given.

Later that year, at a court held on 15 November, when John Smyth of

Nibley was present, the future of two other girls, presumably of that original party, was discussed. The minutes state that: 'There were appointed to take care of the two Virginia maids remaining in the Custody of Mr. William Webb the husband,[10] Vizd Mr. Casewell, Mr. Roberts, Mr. Coninge and Mr. Webb who are likewise desired to place them in good services where they may learn some trade to live by here after from which respect the Company hath promised to bestow somethings with them.'[11] On the 11 June following, a Preparative Court minuted that 'Mr. Webb moved that some course might be taken that the two Indian Maids might be disposed of to free the Company of the weekly charge that now they are at for the keeping of them. Whereupon some having moved that they might be sent to the Somer Ilands at the charge of this Company it was thought fit rather to refer it to the next Court to determine thereof.'[12] Two days later the Company's Great and General Court, at which Smyth was present as he had been at the Preparative Court, on the 11th, having considered the motion of the Preparative Court relating to the Indian girls who had 'been a long time very chargeable to the Company', ordered that 'they shall be furnished and sent to the Summer Ilands whether [whither] they were willing to go with one servant apiece towards their preferment in marriage with such as shall accept of them with that means – with especial direction to the Governor and Counsil there for the careful bestowing of them.'[13] The Court appointed a committee of eight, headed by Sir Edwin Sandys, and including Sir John Danvers, the Deputy for the Company, and Mr. John Smyth, to draw up instructions for the Governor of the Somers Ilands, so that he might be fully aware of his duties relating to the Indian girls. The Treasurer and Secretary of the Company were likewise ordered to arrange the details of their departure.

The above directives were implemented, and Captain John Smith in the following year reported on the marriage of one of the Virginian maids.[14]

It must be pointed out that Sir William Throckmorton, who donated forty shillings towards the sick girl's welfare, and John Smyth, who was present at most of the above Courts and was appointed to a committee instructed to deal with the transportation of the remaining girls, were both, along with George Thorpe and Richard Berkeley, original sponsors of the Berkeley Company. Throckmorton and Berkeley moreover, were also Gloucestershire gentry and kinsmen of George Thorpe.

So far no reference has been made to the young males who were brought over by Sir Thomas Dale to be educated. Amongst the twenty-five entries relating to members of the Thorpe families in the registers of St. Martin in the Fields,[15] are two, both apparently referring to the same person. They are unusual in their presentation. The first, dated 10 September 1619, records that a Georgius Thorp was baptized. On the 27th of the same month an entry stated that Georgius Thorp, *Homo Virginiae*, was buried. The Latinization of the christian name (I noticed no other example so rendered during the period of the search), and the description of the person as an 'Homo Virginiae', demands comment. It raises the question of the connection of this entry with George Thorpe, which in turn calls for a discussion of Thorpe's period of residence in London at this time.

The Thorpe entries as a whole suggest that at least two families of that name used that church during those fifty-one years. The family of Wanswell Court, Berkeley, was one of these, and the two American historical publications mentioned below seem convinced that one at least of the other families of Thorpe (if there were more than one other) were related to those of Berkeley.[16] The linking figure, they suggest, is one Otho Thorpe who was baptized 16 August 1606, whom they equate with the Major Otho Thorpe who appears in Virginia records and, they say, died in the parish of All-Hallows-in-the-Wall, London.[17]

George had five children by his second wife.[18] Their four sons were baptized in Berkeley Church, William (2 September 1612), John (27 September 1615), Richard (3 November 1616) and George (in September 1620 – six months after his father had sailed for Virginia). George was buried on 26 September 1620, i.e., only a few days after his baptism.

Margaret Thorpe was buried at Berkeley in November 1629, and in her will, dated 29 June 1629, and proved in the following February, she mentioned both William and John, – George had died in 1620, and presumably Richard at some unknown date. In addition Margaret mentioned her daughter, Margaret.[19] In the St. Martin's register a Margaret Thorp was baptized on 13 February 1614, a date which would 'fit in' well between that of William (September 1612) and John (September 1615). George Thorpe, their father, as stated above, was still a gentleman Pensioner in 1614, and in that same year became an M.P. Furthermore he had been a member of the Virginia Company of London since 1612 – perhaps even earlier – and may well have been elected a member of the council of that body by 1614. Thus Thorpe would, of necessity, have had to be in London for considerable periods at that time. Consequently, it would appear reasonable to assume that it was his daughter who was baptized at St. Martin's in 1614.

It is clear from correspondence surviving in the Smyth of Nibley Papers in the New York Public Library that Thorpe was operating, if not fully resident, in London for much of the time during which the terms for a land grant in Virginia on behalf of the Berkeley Company were being negotiated, i.e., 1618-19. Indeed, Thorpe's admission to the Middle Temple in February

1598, subsequent to his earlier membership of the Staple Inn, his appointment as a Gentleman Pensioner by 1604/5, and that of a Gentleman of the King's Privy Chamber at some unknown date, shows that Thorpe must have been based in London for many years.[20]

In a letter written by Thorpe to Sir George Yeardley (the lately appointed Governor of Virginia), dated 4 February 1619, relating to the recently procured patent for a plantation for the Berkeley Company, Thorpe stated that the copy of that document, which he was enclosing for the information of the Governor, had been transcribed by 'The Virginia boy of me'[21] – no name was given. This native was, obviously, a trusted and able servant, one who was capable of copying faithfully a grant of importance, legally phrased, which would satisfy the Governor of Virginia himself.

From whence, and when, did Thorpe acquire this Virginian boy? The most probable answer may be found by recalling Dale's Indian contingent and turning back to still earlier events beginning in 1611, which involved Dale and Thorpe. Early in 1611 Sir Thomas Dale, who had been serving in the Low Countries, returned to England for employment with the Virginia Company. In that February he married Elizabeth, a daughter of Sir Thomas Throckmorton, whose great aunt was Margaret Thorpe (née Throckmorton), the paternal grandmother of George Thorpe.[22]

Then in 1616 Dale returned to England in the *Treasurer*, bringing with him a party of Indians, of whom some were to be placed in English homes and educated. Pocahontas, for whom the journey was a 'good will' visit, had been 'educated'[23] during the period of her 'captivity', and had accepted baptism prior to her marriage to John Rolfe in 1614.[24] It is reasonable to suppose, in view of the Dale-Thorpe relationship by marriage, and the known interest of other Gloucestershire relations in the up-bringing and well-being of other Indians, that the latter's Virginian boy was one of the young male Indians brought over by the former. Thorpe's 'Virginian boy' was clearly in London with him on 18 February 1619, when the former wrote to Yeardley. Letters of 10 April, 2 and 20 July[25] either state, or suggest, that Thorpe was at those times in the City, confirming the supposition that Thorpe had a London house.

In ancient Rome the custom of a slave taking his master's name was well established, and in the palmy days of the plantations in British North America it was again an accepted practice. In view of this cumulative evidence, it would be reasonable to suggest that the Georgius Thorp who was baptized at St. Martin's in September 1619, and described in the entry of his burial on the 27th as *Homo Virginae*, was indeed the servant of George Thorpe of Wanswell Court, Berkeley. If this is so, then it may well betoken the first spark of those humanitarian feelings which were seen in full maturity through his regard and labour for the Indian peoples during his all too brief two years in Virginia.

Yet a third question arises from the St. Martin's entries, namely why was Georgius Thorp, probably an adult, baptized just seventeen days before his burial? Several possible reasons might be put forward, but perhaps the simplest may approach the nearest to the truth? Georgius had probably been in Thorpe's employ and household for three years or more, and had become a trusted member of his entourage, where the christian way of life was the accepted norm. Furthermore, no doubt, Georgius had received instruction in the christian faith over a long period, but without taking the final step of baptism. Suddenly illness overtook him and he felt that the end was drawing near. He was far from his home land and native peoples, but in the midst of his adoptive family to whom he has become attached. Why should he not now acknowledge his master's God, so that when death did come he would be accepted into his master's Heaven or Happy Hunting Grounds? Perhaps too George Thorpe may have pressed this course of action when the illness had reached a critical stage for his trusted servant, for whom he would have wished the full rites of christian burial, something which baptism would ensure.

If it is assumed that Georgius Thorp was indeed one of the youthful Indians brought over by Dale to be educated, and if, as it has been suggested, Thorpe himself played a part in educating his Virginian boy,[26] and instructing him in the rudiments of the Christian faith to the point at which he finally accepted baptism, is it not possible that, through this close and long association, a change of outlook or perhaps, as might be more likely, a 'bringing out' of a latent undeveloped leaning towards missionary concern was awakened? This would appear feasible. If however, Thorpe was already interested and active in humanitarian and missionary enterprises – unknown today for lack of clear evidence – then this association with his Virginian boy, and possibly with others being cared for by acquaintances in London, might well have increased that concern.

One other point in the sequence of events between 1616 and 1621 relating to the young Indian 'visitors' merits consideration.

When the plight of the consumptive girl was discussed at the Company's Court, and sick benefit was decided upon, one of the members present offered forty shillings 'out of his own purse' for the same purpose. That person was Sir William Throckmorton, a blood cousin of Thrope, and also a close relation of Dale's wife, who herself was a Throckmorton. Later when the future of the two remaining girls was being decided by the Company in 1620-

1, the Great and General Court elected a small committee to deal with the matter. An examination of the plans decided upon by the latter body shows that they were both practical and generous and, in the case of the one girl of whom later records survive, the outcome was idyllic, for Captain John Smith in his *General History* suggested an atmosphere of wedding bells and high festivity, when he wrote that 'the marriage of one of the Virginia maids was consummated with a husband fit for her, attended by more than one hundred guests, and all the dainties for their dinner [that] could be provided.'[27] The committee and the Governor had honoured their commissions.

On the committee of eight dealing with the two girls from Virginia sat John Smyth of Nibley. Is it not strange, indeed, significant, that in the three cases where the lives of members of that small party of Indian children brought over by Dale in 1616 are recorded in later years – and in almost every instance the subject was welfare – members of the Berkeley Company's founding quartet figure prominently, i.e., Throckmorton (sick girl), Smyth (two remaining maids) and Thorpe *(Homo Virginae)*?

It must be remembered, however, that Throckmorton and Thorpe were not only cousins, but also related by marriage to Dale, and were also cousins of Richard Berkeley, the heir of the cadet branch of Stoke Gifford of the Berkeleys of Berkeley Castle, to whom Smyth was steward. This may suggest that the educational and cultural experiment of Sir Thomas Dale in 1616 had some 'family' backing, for Lady Dale was a Throckmorton and her mother a Berkeley. The interest engendered by the events which followed could have been a factor in the formation of the Berkeley Company in 1618/9, and also a possible reason why Lady Dale herself in 1621 applied for a patent for a 'particular plantation' i.e., one to be founded by private enterprise. This was granted at a court held on 11 June that same year.

In May 1618 Thorpe figured in the early foundation of the Smythe Hundred, and shortly special attention will also be paid to the sharply contrasting attitudes towards religious observances, as seen through the orders of that company and the list of supplies deemed necessary for their thirty-five men, with a markedly differing approach of the sponsors of the Berkeley Company, who included Throckmorton, Thorpe and Smyth, towards the material and spiritual well-being of their party of thirty-five men only a year later. The apparently gradual development of humanitarian and spiritual concern is most marked in the case of Thorpe. And upon his arrival in Virginia the metamorphosis is seemingly complete. Consequently it is not surprising that, after his death, Thorpe was often referred to as that religious or Godly man by contemporaries and later writers.

The reason for this apparent change in Thorpe, if change there was, is not easy to determine. It may be linked to his early training at the Middle Temple, a training which may have been operative, but unnoticed through lack of documentation, during his developing career in the City. If this was not so, however, what other factors may have activated the humanitarian and missionary zeal which was so patent all through his brief but distinguished and varied period of employment in Virginia? Perhaps the most probable explanation is to be found in a combination of two or more agents, namely, the re-awakening of precepts and principles inculcated during his formative years at the Middle Temple, following upon personal experiences between 1614 and 1620. Two such experiences can be suggested:

1. Between those years Thorpe lost one son, possibly two. Infant mortality was at that period so considerable, however, and such an accepted part of life, and in addition Thorpe had several other children, that it would appear necessary to seek some other cause for his seemingly changed outlook.

2. Personally, I believe that, whatever the influence of the Middle Temple may, or may not, have been, the primary cause of Thorpe's new vision of life, giving him fresh purpose, was the return of Sir Thomas Dale in June 1616. Alexander Whitaker, one of the outstanding clergymen of the colonial period in Virginia, described Dale as religious and learned, attributes, so said Whitaker, not always found in eminent soldiers. Dale had taken part in the education of Pocahontas in the Christian faith. He had brought a number of young Indians to England that they might be taught the doctrines of the Church of England, and where they might absorb the civilities which, it was hoped, they would find in the British households where they would be placed.

The more distant objective, no doubt, was that later they should return to their people as missionaries and agents to strengthen the settler – Indian relationship – see footnote 27. It would appear that Thrope's native servant was one of Dale's importees. Dale remained in England for a year and a half. He then visited the Low Countries for a short while, before sailing for the East Indies on 26 February 1618. During the period June 1616 to December 1617 Dale would no doubt have maintained some contact with his Indians, and their foster homes, and most certainly with Thorpe. Here in the tangled web of family relationship, and Thrope's constant contact with his Indian servant, and probably with other young Indians boarded out in London homes, one can see a valid reason why his interest in, and concern for, the Indian peoples in Virginia may first have been aroused, and which, finally, came to fruition in the colony.

2. THORPE'S INVOLVEMENT IN THE NEW WORLD

It has been pointed out by Professor W.F. Craven that 'there has always appeared to be something of an hiatus in Virginia's history from the issuance of the third charter of 1612 to the events immediately preceeding the revival in 1618.'[28] His explanation was that during that period important events relating to the company were taking place in Bermuda, where in 1615 the population was double that of Jamestown as late as 1616.

The date of Thorpe's initial involvement in the affairs and activities of the New World is not known. His name, however, is included amongst those mentioned in the third charter, March 1612, who had become 'adventurers and have joined themselves with the former adventurers and planters of the said Company and society . . . and shall be brethren and free members of the Company,'[29] Thus his membership probably was registered between 1609, the date of issue of the second charter, and the granting of the third. The extent of his actual holding is also not known.

His next recorded participation stemmed from the same charter, one of the main purposes of which was to extend legally Virginia's seaward claims to include the Bermudas or Somers Islands,[30] with a view to a new colonization project by means of a fresh joint-stock issue and company. The Bermuda group of islands had been well outside the limit of settlement authorised in 1609.[31] When finally chartered, the Somers Islands colony was launched on principles that were in sharp contrast with the Virginia policy of communal investment and responsibility. Private enterprise and venture was encouraged. This, however, did not necessitate the physical presence of the investors, for at an early stage a scheme was devised whereby the various land shares were grouped into areas or districts, at first designated 'tribes', but later termed 'parishes,' with a steward or baliff in a supervisory role over each. The colony of the Somers Islands became finally established when, on 29 June 1615, King James granted to a group of more than 100 named adventurers, one of whom was George Thorpe, 'a charter of incorporation.'[32]

The inclusion of Thorpe's name in the above list is confirmation of his intention to invest in the Somers Islands Company.[33] A long letter written on 14 July 1616, to Thorpe from the colony casts some doubt on whether or not he actually paid his subscription for the share. The author of that missive, which began, 'Salutem in Christo', said that he understood that Thorpe had 'been by some discouraged as touching your share, inso much as when you came into the court to tender your money for the supplying of the said share you were informed that your land was nothing worth, but full of rocks, whereupon you reserved your money telling them that when you were

informed the truth thereof you would supply it . . .'[34] The writer, Bryan
Cave,[35] confirmed the poor quality of Thorpe's allotted share, which was plot
number twenty-one in the Harrison tribe,[36] by stating that 'as the old
subdivision stood your ground was little worth . . .' being so narrow that
there 'could be no fences left . .' Cave went on to assure Thorpe that a fresh
subdivision had taken place, and, as a result, 'All your ground lyeth together
your share is as good as any one in all the tribe both for ground, timber, and
fresh water and fishing . . .' He expressed the hope that Thorpe would no
longer be apprehensive, and confidently affirmed his belief that given 'plants
and other necessaries' the holding would be profitable. Furthermore he
offered, in view of the fact that 'your ground lyeth next to our shares', if
Thorpe wished, to 'undertake the overseeing and ordering thereof, and also
our governor will allow me a man for the manuring thereof . . .' The latter
part of the letter highlighted the rat problem,[37] and the suggested measures
being taken to eliminate the trouble.

To this letter the Governor of the colony, Daniel Tucker, took the unusual
step of adding a long postscript. He apologized for 'not having convenient
leasure at present to write you at large . . .' He expressed the hope that 'my
persuasion may prevail . . .' and encouraged Thorpe to take up his share and
'send provision for two or three men, and to that effect I have written to the
Honourable Lady the Countess of Bedford.'

Taken together the letter and postscript are illuminating on two counts. It
is clear that rats had become a major embarrassment in the colony, and that
news of these pests and the destruction wrought by them was being commented on back in England. Cave obviously was anxious not only to assure
Thorpe that his fresh holding was desirable, but at the same time to persuade
him that the difficulties presented by the rats, of which he appears to have
assumed Thorpe would have heard, could be overcome.

Secondly, it is manifest that Cave and Tucker entertained an added fear of
the effect which Thorpe's possible defaulting, through justifiable dissatisfaction, might have upon other investors. Thorpe was evidently an influential
figure in the Virginia Company, and (if Brown is correct in his assumption)
was already a member of His Majesty's council for the parent company. Thus
abrogation by him, following upon the problems caused by the rats, might
well occasion a more general loss of confidence in the whole colonization
project in the Somers Islands.

Whether or not Thorpe took up his intended investment in the Somers
Islands is not known. There is, however, amongst the Ferrar Papers evidence
that Virginia, two years later, was the scene of his involvement in another
settlement scheme. The document[38] records that as a result of Virginia

Company discussions at General Assembly and Committee levels during May 1618, it was decided to select, equip and transport a party of thirty five men to the colony. The settlement, i.e., a particular plantation, was designated the Smythe Hundred after Sir Thomas Smythe, one of the principal investors,[39] who had been Treasurer of the company. Two years later, as a result of a heavy transfer of shares it was renamed Southampton Hundred.[40]

The details of the furnishing of the party, both in clothing for the personnel and in collective equipment to be taken, give an intresting insight into the supplies deemed necessary, and their respective costs.[41]

The requirements of defence and hunting were obviously intended to be covered by such items as twenty breast plates, thirty six head pieces, twenty muskets, forty swords and daggers and two barrels of powder, 'which will allow every man 10 lbs and more . . .', and six hundred weight of lead and three melting pans. The constructional tools included pitsaws and handsaws, hewing and broad axes, a grind stone, hammers, crowbars, iron wedges and sundry smaller implements such as files, chisels, augers and nails. The agricultural requirements listed were, naturally, basic, i.e., a plough 'with all things belonging to it,' picks, shovels and spades, but no hoes or rakes were mentioned. The inclusion of nets, hooks and lines show that fish, of which the rivers and lakes in Virginia were reputed to be well stocked, were recognized as an important potential item of food, and one which, if fully exploited, could well save valuable freight space in the not too frequent supply ships.

When this catalogue of ordnance, personal equipment and stores, and agricultural and building supplies is compared with those specified for the Berkeley Company's party of thirty five men – a similar sized group – one omission emerges prominently, namely, the provision for religious observance. The seeming lack of appreciation of man's spiritual needs in the stores ordered for the Smythe Hundred is in marked contrast with the twelve page list of goods of all kind assembled for the Berkeley contingent. This (Kingsbury III, pp. 178-89) will be examined in chapter 4.

The list of 'the names of such as by order of the Court are entreated to undertake the providing of those men' for the Smythe Hundred is short – thirteen in all. Amongst those sponsors who were 'entreated' to produce the manpower, were Sir William Throckmorton and George Thorpe, each of whom was required to find two men for the party, but their occupations were not specified. Beyond the obvious financial responsibility and the obtaining of two men each for the labour force, it is not known whether Throckmorton and Thorpe took any active part in the affairs of that hundred, even to the extent of a physical presence in Virginia for a time. The reference to Thorpe by the Governor of Virginia as a seasoned settler in 1621, barely a year after Thorpe had landed at Jamestown late in May 1620, might suggest the possibility that he had had previous experience in the colony, but, personally, I think not.

This experience of Throckmorton and Thorpe in colonial investment in the Smythe Hundred may well have been one of the *stimuli* which prompted them in 1619 to organize a company of their own. Perhaps too, the apparent lack of care for the spiritual welfare of the labour force, as suggested by the list of supplies authorized, offended Thorpe and Throckmorton and persuaded them to form their own company, which would have clear humanitarian and spiritual terms of reference. Because of the paucity of documentary evidence of all kinds, e.g., records of the Virginia Company, and those of the Smythe Hundred, as well as of correspondence generally, the above suggestion can only be made under the heading of 'wild speculation', but Throckmorton's generosity towards the Indian maidens, and Thorpe's character as seen later in Virginia, would support such a possibility.

Before this section is concluded it is appropriate to consider one other matter germane, namely the date of the foundation of the Smythe Hundred. This question affects the status of the party of thirty five settlers, i.e., were they the actual foundation party or a follow-up group of colonists? There appears to be no certain answer on this point.

Amongst Argall's special missions when, in May 1617, he returned to Virginia as Deputy Governor, were (1) dealing with the share situation of the old planters, and (2) 'locating new private plantations or hundreds for the adventures in England etc.'[42] Brown added that 'The first plantations located at the charge of private adventurers under the commissions sent by Argall were: 1. "Smythe's Hundred . . . containing 80,000 acres."'[43] 2. two other named plantations. He further stated that a band of eighty settlers for those first three plantations went out in the *George*. Captain John Bargrave claimed to have been the first person to have established a private plantation in Virginia, and Brown inferred that that would have been 'about the year 1618.'[44] Argall officially took over as Deputy Governor of Virginia on 15 May 1617.[45] Several American historians, e.g., A. Brown and C.E. Hatch, state that the *George* took out settlers for the Smythe Hundred.[46] The former gives no date, but Hatch said that this took place in 1617, though he quotes no supportive evidence.

The sailing time-table for the *George* during the relevant period was as follows:

Depart	Arrive	Notes
1. England 31 March 1617	Virginia 25 May 1617	Argall aboard
2. Virginia June 1617	England ? 1617	
3. England December 1617	Virginia April 1618	
4. Virginia 25 June 1618	England October 1618	
5. England January 1618/19*	Virginia April 1619	Yeardley aboard.

*Brown stated that Yeardley 'did not sail until the first part of January; he spent "much time upon our English coast" and sailed therefrom on January 29.'

It would appear reasonable to discount that first sailing, for Argall himself was a passenger on that occasion, and although he might have begun negotiations before he left England, when perhaps he had been appointed Deputy Governor designate of Virginia,[47] he would hardly have been able to bring arrangements to such a point that the foundation party for the Smythe Hundred were able to travel with him; yet Hatch is of this mind.[48] I cannot agree for the reasons given above.

If the first voyage can be ignored, then the Smythe settlers must have sailed on the third or fifth, and to some extent the time factor would have affected by Atlantic crossing.

If it is accepted that Argall began negotiations for the establishment of the Smythe Hundred while still in England, and had brought these to an advanced state before he sailed, then this would leave him time after his arrival in the colony to locate and allocate an area for the company, and to enable a party to be assembled and equipped in time to embark in December 1617.

Thus Hatch's suggestion that the Smythe settlers 'appear to have arrived in the ship *George* in 1617' is near enough to be acceptable. There is however, as far as I am aware, no contemporary record of such a party being sent out on that voyage. But, if they did sail in December 1617, then the details discussed at the Company Courts in May 1618 must relate to a later body of men. All that can be said at this juncture is that the emphasis in the latter's shopping list, on weaponry and armour, added to the types of saws and axes and also the number of spades and shovels in the building and agricultural section, gives the impression that it was a pioneering and not a 'follow-up' expedition which was being mounted.

It must be remembered, nevertheless, that the May 1618 details might well represent an early stage in the arrangements, and that the final instructions and decision of the courts have been lost along with so many other Virginia Company records. In this case the appearance of the 'shopping list' and the absence of females in the itemized catalogue of required personnel cannot be put forward as evidence.

The extent and duration of the involvement of Thorpe and Throckmorton in the Smythe Hundred is a matter of conjecture, as is so much of the details relating to that plantation's early development. Did those two Gloucestershire gentlemen withdraw their patronage? If so, did it result from dissatisfaction, or were they rather encouraged, and desirous of forming their own company which could perhaps be ordered and governed along lines specifically humanitarian and religious, with a code of conduct more congenial and in closer accord with their own individual beliefs and practices than perhaps had been laid down for the Smythe Hundred?

3.   THORPE'S FURTHER ACTIVITIES AS SEEN IN THE FIRST SURVIVING COURT BOOK OF THE VIRGINIA COMPANY OF LONDON

In addition to the aforementioned involvements of Thorpe in the New World by reason of his membership of the Virginia Company, a few allusions are made in the extant company Court Book covering 28 April 1619 to 8 May 1622[49] to Thorpe's activities in the domestic affairs of the Company prior to his embarkation for Virginia on 27 March 1620. These will be cited briefly, before passing on to Thorpe's greatest 'adventure', the one in which he displayed qualities that showed him to be a man of considerable calibre, versatility and depth of character, and which marked him out as one of the leading figures in Virginia at that time.

The minutes for the meetings up to 21 July 1619, when the courts went into the normal summer recess before reconvening for the Michaelmas term, show that Thorpe was present on six out of the eleven occasions, one of which appears to have been an undesignated, special, or may be, a committee meeting, although the latter, to which references are frequent, were not normally recorded in detail.

One interesting item in the minutes of the Court held on 14 June dealt with the application by 'John Woodliefe Gentleman . . . to have a Patent granted to him and his Associates where on to plant the number of 200 persons to be transplanted into Virginia before the end of six years next Coming . . . which the Court hath now granted unto him.'[50] This was the leader of the first Berkeley party who was dismissed less than a year after its initial landing, on the suspicion of dubious practice.[51]

On 7 July at a court at which Thorpe was present, the Company Treasurer, Sir Edwin Sandys, requested an account of the trading affairs of the

Company's Magazine ship which, it would appear, was overdue for presentation: whereupon a bitter altercation followed during which Alderman Robert Johnson,[52] Director of that project, used most unseemly language toward the Treasurer. This resulted in a motion being passed that certain members of the Court should meet the following morning, at Lord Southampton's house, 'to consider of Mr. Aldermans words and censure him accordingly.'[53] At the following court, 13 July, 'It was agreed that for the preventing the like abuse to the Treasurer hereafter, the former committee, that is to say, the Lord of Southampton, the Lord of Warwick, Sir John Danvers, Sir Thomas Gates, Sir Nathaniel Rich, Mr. John Wroth, Mr. George Thorpe, and Mr. Deputy Ferrar to whom this matter was formerly referred . . . should set down in writing to be entered in the court books the justification which the court hath given to Mr. Treasurer . . . [and] the form of some strict Law for the preventing of the like wrong and abuse in the future time.'[54]

At that same court the Treasurer moved, in view of the weight of business to be transacted before the magazine ship should depart, and because he was proposing that the General Courts should go into recess until the Michaelmas term,[55] that a committee 'might be appointed to meet every day for the dispatch of the same.' The motion was approved and a committee, composed of Sir John Danvers, Mr. Deputy Ferrar, Mr. Alderman Johnson, Mr. John Wroth, Mr. Thomas Gibbs, Mr. George Thorpe, Mr. Granmer and Mr. Chambers were appointed. They were to meet at the house of the Treasurer which was 'near Aldersgate'.

The Michaelmas term courts began on 20 October, but it is important to observe that Thorpe's name does not appear on any attendance sheet after that date, unless he is hidden in the obscurity of the 'etc.' with which most tables end, and this, in view of his standing in the councils of the company, is highly unlikely. The reason for this absence may well stem from his growing involvement in the formation of the Berkeley Company. It will be seen later that the costs of this 'adventuring' were heavy, and Smyth, writing in 1639, stated that Thorpe had sold a goodly number of his estates both in Gloucestershire and in other counties before he himself sailed for Virginia.[56] Perhaps the approach of his own departure for the colony, and the negotiations relating to the sale of the various properties, mainly in the west, were the principal factors behind his non-attendance at the company courts. References, however, are made to Thorpe in the minutes of certain of those courts which confirm that he was, and had been, much involved in the company's affairs though absent from London. Such a reference occurred at a court which was held on 3 April 1620, a matter of seven days after Thorpe had actually sailed for Virginia.

For some time an educational project for the colony had been mooted, and indeed considerable sums of money had been donated and collected for the furtherance of this worthy cause.[57] The ways of financing, and the method of developing Henrico, and the appointment of a Deputy to the Governor of Virginia for the management of the 10,000 acre estate set aside for the creation and maintanance of this scholastic dream, had clearly exercised the Company for some time.

> It was announced on the third by the Treasurer 'that the Committee appointed in the last court for the drawing a letter for the Company to the Governor have met and finished the principal points of the same, if the court shall allow thereof, therein mentioning of 2 very sufficient and able men which are to go as Deputies for that company and to take charge of 2 particular governments under Sir George Yeardley for managing and ordering 2 parts of the public land and tenants, the one for the College, and for that have dealt [with] Mr. George Thorpe, a gentleman of his Majesty's Privy Chamber, and one of his Council for Virginia, who hath promised with all diligence to have exceeding care thereof, the other . . . yet to be nameless . . .'[58]

The above quotation is of considerable significance for it both confirms Thorpe's appointment as a Gentleman of the King's Privy Chamber, an office of some desirability, and his membership of His Majesty's Council for Virginia. It appears also to establish beyond reasonable doubt the principal purpose of his voyage to the colony in March: for it will be observed that the Treasurer stated categorically that Thorpe 'hath promised with all diligence to have exceeding care' of the college estate. This makes it abundantly clear that though a sponsor of the Berkeley Company and Hundred, Thorpe had sailed first and foremost to plan for, and supervise, the development of the Henrico estate and its seminary building programme.[59] Letters from his fellow Berkeley adventurers, Berkeley and Smyth, support this view.[60]

On 17 May following, the Treasurer 'signified to the Court the Company's former resolution for entertainment of 2 new officers by the name of 2 Deputies to govern 2 parts of the public land in Virginia, one was Mr. George Thorpe, well known to the Company for his sufficiency who is already gone, and have deputed him to govern the college lands with a grant of 300 acres to be perpetually belongong to that place [office], and 10 tenants to be placed upon the land.' In other words Thrope's stipend, as Deputy, was to be the income from the 300 acres which the tenants, provided by the Company, would work. Probably these were tenants at halves. On 26 June the Treasurer informed the court that the charter for the appointment of Thorpe as Deputy for the college lands, of Mr. Nuse as Deputy for the company lands, and of a Mr. John Pory as Secretary of the Colony was being prepared.

One has only to compare established authorities on the early history of America to realize the conflicting impressions which sometimes may be formed. This is largely due to the paucity of contemporary records which have survived, and the slight differences of interpretation which, on occasion, may be made. Brown, for example, stated that John Pory was offered the post of Secretary of Virginia by 28 November 1618, and that after some preliminary bargaining he accepted the office and sailed for the colony on 19 January 1619.[61] This appears to conflict sharply with the sequence of events recorded above, where on 26 June 1620, the charter for his secretaryship was being prepared, and at the Great and General quarter Court of 28 June that document was read, confirmed and the official seal affixed.[62] The true order of the events, however, is clear. Pory undoubtedly became Secretary of Virginia, at the invitation of the Governor designate, Sir George Yeardley, in 1618/19, and the charter of June 1620 was merely a confirmation of that appointment. That Pory was in Virginia in 1619 and playing an official part in colonial affairs is substantiated by (1) the *Proceedings of the General Assembly of Virginia, July 30 - August 4, 1619,*[63] where on the title page is written 'Mr. Pory out of Virginia 1619,' and (2) a letter sent by him from 'James City in Virginia' on 30 September 1619.[64] Other letters of an official nature were also sent by Pory in 1620 prior to the date of the sealing of the charter.[65]

At the General Quarter Court two days later came the approval and sealing of the above charter, and the announcement of a fresh, and for Thorpe an additional appointment. It was minuted that 'upon notice from Sir George Yeardley that the Councillors in Virginia must be supplied, The Court hath now chosen Mr. Thorpe, Mr. Nuse, Mr. Pountus, Mr. Tracy, Mr. David Middleton and Mr. Bluett to be of the Council of State in Virginia.'[66] The above Mr. Tracy of Hayles in Gloucestershire, and his associates had on the previous 2 February been granted an indenture for transporting 500 persons to Virginia (Kingsbury I, p. 303), and on 7 May had bought Sir William Throckmorton's quarter share in the Berkeley venture (Kingsbury III, pp. 271-4). Soon afterwards Tracy was heavily involved in assembling and catering for a follow-up party to expand the activities at Berkeley Town and Hundred.

NOTES

1. Diego de Molina, a Spanish spy in Virginia, who attempted to encourage the King of Spain to take over Virginia, because of the supposed existance of a silver mine in the colony.

2. Francis Lymbry, an English spy in the pay of Spain.

3. Published in Camden Society Publication no. 76, p. 36; also in Purches IV.

4. Published in 1869, and reprinted in 1968.

5. *History of the Colony and Ancient Dominion of Virginia*, Philadelphia 1860, reprinted, Spartenburg, S.C., 1965, p. 116.

6. Bemiss, op.cit., pp. 2, 15, 21, 73, 76, 100, 111.

7. The story of the incorrect name under which she was buried, and the account of her son, Thomas, and his descendants amongst whom are numbered many of the leading figures in American history, past and present, may be read in most American histories, but have no relevance for this study.

8. Kingsbury I, pp. 338-9. Neill (op. cit., p. 102-3) suggests that Gouge of Black Friars was the eminent Revd. Wm. Gouge, D.D., a cousin of the Revd. Alexander Whitaker who went out to Virginia with Dale in 1611, and was a minister at Henrico City. Whitaker was drowned in 1617. Gouge served at Black Friars for forty-five years before his death in 1653 (aged seventy-nine).

9. Kingsbury I, p. 339; also Neill, op.cit., p. 103.

10. A manager of property, one who has care of another's belongings or interests, a steward. A post of trust and importance as can be gauged by the scale of payments made.

11. Kingsbury I, pp. 427-8.

12. Ibid., p. 485; Neill, p. 104.

13. Kingsbury I, p. 496.

14. Smith's *General History, etc.*, London, 1632, pp. 197–8; Neill, op.cit. p. 104-5.

15. Microfilms of these registers may be examined at Westminster Public Library, London. Those Thorpe entries have been extracted and published in *WMQ*, series I, vol. 9, p. 211, and also in *VMHB*, vol. 12, pp. 171-2.

16. *WMQ*, and *VMHB* ibid.

17. Ibid.

18. Marriage entry, see Guild Hall Library MS 5015 unfoliated, i.e., the original church register. See appendix 5 for some details of the marriage settlement.

19. Jeayes, op.cit., p. 260; also in *VMHB* vol. 17, pp. 398-9, and appendix 7.

20. Despite this heavy London orientation, Berkeley was always their principal domicile.

21. Smyth I, 4; in Kingsbury III, pp. 136-7.

22. See genealogical tables in appendix 11. Further details of Dale's career from 1611 to 1616 will be found in chapter 5.

23. 'Sir Thomas Dale, Mr. Whitaker, Minister of Bermuda-Hundred, and Mr. Rolfe, her husband, were very careful and assiduous, in instructing Pocahontas in the Christian Religion.' Stith, p. 136.

24. Brown I, p. 967; Stith, p. 130 and Campbell, p. 123, both give 1613 as the date of the marriage.

25. Kingsbury, III, pp. 138-9, 148, 151.

26. Might the Virginian's ability to deal with the above mentioned legal document be related to Thorpe's education at Staple Inn and the Middle Temple?

27. Published in London in 1632, pp. 197; Neill, op.cit., p. 105. Neill quotes Smith as saying that after the maids had been converted, married and had had children they 'might be sent to their country and kindred to civilize them.'

28. W.F. Craven, 'Lewis Hughes, Plain and True Relation of the Goodness of God towards the Sommer Iland; *WMQ* series 2, vol. 17, pp. 58-9.

29. Bemiss, op.cit., p. 84.

30. It was specified that 'all and singular the said islands situated and being in any part of the said ocean bordering upon the coast of our first Colony in Virginia and being within three hundred leagues of any of the parts heretofore granted to the said Treasurer and Company in our former letters patent as aforesaid,' *See P.R.O. Chancery Patent Rolls (c.66), and printed versions in (i) Bemiss, pp. 76-94; (ii) Stith, appendix, 23-32; and (iii) Hening, vol. 1, pp. 98-110. Other clauses in the charter greatly benefited the parent Virginia Company, for it gave that body virtual autonomy, with power to elect its own officers in both companies, and even to appoint 'worthy and discreet persons fit to serve us as Councillors to be of our Council for the said plantation,' i.e., Virginia. The King, however, retained the right of veto. Their General Courts were to assume full directive powers, as against the Sovereign's hitherto nominated Council, which though retained, became in practice the administrative agent of the full Company.

31. See the second charter granted by King James to the Virginia Company, e.g., Bemiss, pp. 27-54.

32. Brown I, pp. 770-1. Based on *Colonial Entry Book*, vol. xvii, p. 1-46.

33. Most members of this Company were also members of the Virginia Company of London, which was in every sense the parent body.

34. Smyth I, 2. It is published in full in the *NYPLB*, 1899, vol. III, pp. 160-1. It is not mentioned in Kingsbury.

35. Probably one of the two Bryan Caves who were admitted to the Middle Temple in 1596 from Leicestershire and in 1600 from Coventry, respectively.

36. See map printed in General Lefroy's *The History of the Bermudaes or Summer Islands*, Hakluyt Society, 1882.

37. George, Lord Carew, in a letter of June 1616 to Sir Thomas Roe, also referred to this plague of rats. He wrote 'In the Bermudas little good is to be expected; they make some tobacco, but of other industry, I hear nothing. Since our plantation there the rats are so multiplied, whereof that island was free, as that they destroy whatsoever is planted.' Brown, I, p. 789, in Camden Society Publications, no. 76, 1860, p. 36. Also included in Purches IV, 1874.

38. Magdalene College, Cambridge. Published in Kingsbury III, pp. 94-8. Mentioned in Kingsbury I, p. 129.

39. Sir Edwin Sandys and the Earl of Southampton were also members of the subscribing body.

40. The date of the change of name was 17 May 1620 – Brown I, p. 1015.

41. It is unfortunate that the Court Books of the Virginia Company prior to May 1619 have been lost. Consequently the full details of the discussions relating to the indenture and actual formation of this very early, perhaps the first, particular plantation cannot be quoted.

42. Brown II, p. 256.

43. Ibid., p. 256.

44. Brown I, p. 824.

45. *A Hornbook of Virginia History*, Virginia State Library Publications, no. 25, 1965, p. 103.

46. Brown II, p. 256; C.E. Hatch, *The First Seventeen Years*, Virginia 1607-1624, *Jamestown 350th Anniversary Historical Booklet*, no. 6, 1957, p. 39.

47. Yeardley, who succeeded Argall, began negotiations concerning the Berkeley Hundred while he was still in England as Governor designate late in 1618.

48. Hatch, op.cit., 'The first settlers to come over in the venture appear to have arrived in the ship *George in* 1617.'

49. At the end of this volume, on an unnumbered page, is a certification, signed by the joint secretaries, Edward Waterhouse and Edward Collingwood, that the present manuscript was an exact copy of the original, now lost (see Introduction), and that the minutes of the 20 May 1620 and the early part of the minutes of the quarter Court held on the 22nd were missing.

50. Thorpe, one of the sponsors of the Berkeley Company, was not present at that Court. He might well have spoken against the grant had he been there.

51. The trouble may well have resulted from a too great attention to his own grant, which was south of the James river, and a neglect of his duties at the Berkeley Hundred. At an extraordinary Court held on 3 April 1620 (Kingsbury I, p. 331) it was reported that Martin's Hundred had suffered under an unfaithful manager, 'one Boyse entertained there to be a Bayly of their Hundred who contrary to covenants hath forsaken their Plantation and settled himself elsewhere'.

52. Alderman for Cornhill Ward, 1618.

53. Kingsbury I, p. 242.

54. Kingsbury I, p. 243-4. A copy of the minutes to the censure of the Alderman by the Committee forms no. 250 of the Manchester Papers and published in HMC, 8th report, part 2, p. 33.

55. Kingsbury I, p. 245. He proposed this 'in regard the time of the year passeth away, and most of the Company retireth themselves into the country.'

56. Smyth III, Vol. 3 p. 376.

57. Henrico College and University.

58. Kingsbury I, p. 332.

59. Ibid., p. 234. This lists the craftsmen needed for the erection of the required buildings, i.e., smiths, carpenters, turners, husbandmen, potters, brickmakers and bricklayers.

60. Smyth I, 3 (23-25); in Kingsbury III, pp. 374-81.

61. Brown I, pp. 969-71.

62. Kingsbury I, p. 382.

63. Edited by William J. Van Schreeven and George Reece, Jamestown Foundation Virginia 1969, where, on the title page, is printed 'Writeen and Sent from Virginia to England by Mr. John Pory, Speaker of the First Representative Assembly in the New World.'

64. Kingsbury III, pp. 219-222.

65. Ibid., (i) pp. 249-253 (13 January 1620), (ii) p. 254 (24 January 1620), (iii) pp. 255-8 (16 January 1620), (iv) pp. 300-306 (12 June 1620).

66. Kingsbury I, p. 383. Mr. Horwood of Martin's Hundred was also added to the list of new Councillors.

4

The Berkeley Company

1. ITS BACKGROUND – LOCAL AND NATIONAL

There are cogent reasons why the Berkeley Company entered at so early a date, and embarked so enthusiastically upon, the private settlement project in Virginia. Some of these influences were common throughout Britain, and also in parts of Europe, while others were essentially local in provenance.

Professor Bridenbaugh has discussed in some detail the general social and economic situation in Britain during the stated period, and suggested that certain factors were mainly instrumental in encouraging the emigration from this country.[1] It began as a tiny trickle in the closing years of Elizabeth's reign, and rose almost to flood proportions during the middle years of the reign of Charles I.

These *stimuli* are dealt with more succinctly by G.M. Trevelyan in his *English Social History*. The latter also put forward other non-economic reasons why the early years of the Stuart dynasty saw the commencement after a slow start of substantial colonial expansion.

The Elizabethan attempts at settlement in the New World had failed largely because of war conditions. When, however, King James I, early in his reign, had negotiated peace with Spain – precarious though this was at times – the first pre-requisite for possible colonization in the west had been achieved. The maritime experiences of British sailors during the struggle with Spain and her colonies had produced a body of men, mainly recruited, so Trevelyan suggested, from the colliers engaged on the London to north of England run and from the fishermen of Cornwall and Devon, to whom in some degree the expanse of the Atlantic had lost its terror.

The peaceful conditions encouraged also the growth of such bodies as the Bristol Merchant Venturers and the Virginia Company of London to finance and organize emigration, while seeking the rewards of exploration and exploitation of settlement in a new land, and the pecuniary advantages of an expanding overseas market for home products. That alone does not explain the rapid growth of the trading companies. Hand in hand with this desire for opening up new markets for English goods in foreign countries and in the infant, but it was hoped, growing settlements in North America, went the opportunities, as demonstrated by the Turkey, Muscovy, and East India Companies, for general trade and the acquisition of luxuries and finished products from such established trading areas as the Mediterranean and the middle and far East. There was also the possibility of obtaining fresh sources of badly needed basic essentials from both the new and old world, e.g., timber to satisfy the home demands of the slowly developing industries such as iron and charcoal, which the shrinking forests of this country had some difficulty in satisfying.

Side by side with this colonization and mercantile expansion went the necessity of establishing naval and later military bases, strategically sited for the protection both of the new trade routes and the colonial settlements, and also, if occasion demanded, of harassing Spain and her colonies, or any other possible aggressor who might threaten Virginia or similar settlements and trading areas.

Thus the conditions and means for 'foreign' settlement had been created; but what of the human element in colonization, the men and women eager, or at least prepared, to embark upon that venture of faith, the leaving of their native land in the hope of establishing a new home in a strange and distant country?

Conditions here too were propitious, brought about by several factors. Firstly, there was the problem of over population, resulting from the changing social conditions to which the country had not yet adjusted itself.[2] Then came land-hunger, especially amongst the younger sons of peasant, yeoman and country gentlemen alike, which resulted in keen competition and rising rents. Unemployment was rife, and many, especially craftsmen, felt that their labour and skills would be much in demand in the new lands. These had been well publicised by Hakluyt in *The Principall Navigations, Voyages, and Discoveries of the English Nation*, and also brought to peoples' notice through the occasional broadsheet. The spirit of adventure, which had blossomed in the Elizabethan era, also influenced the rise in emigration, especially amongst the middle and wealthier sections of the community. Indeed Virginia held out for many the promise of future release from burdensome, even acute, current problems, the somewhat restrictive conventions in England, and the possibility of personal fame and fortune. Lastly, there was for some, including, I believe, George Thorpe, the religious motive, the urge to convert and educate the native, and later in the century to obtain freedom of worship. The early planning for the University or College of Henrico, near the site of present day Richmond, symbolized that missionary desire.

In some parts of Britain there were additional specific factors which greatly encouraged – or discouraged – the preparedness of people to stake their all, and to seek a fresh start, and possible fortune, in that vast new world many weeks voyage across the generally awe-inspiring Atlantic Ocean. The Berkeley Vale, the banks of the tributaries of the Severn which rise along the Cotswold Edge from Stroud and Dursley to Kingwood, and also the district between Tewkesbury and Winchcombe were areas where local conditions, some of contemporary date, others of ancient origin, demonstrably affected the number of people ready to accept the risks of 'adventuring' westward to America.

When the economy of the Berkeley and Severn Vale and the parishes along the Cotswold Edge during the sixteenth and seventeenth centuries is examined, it is seen that the precarious and vacillating nature of the woollen industry, especially from the point of view of the labour force, was disturbing. The prospect could be said to have varied almost decade by decade from fair to frightening. Gloucestershire in general, and particularly the Stroud valley and the Cotswold Edge leading down to the river Severn, in the sixteenth century were noted for the number of woollen mills in which the broadcloth and similar products were manufactured; even so the employment graph fluctuated with discomforting frequency, producing a feeling of discontent and at times deep depression.

Dr. Jennifer Tann, in *Gloucestershire Woollen Mills*, reviews the rapid changes of fortune through which the woollen manufactury passed during the reigns of the later Tudors and the early Stuarts. Dealing with Gloucestershire as a whole, Dr. Tann stated that the number of fulling mills within the county increased during the first half of the sixteenth century, but that a serious depression occurred in the 1550s-60s. Variations of fortune continued on into the seventeenth century. Comparative prosperity returned to the local industry during the early years of King James' reign, but from about 1614 signs of impending disaster reappeared on the economic horizon, and by 1616 'Sir Julius Caesar noted grimly in Gloucestershire, Wiltshire and Worcestershire a half or a third of the local looms were out of use'.[3] When it is appreciated that there were approximately 1,500 looms in Gloucestershire, each giving employment to sixteen people, this would represent an unemployment figure of 8-12,000 in the local woollen industry. By 1620 the situation appears to have worsened, a trend which continued until by the turn of 1621/2 there was 'great distress' and 'in the clothing counties the poor assembled in troops of forty or fifty . . . demanding money and meat'.[4] Such was the potential danger, that the Council of State wrote a letter of warning

78

and advice to the Sheriff of Gloucestershire.[5] The main catchment area of the Berkeley Company would thus obviously have been greatly affected by the depressed state of the woollen industry from 1614 onwards.

Berkeley, until the seventeenth century had been a cloth manufacturing centre. In Leland's words 'It hath very much occupied . . . clothing.'[6] Leland wrote of other local towns and villages thus: 'there hath been good clothing in Thornebyry but now idleness much reigneth there.' Wotton-under-Edge was a 'praty market town well occupied with 4 clothiers', and Alderley was a 'clothing village'. Dursley was 'a praty clothing town . . . and is the principal head of the brook serving the tucking mills about the town.'

Indeed, when the locations of Gloucestershire's woollen mills are plotted it will be seen that a large percentage of the mills were sited in the watershed of three Cotswold Edge tributaries of the Severn – see map:
(1) the Little Avon which empties into the Severn at Berkeley; (2) the Cam which enters the river six miles further north at Slimbridge; (3) the Frome which drains the Stroud valley and flows into the Severn at Framilode a few miles north of Slimbridge.

The first two streams hardly merit the title of river, although the Little or Berkeley Avon gave access to the medieval port of Berkeley, and was navigable for the Severn trows as far as the town coal and stone wharf at Stock Lane as late as 1900. These two small rivers and their various tributaries, rise on the Cotswold escarpment and flow through the small towns of Berkeley, Dursley and Wotton and a large number of villages and hamlets, e.g., Cam, Cambridge, Coaley, Damery, Ham, Kingswood, North Nibley, Stone, Uley, Wanswell and Wick, all of which are within the Hundred of Berkeley, and several within the extensive ecclesiastical parish. Thus in the fifteenth to seventeenth centuries they provided considerable water-power for the woollen mills operating in that area.

When the 161 page gazetteer of *Gloucestershire Woollen Mills* in Dr. Tann's treatise is studied it will be appreciated how devastating must have been the affect of the depression in the woollen industry upon the local economy. The mills of the Berkeley Avon watershed occupy thirty one pages, the Cam twenty-three, while the Frome, which drains the Stroud and Slad valleys, and flows on through the Stanleys and Stonehouse on into the Severn at Framilode, takes up 103 pages, thus leaving four pages for the rest of Gloucestershire. The number of mills in one township may be judged from Smyth's words in his *Lives of the Berkeleys* 'In the eastern part of the village of Nibley arise springs of excellent sweet water; where on are seated seven tuck mills and grist mills, most of them double mills before the said stream be passed through the village.'[7]

Thus the diastrous state of the woollen industry in Gloucestershire could have been a major factor in the conception and birth of the Berkeley Company in the winter of 1618/19, and the formation of the strong contingents sent out to Virginia in September 1619 and again in September 1620. A number of Berkeley, Nibley, Uley and Wotton-under-Edge persons can be identified in one or other of the parties.

It was another, and possibly equally powerful factor, which brought Virginia to the attention of people living more than thirty miles north east of Berkeley, and which undoubtedly played a major part in the recruitment of personnel for the second large group of emigrants for the Berkeley plantation in September 1620.

Dr. Joan Thirsk reviewed, in two essays[8] upon which I have drawn heavily, the economic conditions and changes in the Tewkesbury Vale, and especially the eastern half, during the early seventeenth century. She made special reference to the introduction, at a particular moment in time, of a singular, agricultural experiment, in the district around Winchcombe, and made this pertinent observation. She wrote, 'The Virginia plantation [colony] first aroused the enthusiasm of Gloucestershire gentry from another part of the county before those in the Winchcombe district took any serious interest.' The explanation for this apparent lateness of involvement in colonial settlement lay in the timing of the cultural, social and economic vicissitudes through which much of the Tewkesbury Vale passed during the first two decades of that century.

Dr. Thirsk pointed out that early in the seventeenth century poverty in the eastern half of the Vale of Tewkesbury 'was a byword.'[9] Industry except for a little of the cottage variety, e.g., glove and clothmaking etc., was virtually non-existent, while arable land in no small measure had given way to livestock pastures. The Winchcombe district had become 'a pastoral region with an excess of unused or under-used labour.'[10] The small towns too 'suffered the same poverty' as the neighbouring countryside.

Between the dissolution of the monasteries and the early years of the seventeenth century a number of wealthy members of the Livery Companies had bought properties in the Tewkesbury – Winchcombe area, e.g., Hicks, Hayning and Whitmore. They in conjunction with some of the less affluent gentry, e.g., Giles Broadway (Postlip) John Ligon (Arle Court, Cheltenham), the Tracys of Toddington and Hayles and John Stratford[11] of Farmcote launched in 1619 – possibly even in 1618, a scheme for tobacco growing in the area.

Some also had embarked upon other agricultural manufacturing projects, e.g., oil from cole-seed, wine and salt[12] production and soap making, all of which, incidentally, outlasted the tobacco experiment as stable local enterprises.

These new agricultural occupations, especially the tobacco growing, gave promise of brighter prospects for the hitherto unemployed labour force, and at the same time held out the possibility of financial gain for those 'farming' the new ventures, particularly the tobacco growers, and those who had rented land for its cultivation. The success of this Gloucestershire tobacco experiment was shortlived, for the Virginia Company and colonists and the King feared that the continued successful cultivation of tobacco in England might well have an adverse financial affect upon them, and steps were taken to prohibit tobacco growing in this country.

At a Virginia Company Court on 8 January 1620 tobacco figured prominently in the discussions, and it was reported 'by Mr. Treasurer that his Majesty out of love and affection to the Company have given order for the inhibiting of the planting of English Tobacco for these five years . . .' [13] Certain strings were attached, that have no relevance for this study. In that royal proclamation the King was frank about his personal antipathy towards tobacco, and gave certain sound financial reasons why its cultivation in England, must, at least for a period, be banned. He wrote 'It is not unknown what dislike we have ever had of the use of tobacco, as tending to a general and new corruption both of men's bodies and manners; nevertheless it is of the two more tolerable that the same should be imported amongst many other vanities which come from beyond the seas then permitted to be planted here within this realm, to abuse and mis-employ the soil of this fruitful Kingdom . . . The Colonies of Virginia and the Somers Islands are proper and natural climates for that plant, and receive much comfort by the importation of it into this Kingdom, and it tends to increase our Customs.' [14] That proclamation sounded the death-knell of legitimate tobacco growing in this country, although its unlawful cultivation continued on a small scale for many years. [15]

It was without doubt this legislation, which brought back again to the above area the spectre of unemployment, which was a principal reason why, when the 1620 follow-up party for the Berkeley Plantation was being assembled, a considerable number of volunteers – men, women and children – came from the Winchcombe, Hayles and Postlip area. This recruiting was undertaken by William Tracy of Hayles who on 2 February 1620 had his Indenture 'allowed and sealed' by the Great and General Quarter Court of the Virginia Company, to transport and settle 500 persons to Virginia. [16] On 15 April following Tracy wrote a letter to John Smyth [17] in which is seen the first real hint that he intended to join the Berkeley Company. This became an actuality when he bought Throckmorton's share in that body on the 7 May following. [18]

Those interested in the background of tobacco smoking and its introduction into Europe, and the mixed reception it received, might consult the latter part (pp. 81-120) of James VI of Scotland, I of England, *A Counterblast to Tobacco*, London 1604, reprinted and edited by Edward Arber, London 1869.

Those forty pages, in addition to the 'Counterblast', contain a brief history of the introduction of tobacco into the Old World in the sixteenth century, and also a series of interesting descriptions of methods of tobacco smoking – termed by Henry Bultes, a Fellow of C.C.C. Cambridge, in 1599, 'Dry Drink', and also varied opinions, both medical and lay, as to the properties and effects of tobacco upon man's mental and physical health. Indeed the anti-smoking lobby today have here almost all the ammunition they require to mount a major campaign against the pernicious weed of the 'Counterblast'!

Yet a third local factor may have encouraged local volunteering when the Berkeley Company was launched, namely Berkeley's long maritime tradition. Smyth records that charters from the time of Henry III show that through 'warfage and Toll' in the past 'Great profits came to the lords of this borough town.'[19] Maurice IV, Lord Berkeley (1361-8), maintained a vessel which traded with France, taking out corn and wool and bringing back wine. His son, Thomas IV, Lord Berkeley (1368-1417), in March 1404 was appointed Admiral of the King's ships from the mouth of the Thames to Lands End, and also a Privy Counsellor. He was instructed to be afloat that year for three months. He led in his own retinue five Bannerets, eleven Knights, 285 Esquires and 600 Archers, and it was laid down that his twenty-one ships had to be double manned with mariners. In the following year Admiral Berkeley's fleet attacked 140 'tall ships' sent by France to aid Owen Glendower. The engagement was an English victory, for they burned fifteen ships and 'took fourteen others stuffed with men, armour and victuals. And so returned with honour and profit.'[20] During the reign of Henry VIII the *George* of Berkeley traded at least as far south as Bordeaux, while the sixteenth century South Wales port books record Berkeley merchants transporting cargoes which included oranges, lemons, wheat and barley malt. Berkeley continued as a small port to within living memory. The last Severn trows to use the town wharf were the *Lavender* and the *Industry*.[21] Thus with Berkeley having an extensive frontage on the Severn (a mile wide for much of that length), and with its men, some also no doubt recruited from neighbouring towns and villages, engaged in coastal and overseas trade, and from time to time in naval warfare too, local people would have a familiarity with the sea that lessened the natural dread of ocean travel.

In consequence of the above conditions the four initial sponsors of the

Berkeley Company, Berkeley, Smyth, Thorpe, Throckmorton, and later Tracy of Hayles, probably saw the Virginia venture as socially desirable, giving land-hungry or unemployed members of the local workforce – especially in the Berkeley Vale, Cotswold Edge and Winchcombe areas – the hope and opportunity of employment, of acquiring land, and, maybe, of making their fortune.

The repercussions of the industrial conditions can clearly be seen in the *Margaret's* bills of lading,[22] the nominal rolls of the Berkeley parties and in Tracy's claim that he could find twenty 'promised' people prepared to make the voyage to the New World.[23] Tracy's boast was not without foundation, for on his first and only voyage – he died less than three months after landing at the Berkeley plantation – he was compelled to leave behind a number of those wishing to embark with him.

These then are some of the local reasons for the success behind the formation of the Berkeley Company.

2. THE BERKELEY COMPANY – ITS GENESIS

Before the formation of the Berkeley Company is considered, it would seem advisable to examine the instructions relating to land tenure issued to Sir George Yeardley on 18 November 1618 before his departure to take up his office as Governor of Virginia. This document, commonly termed 'The Great Charter' of the Virginia Company of London,[24] reveals the extent of the policy changes in colonization methods which had slowly been evolving over several years in relation to the status of settlers. This re-orientation has been called 'a triumph of the colonization over the purely exploitative viewpoint.'[25] In other words, private enterprise had been allowed in some measure to replace the discredited and bankrupt communal policy of the earlier days.

In the Great Charter the ancient planters[26] were now allocated, when the 'time of their service to the company . . . shall be expired',[27] 100 acres of land in the colony free of all quitrent.[28] This applies both to those who had ventured at their own expense and also those who had come over at the cost of the Virginia Company. It was Sir Thomas Dale who had fostered the principle that private incentive should replace the hitherto company-controlled labour force.[29]

Those settlers, who had arrived in the colony after the departure of Sir Thomas Dale, received, or had the prospect of, land in varying acreages and on differing terms. The 'new' arrivals, not being stockholders of the company, who financed their own equipping and transportation, received fifty acres for which an annual quitrent of one shilling was to be paid. In addition they would receive fifty acres for each person they transported and equipped at their own expense within seven years. Here too the quitrent was to be one shilling per fifty acres. Those who went at the cost of the Company as Tenants at Halves for a period of seven years were to receive no outright grant of land, but were allowed to rent land with no specified acreage laid down.

Shareholders of the Company,[30] understandably, were treated more generously, and were to receive 100 acres for each paid up share held by them, and fifty acres for each person whom they brought over and financed, provided that that person resided in the colony for three years (though the residence need not be continuous) or died after embarkation had taken place. In each instance no quitrent was to be paid. It was under this last system of grants that the Berkeley Company was formed, for all its sponsors were share holders of the Virginia Company.

The date of the commencement of the negotiations between the Berkeley adventurers and the parent body, the Virginia Company of London, is not known. The indenture itself, the references made by Thorpe to incidents in the preliminaries in a letter of 18 February 1619, and the movements of Sir George Yeardley in 1618 to January 1619 suggest that they had probably begun by the Michaelmas term of 1618, bearing in mind the time required for the passage of the grant through the Company's Courts and committees to its final promulgation.[31]

The indenture itself is the earliest known surviving official document relating to the establishment of the Berkeley Company and its plantation in Virginia. It is a contemporary copy and is numbered 3 (4) amongst *The Smyth of Nibley Papers* in New York Public Library.[32] The conciseness of declaration and detail in the opening lines merits quotation in full:

'This indenture made the third day of February in the year of the reign of our sovereign James by the Grace of God of England Scotland France and Ireland King Defender of the Faith etc. That is to say, in the year of his reign of England, France and Ireland the sixteenth and of Scotland the 52nd. Between the Treasurer and Company of Adventurers and Planters of the City of London for the first colony in Virginia with the advice and consent of the Council of the same of the one part, And Sir William Throckmorton of Clowerwell[33] in the County of Gloucester Knight and Baronet, Sir George Yeardley now Governor of Virginia Knight, Richard Berkeley of Stoke [Gifford], George Thorpe of Wanswell [Berkeley] and John Smyth of North Nibley in the said county of Gloucester, Esquires, free of the said company of Virginia and who have severally adventured for their several shares here after mentioned and for every of the said shares, either they or those whose estates they now have or shall have, have paid or are to pay within one year after the date hereof £12. 10s. 0d.

Gloucestershire men had contracted for ten shares each and Yeardley for five,[34] thus securing for the Berkeley Company a basic 4,500 acres of land. They in their turn pledged themselves 'to transport at their own cost and charge divers persons into Virginia, and there to erect and build a Town and settle and plant divers inhabitants there for the advancement of the general plantation of that country'. Furthermore they promised to 'place preachers, build churches, schoolhouses and suchlike works of charity . . .'. In consideration of this undertaking a further 1,500 acres were allotted to them, an allocation similar to that made to the four cities or Boroughs of Jamestown, Henrico, Charles City and Kiccowtan[35] in the Great Charter of November 1618, and designated the common lands of the respective city or borough.

The wording of the indenture shows that the selection of the land for settlement was, technically, in the hands of the Berkeley officials, but there were certain specific limitations, e.g., it must be an area 'not already or heretofore inhabited by any English and wherein no English person or persons are already placed or settled, or have by order of court made choice of, nor within ten miles'[36] unless separated by a river. Furthermore the choice had to be made 'with the privity and allowance' of the Governor and Council in Virginia. Obviously the local body would have to make some sort of preliminary selection, but it would appear that the proprietors had some say in the matter, as is evident from subsequent correspondence. Sir George Yeardley, writing to John Smyth on 10 January 1620[37] said that he had 'planted' the Berkeley party 'in a very good and Convenient place.' He went on to add that the selection was disapproved of by Captain Francis West, brother of the late Lord Delaware who had been Governor of Virginia, 1610-18. Captain West, it would appear, had plotted land for members of his family, but had not before his departure 'obtained any grant from me of that which he did lay out.' In the same letter Yeardley announced his final withdrawal of his partnership in the Berkeley venture, giving as his reasons 'my public employments, and partly my engagement to bring out of England at my charge twenty-five men this year to furnish Smythe hundred . . .'. He also expressed his desire to offer every assistance needed to Captain John Woodleefe and his settlers. In conclusion he wished those of the Berkeley Company in England and in Virginia 'Your happiness of a New Year.'

The indentures also outlined the fifty acres land grant policy for each member of the Berkeley plantation party. Furthermore it confirmed the fact that the company was to all intents and purposes autonomous, provided that their local laws and directives conformed to those of England and of the Virginia Company. Finally it was laid down that a record of every person transported for or by the Berkeley Company should be entered in a register specially kept for the purpose.

Stoke Park, Stoke Gifford, by J. Kip – the home of Richard Berkeley

Nibley House by J. Kip – the home of John Smyth

The declaration 'to erect and build a Town and settle and plant divers inhabitants there for the advancement of the General plantation of that country' suggests that from the very start, the Berkeley Company's concept of colonization was that of a Gloucestershire village being transported to a new site where it would thrust down its roots and become a self-supporting and self-sufficient community. It will be seen that this idea is fully borne out when the passenger and shopping lists of the 1619 and 1620 emigrant parties are examined.

The next mention of the newly formed Berkeley Company comes in a letter dated in London 18 February 1619 and addressed to Sir George Yeardley, the recently appointed Governor of Virginia. This is a contemporary copy, and is over the names of the four Gloucestershire adventurers Wm. Throckmorton, Rich. Berkeley, Geo. Thorpe and John Smyth, and was obviously written with the knowledge and consent of all four. The originator clearly was Thorpe. This brief letter merits careful analysis, for it contains three casual remarks, each of which is of significance.

Thorpe, as has been pointed out, appears to have been resident in London, at least business-wise, for some years, while the other three, judging from surviving letters to and from them, came to London from time to time but dwelt principally in Gloucestershire. Bearing this in mind and that Thorpe was a member of the council of the Virginia Company, it is understandable that he should write to the Governor to inform him that the awaited Berkeley indenture had finally been sealed and received.

The first paragraph is full of interest, for, having announced that they had procured their patent for plantation in Virginia, Thorpe stated that a copy of that document was enclosed, 'written by the Virginian boy of me George Thorpe, wherein according to your agreement with me George Thorpe your name is used for five shares . . .'. Thorpe obviously felt that Sir George Yeardley, both as a participant in this venture and also as one with whom details of the grant had been discussed, should be fully aware of its promulgation, and its final terms. These comments of Thorpe establish his authorship of the letter and the fact that he had been personally involved in the negotiations. It was at the time when Yeardley was Governor designate, and so Thorpe had both a personal and official interest in the formulation of the application for a grant and its passage through the committees and courts – at least until his departure for the colony.

The significance of the transcription of the grant by the Indian servant of Thorpe, having been aired in the previous chapter, needs no further comment. The letter also contains reference to a transportation ship being wind-bound in Ireland. This has caused speculation, and needs to be looked at carefully.[38]

What are the facts and the implications? A cursory reading suggests that a Berkeley pioneering party had been prepared, which, but for the misfortunes of weather, would already have been launched upon the great adventure – 'We had also sent our men and ship at this time,' seems to imply such a state of readiness. Weight however, must be given to subsequent statements.

1.   The ship had been held up in Ireland 'since before your departure to this present'. Sir George Yeardley sailed for Virginia in January 1619.

2.   '[we] do intend (god willing) that she shall leave the coast of England, by the first of August . . .'

3.   '[we] desire before that time (if possible) to understand from you what proportion of victually and munitions will be fit to send with them.'

In a measure (1) and (3) appear contradictory, for, in the first, Thorpe is saying that but for bad weather they, the Berkeley Company, would already by 18 February have sent out their initial pioneering party; while in (3) the Governor is being informed that they will not be sending out their settlers in August until, if possible, Yeardley has had time to advise them on what food supplies and weaponry will be necessary for the colonists to take with them. This was said in the knowledge that the Governor, having left English waters on or about 29 January could not reach Virginia before March at the earliest, and probably April,[39] and that a letter of information and instruction could not reasonably be expected to arrive back in England before May or June. That might just leave time for the final assembly of men and material by 1 August, the new date of departure proposed in (2).

Even supposing that Thorpe and his fellow Berkeley adventurers had in their preliminary negotiations with Yeardley obtained a 'wants list' for their members, it would appear improbable that their expedition would have been equipped to the point of sailing by 18 February.

What Thorpe may well have been attempting to do was to offer the weather as an excuse – a very real one indeed – for the now obvious delay in the departure of their party and the consequent inability to meet a possibly previously discussed schedule. Had a genuine attempt been made to launch their expedition by or before 18 February it is strange, Smyth being so efficient a recorder and retainer of documents,[40] that not a single manuscript relating to the preparations has, to my knowledge, survived. The identity of the wind-bound ship is not known. The last two paragraphs of Thorpe's letter of February 1619 relate to (1) an offer to Sir George to take up a full fifth share in the expedition, with the enjoiner that if this invitation were accepted, then he would, by the ship bearing this letter, send 'so much merchantable commodities as doth amount to a fifth part'. No actual figure is given. (2) A request that Sir George would select a suitable site for their plantation, i.e., '[I] do entreat your effectual furtherance in choice of a place where we shall sit down,'

Six weeks later a letter from Richard Berkeley to John Smyth[41] reveals that planning was under way. The main subject was that of a leader for the Berkeley colonists. The writer put forward the name of a kinsman named William Chester whom he considered 'worthy and fit', and who seemed 'willing to undertake the command of our men and care of our common business there.' Berkeley also recommended a surgeon from Bristol who was 'well reported of for more than ordinary skill,' He ended by reporting that he had written of both to Throckmorton and 'my cousin Thorp', and that when he received favourable replies from them and from Smyth himself he would sign up both Chester and the surgeon.

One short part sentence, in which Berkeley writes about Chester, has quite startling implications. He said that Chester was prepared 'to accept a share for the years we continue a joint course, and those ended, a man from each of us with land for himself and those men.' The purport of that remark could be that from the very planning stage there was an understanding that at some time in the future, presumably when the town and hundred of Berkeley in Virginia had been fully established, the sponsors would dissolve their partnership, and each set up his own estate, presumably under the common umbrella of the original indenture. This possibility will be considered again when William Tracy's grant, issued in 1620, is evaluated.

This letter, which begins 'Mr. Smith', and ends 'Your assured loving friend, Rich: Berkeley', demonstrates the relationship between Smyth and the other three. The latter in various letters term one another 'cousin', while Smyth is either 'Mr. Smyth' (as here), 'Sir', or 'Dear Friend.' It is interesting to look forward eighteen years and to note that Smyth at long last became one of the 'family' when his second daughter, Ursula, married Thorpe's eldest son, William.

On 10 April Throckmorton wrote from Clearwell to Smyth,[42] beginning 'Sir', and referring to Berkeley and Thorpe as cousins. He understood, he said, that Smyth was going to London on the following Monday, and expressed the intention of being there himself a week later. He asked Smyth on his arrival in the city to remind Thorpe to answer a letter which he, Throckmorton, had sent some time earlier 'concerning our forest business.' The writer next said that he would be leaving orders that £10 should be forwarded towards the repairing and furnishing of our ship for Virginia. This sum represented, it was hoped, a quarter share of the believed cost. Did this mean that the previously mentioned ship windbound in Ireland had returned and was undergoing repairs in some English port? If so, was that port Bristol?

In the same letter Throckmorton also requested Smyth to assist him in obtaining twelve men 'for my part according to your promise; for that these parts are so barren of men fit for that complement that I must rely wholy upon your help therein.' This request that Smyth should find twelve men for him, and the letter of 18 February giving fifty as the expected strength of the initial settlement party seems to suggest that either Throckmorton was not very energetic in trying to raise a quarter of that complement or that the Forest was an extremely unresponsive area. In view of his ultimate withdrawal from the company thirteen months later the first alternative might well have been the reason.

Throckmorton finally passed on to the subject of Will. Chester, and expressed the hope that they, the four Berkeley adventurers, would all be of one mind in that appointment because of his suitability: 'And I think that the sparing him one man out of each of our parties will be plentifully recompenced with the service he will do us there.' This sparing a man by the four sponsors (as suggested by Berkeley in his letter of 3rd April) appears to envisage that this was one of the terms demanded by Chester, and that it would have an immediate operative date, at least from the moment of landing at their grant.

The letter has two endorsements. The first by Smyth merely noting that it was from Throckmorton and related to 'Chester to be our Cheefe'. The second (hand unidentified) runs 'Mr Effington a pertens [= appertaining to] Mr. Woodleefe's letter and proposit[ions] the copy of the invoice and money about Walter Copy and others. tools and implements.' This is puzzling. It ignores Chester and introduces the name of John Woodleefe who actually headed the first Berkeley party. It seems to suggest that someone – probably Smyth – had already been in touch with Woodleefe, who, it would appear from the mention of invoice, money, personnel and implements, had some connection with the preparations already established. I believe that Smyth had already begun negotiations with Woodleefe, and that this fact was known to Throckmorton and caused him to express the hope that all might be in agreement on the matter of Chester, i.e., an attempt to influence Smyth in Chester's favour.

More than two months passed before the date of the next surviving letter from any of the Berkeley adventurers. This missive, dated 2 July,[43] was written by Thorpe, presumably from London, to Smyth at Nibley. The preparations were well under way, for the letter begins 'I have received all our muskets for Virginia and the mills are almost ready. I have likewise bought divers . . . other things' and added that he would shortly be sending all the things which he had obtained. Thorpe then stated that he had arranged with Thomas James and 'my servants at Wanswell to pay presently unto you £50 which I hope with what I have formerly laid out and shall lay out here will go near my part [share] of the Voyage.' Finally Thorpe asked Smyth, if he believed that Throckmorton was displeased with him (Thorpe) – which he doubted – that he would assure him that 'according to my letter herewith' Throckmorton's accounts would soon be settled.

A few days later Thorpe, as has been stated, was appointed to and served on, the committee of the Council of Virginia which had been instructed to consider and deal with Alderman Johnson's outburst against, and abuse of, the Company Treasurer, Sir Edwin Sandys. These committee meetings and the Courts probably took up time which he could ill spare.

Thorpe on 20 July again wrote to Smyth.[44] The original is badly mutilated with many missing words, some of which have been added in a transcript made by a Mr. Lydenburg of the New York Public Library.[45] Because of its condition, and because Thorpe was, obviously, writing under some stress both of time and circumstance, it is not possible to be certain of the full message in the letter. He begins, 'I am an ill writer', which, judging by his other surviving letters, he was not, 'and therefore I pray pick my meaning out of the general letter.' This could suggest that this existing letter was a covering one for a longer and more informative epistle which has been lost.

The first part of the letter appears to centre round one by the name of Partridge. Whether this was Richard or Thomas – both of whom appear in Berkeley records – is uncertain; I follow Kingsbury, because of circumstantial evidence, in assuming that it is the former, who figures frequently in the shopping lists of the first Berkeley colonists, and who embarked for Virginia with Thorpe on 27 March 1620, and died there.[46] He is included in two surviving lists of subscribers to the Virginia company, the first of which[47] is conjecturally dated at 1618, while it is stated that the second[48] (both quote £25 as the subscription figure) represents payments made while Sir Thomas Smythe was Treasurer of the Company, i.e., before Sir Edwin Sandys replaced Smythe on 28 April 1619.[49]

Thorpe expresses sorrow that Partridge 'hath so behaved himself, that he is lost'. He adds that he has sent for his (Thorpe's) horses, and that Partridge is to bring them. It appears that the purchase and transportation of goods for the expedition lay behind these fragmentary and disjointed remarks. The closing portion of the letter contains two interesting and personal statements by Thorpe. He says firstly that he will speak with Lady Dale herself (a relation) 'concerning her promise to you', i.e., Smyth. Lady Dale, a little later, herself became an adventurer, so perhaps she was at that time contemplating a stake in the Berkeley Company? Alternatively the promise may have relevance to a transfer of cattle which became the subject of a court case after the Indian massacre. Secondly, Thorpe assured Smyth that his delay in coming to Berkeley (or was it Bristol?) was caused entirely by his efforts 'to hasten Mr. Woodleefe and the mariners.'

On 3rd August Sir Edwin Sandys, Treasurer of the Virginia Company, dispatched a letter to the Governor of Virginia, Sir George Yeardley, commending the Berkeley Company to him.[50] Although short it is quite remarkable, whether viewed as an official missive or a plain reference, for here is the head of the Virginia Company writing direct to the head of the colony requesting him to accord the Berkeley settlers privileged treatment. So deliberate and so personal is the appeal, coupled with a reminder of Thorpe's standing in the Company, that the inclusion of the letter would seem proper.

> To my honourable friend Sir George Yeardley knight governor of Virginia.
>
> Sir, I commend unto your good favour and care, the beginning plantation of Sir William Throckmorton and Mr. George Thorpe (who is of the Council) with other gentlemen their associates, who send to you by this ship fifty persons to that end. Their desire is that they may be well placed, and have such other assistance as their case shall need, and your place with your experience[51] can best afford. You shall hereby much bind them in love to you and make me also beholden to you for their sakes. So with heartiest commendations I rest
>
> Your assured loving friend
>
> London 3 August 1619.   Edwine Sandys'.

Dr. Susan Kingsbury, following the pagination of the Smyth of Nibley papers in New York, has rightly run Smyth I, 3(13-16)[52] together. These are dated in July, August and September, and are the shopping lists of the goods and equipment purchased for the Berkeley colonists, and certain other expenses incurred in mounting the expedition. It would seem sensible that these should be considered as a whole and not chronologically, for thus a fuller appreciation of the careful and detailed planning behind the dispatch of the Berkeley party will be possible. This important composite account will be considered immediately before the departure of the settlers is discussed.

The next official document featuring the Berkeley Company deals with the chartering of a ship for the transportation of their party to Virginia, and is dated 18 August 1619.[53] The respective negotiators were an Edward Williams 'of the City of Bristol marchant owner of the good ship called the *Margaret* of Bristol of the burden of 45 tuns or thereabouts' . . . and John Woodleefe 'of the Town of Buckingham Esqre Marchant lader . . .' One Henry Penry was the Master for the voyage.

The chartering of the ship

The terms, in brief, were as follows:

1.   The party would sail 'with the first fair wind and weather . . . after the XVth day of September next,' from the port of Bristol called Hungrode 'as directly as wind and weather will permit' to any port in Virginia that Woodleefe 'or his factors or assignees' shall decide.

2.   The ship would discharge its 'burden' and remain in Virginia as long as required before returning, reladen at the pleasure of the said leader to Hungrode.[54]

3.   Hire. Within fifteen days after the ship's return to Bristol the owner would be paid £33 per month of twenty eight days, reckoning from the day of sailing.

4.   Duration in Virginia – limit of fifty days.

5.   The owner was to ensure that, at his own cost, the ship was fully seaworthy and 'well apparelled, and victualled and sufficiently furnished as well with able Master and seven other sufficient men and one boy' to man the vessel.

6.   The Master his crew and mariners were to give Woodleefe and his party all reasonable service.

7.   Woodleefe was to be 'ready with his men, goods, provisions and other things aboard' by 15 September.

8.   That if '(which god forbid)' the ship 'shall be robbed or spoiled on the sea salt or fresh [during the voyage] of any manner of goods wares provisions or marchandizes' then the owner and Woodleefe 'shall stand to his own loss . . .'

9.   A bond of £400 was to be given by the Berkeley Adventurers and Woodleefe. The last requirement has 'cancelled' written alongside in the margin.

Early in September four documents were issued by Throckmorton, Thorpe, Berkeley and Smyth to Captain Woodleefe. The first, undated, was headed 'Remembrances', and contained explicit instructions relating principally to his specific obligations to those Adventurers. The remainder, all dated 4 September 1619, were 'A Commission to Captain Woodleefe', the 'Agreement' between the Adventurers and Woodleefe, which was largely concerned with the financial details of responsibilities of both parties; while the last – the most important from the point of view of this essay – is entitled 'Ordinances directions and Instructions to Captain John Woodleefe.' These and especially the 'Agreeement' and 'Ordinances' are long. They will therefore be considerably shortened, but the principal points will be made clear.

This group of five documents,[55] along with the purchasing and expenditure lists,[56] and the roll-call and details of the settlement party,[57] plus the four records which follow them in Kingsbury III, and dated September 7th,[58] 9th,[59] 15th 1619,[60] and 16 September 1619 – 16 September 1620,[61] all preserved amongst *The Smyth of Nibley Papers* in New York, constitute a collection unique in the annals of any early seventeenth-century 'particular' (private) plantation in Virginia, and in as much as they reflect decisions by Thorpe amongst others, they are of inestimable importance in this study. They need to be considered carefully.

Documents relating to Woodleefe and the Berkeley Settlement

I.   Remembrance to Woodleefe

Ten personal tasks, over and above the routine duties connected with settlement organization, are tabulated in this first document, concluding with general instructions:

1.   Woodleefe must inform the Adventurers of the details of the follow-up party, i.e., number of men and women required, date of their departure and the necessary equipment and stores to be sent with them.

2.   He is to deliver all letters carried (including one from Sir Edwin Sandys) to the Governor, copies of which were enclosed for Woodleefe's information, He must also obtain and despatch the Governor's reply.

3.   Tobacco seed must be sent to Mr. John Smyth. This, in view of the tobacco growing experiments then beginning in the Winchcombe area, is interesting, and suggests some intercommunication, if not co-operation, between the Winchcombe and Berkeley districts.

4.   Partridge – if the same as in Smyth I, 8; (in Kingsbury III, p. 151) – again appears to be troublesome, and Woodleefe is required to ascertain whether or not Partridge will be joining the Berkeley party. Confirmation comes later that Partridge was already in Virginia.

5.   A certified list must be obtained from the Governor or his deputy of the number and names of the party who actually landed in Virginia. Thus the names of those who (as did occasionally happen) disembarked in Ireland, or who (as frequently occurred) died at sea, might be known.

6.   Woodleefe must verify whether (or not) the Governor was taking up the option of a fifth share in the enterprise.

.7.   Woodleefe was to make the 'best speedy use' of the 'trucking stuffs' (trading goods?) taken with them, i.e., 'beads, hatchets, copper, shoes, knives'. Most of these items obviously would be used for barter with the Indians.

8.   He was to ensure that all seed planting was undertaken at the correct

time so that the development programme would not be upset.

9.　Young Thomas Peirse, as his father requested, was to be trained as a carpenter. This lad may have been the son of Henry Peerse, Gent, who was also a member of the Party, amongst whom there were three carpenters and two joiners.

10.　The ship's carpenter shall 'upon arrival fall in hand with making our boat, otherwise we lose the charge laid out for the materials and you the needful use and hope of profit.'

From this last short sentence two points emerge. Firstly, a 'professional' in the person of the ship's carpenter was being used for the designing and building of their own small craft for the plantation's use. This was understandable, despite the fact that one or more of the three carpenters in the party, drawn no doubt from the Berkeley Vale or the adjacent Cotswold Edge, probably had some knowledge of boat building. Secondly, it throws light on the normal location of the various Virginian plantations and their trading practices. Most of the plantations then established were sited, ribbon fashion, along the north and south banks of the James river or one of its tributaries. Water was the principal and most practical means of communication between plantations and other centres of population such as the capital, Jamestown, and when possible, the easiest method of carrying out trade and barter with the Indians. Extant grants and charters show that some individuals, if their vessel was of sufficient size – and ships of but ten tons successfully crossed the Atlantic – sailed north to fish for food and profit, and southward to the West Indies. A boat therefore was essential to the life and prosperity of most plantations.

The final paragraph of the *Remembrances* dealt principally with the cost of mounting the Berkeley project up to the moment of departure from England – a matter of £1040 'and upwards'. The Governor, if he wished to become a fifth shareholder, was requested to forward his share quota '£208 at the least' by the *Margaret* on its return voyage.

II.　Commission to Captain Woodleefe, dated 4 September 1619

This second document opened with a declaration of intent by the four Adventurers. They purposed to send an initial party of about thirty settlers to Virginia that September, and the same number of men to increase at subsequent voyages. There they were to erect and build 'a town to be called Berkeley and to settle and plant our said men and divers other inhabitants there, to the honour of almighty God, the enlargeing of christian religion . . . and the particular good and profit of ourselves men and servants . . .'.

The Adventurers outlined their legal right to the land, and with the advice and counsel of the Virginia Company, stated that we 'do nominate authorize and appoint the said Captain John Woodleefe to be Captain and governor of the said people and servants . . .'. He was also given authority to 'trade either with the natives of Virginia or the English there residing . . .[and] to be our chief marchant . . .'. Limitations, present and future, are mentioned, which may have been intended to refer to the *Agreements* dated that same day.

III. Agreement

This third document, dated 4 September, begins 'Covenants and agreements had and made by and between' the four Adventurers and Woodleefe. Then follow a summary of title and purpose similar to that given in the above Commission, and eleven considerable paragraphs.

1. The site selected and built upon shall be named Berkeley, and their lands and territories about shall be called Berkeley Hundred. If later more land is allotted or bought it too, unless far distant, shall also be so designated.

2. All costs and profits are to be shared equally between the four Adventurers.

3. The four agree that policy and direction shall at all times be ordered by a majority decision.

4. The ownership of shares in the Virginia Company, past and future, by the four adventurers is outlined, and future purchases 'Jointly or severally' shall be paid for and enjoyed equally. A limit of ten in addition to their present holdings is stipulated. It would appear that whereas Throckmorton, Thorpe and Smyth had previously invested in shares in the Virginia Company, Berkeley had not.

5. Woodleefe, it would appear, had, at his own expense in April last 'transported four men into Virginia being in his family now there abiding with his wife and children . . .'. Therein lay the seeds of future trouble which resulted finally in the dismissal of Woodleefe from the leadership of the Berkeley plantation. Seemingly those four persons already transported and others, native or English, whom Woodleefe might in the future engage for the Berkeley plantation, were to be treated as Berkeley servants in all respects, and Woodleefe's expences in those connections will be allowed.

6. Woodleefe was not to establish a private settlement on the north bank of the James river unless it was at least ten miles distant from the Berkeley holding. He must live with the Berkeley 'family' and further their interests.

7. Within a year a second Berkeley party was to be sent out, having William Chester as leader, possessing similar authority to that enjoyed by Woodleefe. Each community was to enjoy its independence, but would be supported from England equally. Woodleefe and Chester were to continue to

exercise their separate commands 'till a Division be made by' Throckmorton, Berkeley, Thorpe and Smyth or three of them, and were to have 'a full XXVth part apiece of the whole clear gains and profits from time to time . . .'

8.   When a partition of 'lands, men, goods and chattels shall be made . . . each man [master or Adventurer] shall first make choice of such three men' out of either parties 'as were by himself drawn into the journey and provided to be sent over.' The rest or majority of the partners were to have some say in the matter.

It is clear from the use of the words 'town' and 'Hundred', and the thought behind such phrases as 'similar numbers of men at subsequent voyages' and 'divers other inhabitants', that a considerable settlement was, from the beginning, envisaged. Looking into the future for a moment, one sees that the same conception must still have been in mind when William Tracy became involved. He was related by blood or marriage to all but Smyth of the Berkeley Adventurers, and in 1620 applied for and obtained a grant to settle 500 in Virginia. Later that year he bought a share in the Berkeley Company.

These references would explain the occasional allusions to a division of the parent Berkeley Company into several separate bodies or groups. This plan, presumably, would have become operative when the Berkeley settlement had reached a certain stage of development, and had become fully viable, though in fact that moment of hoped for expansion never arrived.

9.   In this paragraph the possibilities relating to the fifth share offered to the Governor were considered, and a conference between Yeardley and Woodleefe was proposed. The latter was prepared to take up the share in the event of a relinquishment by Yeardley.

10.   Woodleefe was to purchase one third of Throckmorton's share, 'besides his fifth part from Sir George Yeardley if it accrue to him,' All adventurers agreed to pay their dues at the correct time.

11.   Details of the hire of the *Margaret* (£33 a month) and the wages of the pilot, Toby Felgate, (£4.-10s.-0d.), were confirmed. The four Adventurers would each deliver, before 20 January next, £50 to Mr. William Yeomans, vicar of St. Phillips, Bristol. the acting treasurer for the first voyage, and a penal clause was included if they failed to do this. The vicar, presumably, was to pay the *Margaret's* owner monthly from the £200, while possibly holding Felgate's wages until his return, or paying his wife, if she lived locally.

IV.   Ordinances Directions and Instructions

These directives were both extremely interesting and important, for the document set out clearly the emphasis placed by the Adventurers upon daily and regular religious observances, and also the care and thought which had gone into the planning and preparation for the establishment of the new Berkeley Town and Hundred.

These charges were issued to Woodleefe in the name of all four Adventurers, and began with the remarkable order legislating for an annual Thanksgiving Service to be held at the Berkeley Plantation:[62]

1. 'Impr We ordain that the day of our ship's arrival at the place for plantation in the land of Virginia shall be yearly and perpetually kept as a day of thanksgiving to Almighty God.'

2. (a) Sunday was to 'be kept in holy and religious order', and 'All bodily labour and vain sports and scandalous recreation' were forbidden.

(b) Morning and Evening Prayers – *English Book of Common Prayer* rite – were to be held daily and attended.

(c) Such other divine exercise of preaching and reading were to be on the said day used 'as the minister for the time shall be able to perform'.

(d) All festivals and holy days as appointed in England must be observed.

(e) The uses, rites and ceremonies and prayer book used by the 'Church of England' would be 'in all things observed and kept,'

3. The plantation Governor and all the people, including servants, would attend prayers once a day. These were to be held immediately after the forenoon labour ended and before dinner. Absentees, unless they had a valid excuse, would forfeit their supper. The Governor and his assistances however could be exempt.

4. The site chosen for settlement must be 'healthy for air,' 'accomodiate with fresh water', accessible for the ship's pinnace or barge, and rich 'in mould and soil and most likely to bring fourth the best commodities of that country . . .'.

Then follow a considerable list of crops, e.g., flax, vines and wheat, and natural products, e.g., iron ore, timber and meadow grass, which it was desirable that the locality would support or yield. Woodleefe was required to seek and follow the advice of his assistants and be guided by Sir George Yeardley.

5. Directly the site had been selected houses were to be built 'homelike and to be covered with boards.' Particular attention was to be paid to two buildings, the store house for tools, powder, shot, armour and food, and a common hall for prayers and eating. If those two buildings could not be erected before the ship was unladen then the goods aboard must be stored in the warehouse at Jamestown or the 'Bermuda granary', leave from the Governor having been obtained.

6. 400 acres were to be secured speedily with a seven and a half foot fence for the protection of crops and cattle.

7. Woodleefe's assistants were named – Ferdinando Yate, John Blanchard, Richard Godfry, Rowland Panter and Thomas Coopy – and he was required on all matters of importance to seek and take their advice; a majority decision would suffice. These five were to eat at Woodleefe's table. The remainder of the party would eat together.

8. Guards must be mounted nightly. At first these should be five in number, but would be increased as opportunity and numbers directed – to about seven, it would appear, when one of the number would be deputy and termed captain of the watch.

9. The following appointments, 'for the more decent and comely government' of the settlement, were ordered. Yate 'to be ancient' (standard bearer or ensign) and also in charge of the armour and 'tools of husbandry.' Paynter (the Panter of paragraph 7) was to be 'Sargeant' of the Company, and 'clerk of the kitchen' with two assistants '(as Caterers or country purveyors)'. Blanchard was nominated as 'Steward of the household and clerk of the store of apparel and bedding.' Perce was to be Usher of the Hall. Tho: Partridge, 'now abiding in Virginia', if he joined the party was 'to be bailiff'. If he did not, another must be selected by Woodleefe and his assistants.

10. If Woodleefe should die before Chester arrived then the assistants would jointly exercise the office. If, after the arrival of Chester, either leader should die the survivor with the two sets of assistants would govern the whole settlement and the two parties.

Before scrutinizing the vital departure documents, i.e., the nominal roll of the first Berkeley settlers certified by the Mayor of Bristol,[63] and the considerable catalogue of stores and equipment with the accompanying comments and observations by various Adventurers, a surviving indenture and a letter from the Adventurers to Sir George Yeardley must be examined.

The indenture, dated 7 September 1619, is between the Berkeley Adventurers and a Robert Coopy,[64] who is described as a husbandman of North Nibley. He covenanted to serve the Adventurers for three years on 'lawful and reasonable works', and to be obedient to the appointed leaders. In return the Adventurers undertook to transport him to the colony and there to maintain him with 'convenient diet and apparel meet for such a servant,' and at the end of three years to make him a free man with the recognized 'freedoms and privileges,'. He would then receive for the period of three lives a grant of thirty acres within their 'Territory or hundred of Berkeley' at a rent of twelve pence per acre, and under 'such other reasonable conditions and services' as shall be agreed before sailing. Coopy's wife was to be paid ten shillings per quarter during his indenture period – 'if he so long live.' Thirty shillings had already been paid to her.[65]

This type of servant's indenture, with variation of terms, represented the usual conditions of service for servants to the private plantations during the closing years of the Virginia Company's life. This particular indenture is signed by Richard Berkeley, George Thorpe and John Smyth, and bears the seal of each.

The letter to Yeardley, dated 9 September, touches upon several subjects. Firstly, reference is made to an enclosed copy of the letter sent by the Adventurers to him on the previous 18 February 'lest the same should not yet be come to your hands'. Secondly, the writers announced the departure of their party of thirty-five colonists under Woodleefe, and requested the Governor's assistance and patronage for them. They then inquired whether he, now that he had achieved high office and great responsibility, would be accepting the fifth share in the partnership. They expressed the hope that he would take up the original offer, and, in anticipation of this, they appended a suggested method whereby he could settle the payment of his share. Finally, they apologized for the lateness of the party's departure, and assured the Governor that they proposed to send the follow-up party by April next.

It has already been mentioned that three documents, vital to a proper appreciation of the muster of men and material for the pioneering party of the Berkeley Company, have been printed in full in volume 3 of Dr. Susan Kingsbury's work on the Virginia Company of London. The first to be examined, represented by *The Smyth of Nibley Papers* 3 (13-16),[66] is a consolidation of several lists of stores and items of equipment purchased by, or on behalf of, the Berkeley Adventurers. The prices too are recorded, and also certain other financial outgoings,[67] as well as some details relating to personnel, materials and the areas from whence they came. The final page (Kingsbury III, p. 189) is a tabulation of the involved financial positions of the four Adventurers. This was made more complicated by the uncertainty over Sir George Yeardley and his proposed fifth share.

The remaining two documents are nominal rolls of the settlers who formed that first Berkeley party. The shorter and presumably the earlier – it is dated 15 September 1619 – is a certificate 'of the Men who Shipped in the *Margaret* under Captain Woodleefe.'[68] It was issued by John Swye, mayor of Bristol, and addressed 'To the Treasurer Company and Council of Adventurers and Planters of the City of London, for the first Colony in Virginia.', and avowed that 'John Woodleefe Esq.' and 'thirty six persons whose names ensue . . . forthwith proceeded in their voyage accordingly' from Bristol. The list which follows gives no information relating to the individuals save that the first four are designated 'gent' and the two named Richard Sherife are differentiated by the words 'thelder' and 'the younger'.

The second roll, merely dated September 1619, is heavily annotated with many later entries, and would appear to have been Smyth's own working copy.[69] Its importance lies in the fact that considerable details relating to the men are added, e.g., the length of their indentures, which varied from three to seven years, and the acreage which would be allotted to them at the end of their indenture – from fifteen to fifty acres. In most instances the fate of the individual settler, e.g., 'dead', 'slaine', 'returned' (to England) is recorded in the handwriting of John Smyth. There are, in addition, the names of two other parties of Berkeley settlers. The first, four in number, were those sent over by Woodleefe in April 1619 – perhaps as an 'advance guard' or maybe they were shipped before it was realized that the departure date of the main party would be so long delayed. The second group, also four in number, 'went after with Mr. Thorpe, 27.mtij [March], 1620.'

The document ends with a few details relating to the terms of some indentures and the financial assistance given to certain members of the party, e.g.,

1. 'Thomas Coopy hath XL ^{s} per Ann. paid to his wife.'

2. 'John Singer the Surgeon hath 50 ^{s} in hand towards furnishing of his chest, And thirty shillings the month, beginning monday 13. September. 1619.'[70] It would appear that normally the indentured servant had a wage of 40/- p.a.

To return to Smyth I, 3 (13-16). These lists of commodities, the movement of goods and the overall financial picture as seen through those twelve packed pages merit careful examination by a social historian. It will not be possible in this survey to do more than draw attention to certain unusual entries amongst the purchases, the movement of certain pieces of equipment, stores or items of merchandise and the activities of some Adventurers or members of the settlement party, and finally to suggest possible, or positive, conclusions.

On the first page of this long document is a list of things bought for the Berkeley Company by Thorpe in London during July 1619. Amongst a variety of purchases – there are twenty-nine entries (three of which relate to expenses of two members of the party) – two groups stand out. The first comprises items essential for the defence of the proposed town and hundred of Berkeley in Virginia against possible attack by Indians or Spaniards. The list begins with twenty-four muskets at one pound each. Later come three barrels of gunpowder and sixteen swords. Lead for the bullets and the melting ladles, however, were bought at Bristol, presumably to save transportation costs. Undoubtedly the reason why the twenty four muskets at one pound each and the sword were bought in London, while the other defensive equipment, pike heads, corselet, calivers furnished, 'armours' and one musket (at fifteen shillings) were obtained in the Bristol areas, was that better steel was obtainable in the City than in the provinces, and that in the seventeenth century, as in the nineteenth and twentieth, London-made guns were considered better than those obtainable in the provinces, and commanded a higher price. Maybe Charles Coyle, one of the Berkeley settlers and himself a 'gunmaker and smith', advised Thorpe on this matter.

The second group of purchases made by Thorpe also stand out, and bears the stamp of that 'religious gentleman'. The items were two Church Bibles at £3. 6s. 8d. the two, two copies of the *Book of Common Prayer* at 14s., and six books of religious devotions. These were three copies of *The practice of piety* (7s.) and three of *The playne mans pathway* (3s. 6d.). It is interesting to observe that, when in May 1622, four fresh colonists were sent out on the *Furtherance* to the Berkeley Plantation, Smyth recorded that 22d. had been expended on 'a Testament for one of them much desiring the same'.[71]

When the remainder of the stores and equipment is considered the wide variety of those goods, and their quantity seems remarkable,[72] especially when this catalogue is compared with the 'shopping list' of the similar sized party (thirty-five) which had been scheduled to establish the Smythe Hundred a year previously.[73] These entries will be considered under three main headings, i.e., provisions, domestic requirements, and constructional and agricultural tools and material.

Provisions " a selection
8,000 biscuits, bread, 160 lbs. butter, 50 lbs. suet, oatmeal, 127 lbs. bacon, 'horsemeat', two lots of cheese – one of 224 lbs., the other of '300 quarters and 25 lbs.', 5 ropes of onions, 33 lbs. of soap, pepper, salt, ginger, a barrel of vinegar, 11 gallons of oil, 20 bushels of wheat, 60 bushesl of peas, 5½ tuns of beer, 6 tuns of cider, 11 gallons of sack, 15 gallons of aqua vitae, etc.

Domestic Requirements
Suits (made), shirts (made), caps and bands, 200 pairs of shoes, stockings, 5 doz. handkerchiefs and falling bands, sheets (made), bolsters (made), 586 ells of canvas of differing types, 27 ells of dowles for sheets, 145 yards of 'gray welsh frise' (flannel), nearly 2,000 buttons (various types), quantities of thread, 200 needles, taylor's shears etc.

Kitchen Utensils
48 trenchers, wooden platters, dishes, bowls, spoons, horn cups, skimming dishes and saucers, dripping pans, frying pans, kettles, bellows, 'pot hangings', pot racks, 'tongs and side shovels', knives, candlesticks, 'lanthorn', 'quarter cans and small cans', scales, etc.

Constructional and Agricultural Tools and Material
Axes and Hatchets, (dozens of them, some for trade and barter no doubt), many types for felling, squaring, cleaving, coopers, adzes. Saws, again many and various: 'long', 'tenant',

'hand', 'long thirt' Hoes, many and various for 'weeding', 'hoeing', 'long', 'short'. Spades (dozens), shovels, pickaxes, crowbars, bill hooks, reaping hooks, hammers, chisels, pliers, pincers, files, awls, spokeshaves, vice, iron wedges, 'cawking and planing irons', whetstones. Over 20,000 nails of differing sizes and purposes, e.g., hob, sparrow, bushell, stove, overlop, culford, and the usual 3^d to 10^d variety; locks, latches, padlocks, staples for doors, 6 lbs. of glue, wain ropes, 'fishing tools', seine net and ropes.

Trade with the Indians is clearly indicated by two entries in Thorpe's list recording the purchase of 6,000 beads – 4,800 'of the smaller sort', while correspondence and the keeping of records were clearly in mind when half a ream of paper, two quires of paper, 4s. worth of ink, 'ink' (separate entry), wax, parchment, and silk string were bought. Thorpe plainly considered that the garden was one of the keys to physical survival when he bought '30 sorts of garden seeds' – item 15.

Costs of transportation and similar accounts include:

i 'To Mr. Felgate for carriage of 700 lb. weight from London, for the hire of a horse, his own charge and his man's to Bristol and for his man's work there as by his bill appeareth besides 22^s paid by Mr. Thorpe . . .' — £4. 6s. 3d.

ii 'charges of plowmen and others at Barkly with 3 wains and 4 horses laden with peas, cider and London provisions from Cam Nibley and Wanswell' – 5s.

iii 'To the boatmen of Barkly for cariage of divers things from Barkly' 15s.

iv 'Payd for the Ship' – £120.

v 'Laid out by Richard Partridge in Ireland for provisions and other expences there over and besides £14 freight by him received' – £41. 5s. 4d.

vi 'Laid out by Richard Partridge at Gatcombe about the ship as appeareth by his bill of accompt given by Sir William Throckmorton' – £52. 10s. 7d.

There appears to be no supporting evidence as to whether these last three entries refer to the ship windbound in Ireland in the February which had so delayed the departure of the Berkeley party, or the *Margaret* on which the settlers finally embarked.

The lading list with its many supplementary details is a remarkable record revealing in no small measure the character of the Berkeley Adventurers, at least collectively. The first point which impresses is the detailed planning which lay behind the assembling of such a selection of goods. Perhaps here may be seen the influence of Woodleefe, an experienced and seasoned planter, while it must be remembered that Thorpe, even if he had not physically landed in Bermuda or Virginia — but he may have done so, had had investment experience in both colonies. Throckmorton too had ventured (1618) in the Smythe Hundred, but, as far as is known, never sailed to Virginia.

Secondly the humanitarian overtones are clear. The sponsors – and Woodleefe too maybe – were fully conscious of their obligations to equip their settlers in a proper manner and so to ensure their well-being. A comparison between the Berkeley list and that drawn up for the pioneers of the Smythe Hundred in May 1618 gives evidence of the feelings of the Berkeley quartet towards their servants. It was as if they said 'You are taking the physical risks, we will equip and protect you to the best of our ability.'

Thirdly it is evident that the Berkeley party intended to lay the foundations for a permanent and expanding settlement, and one in which the 'family' element was well to the fore in the minds of the planners. The instructions to Woodleefe to report on the numbers of men and women deemed desirable in the next party – scheduled for the following April, and the reference to schools took growth of settlements one step further. This too is seen in the skills and trades represented in that initial party – carpenter, cook, cooper, fisherman, fowler, gardener, gunmaker, joiner, sawyer, shingler, shoe-maker, smith, surgeon, tailor and turner. Some men combined two such skills. Finally, the naming of the plantation 'The Town and Hundred of Berkeley' showed clearly that the sponsors had in mind a genuine re-creation or transplanting of the borough of Berkeley surrounded by the villages of the Hundred along the Severn Vale and the Cotswold Edge from Gloucestershire to the tidewater in Virginia. The reference to the splitting up (outward expansion might be a better phrase) of the original settlement, and Tracy's charter in 1620 to settle 500 persons on the Berkeley grant is further confirmation of this basic but grandiose scheme. It is evident that from the start the economy of the new Berkeley was, like its parent, to be based upon agriculture.

The final characteristic of the private plantation of Berkeley, and one which, judging from the available evidence, set it apart from others was the great emphasis placed upon the spiritual welfare of the settlers. It is clear that the sponsors were deeply concerned that the transporting of Gloucestershire people to a distant land should not deprive them of the solace of religion and the opportunities for spiritual development and growth, and that the loss of their ancient parish churches should not result in a weakening of their christian consciousness.

The instructions to Woodleefe were specific and detailed in the first three of the ten-paragraph manifesto of Thorpe, Smyth, Berkeley and Throckmorton. Those orders laid down that the settlement they were about to found should be run on strict Christian principles, and in due conformity with the practices of the English Church. Rules spelt out precisely the observance of Holy Days and daily prayers and worship; and attendance was of obligation. Those who, without valid excuse, absented themselves were to be deprived of their 'supp'. The annual Thanksgiving Service, the subject of the first paragraph, will be discussed in appendix 1.

It was no doubt, with these instructions in mind, that Thorpe, who almost certainly had a hand in drawing up the above regulations, bought the Church Bibles, Prayer Books and devotional literature, all of which would have been used daily by the reader in their dual-purpose hut until a church was erected. A minister was scheduled to come – and came, with the follow-up party. Two entries in the above mentioned lading list and financial statement show the continuity of this theme. The first records the purchase of bread and wine for communion. The second stated that before the party set sail a Mr. Huggins 'gave the Communion and a sermon to our people' (p. 188).

Thus in conclusion, comparing the lading catalogue of the initial pioneering parties of the Berkeley and Smythe Hundreds, it would appear that the sponsors of the Berkeley Plantation were the more considerate of the physical well being of their members and were prepared to lay out large sums of money to try and ensure their health and happiness. Furthermore, they seemed deeply concerned also for their spiritual health. These sharply delineated characteristics seem to have placed them apart from their peers. One of their number, Thorpe, during his two years in Virginia (1620-2) gained – for a layman at least – a reputation second to none for humanitarianism, devotion and missionary zeal. In consequence, it would appear reasonable to suggest that the particular orientation of policy of the Berkeley Company was in no small measure attributable to Thorpe and Smyth, who, it is said, also was a religious man.

NOTES

1. Carl Bridenbaugh, *Vexed and Troubled Englishmen 1590-1642*, O.U.P. Paperback, 1976.

2. Ibid., p. 48.

3. J. Tann, op. cit., p. 31, referring to A. Fries, *Alderman Cockayne's Project on the Cloth Trade*; T. Exell, *A Brief History of the Weavers of the County of Glos.* G.C.L., HC 12.5.

4. T.S. Ashton, *Economic Fluctuations in England, 1700-1800*, pp. 26, 128, 158.

5. J. Tann, op. cit., p. 31.

6. J. Leland, *The Itinerary*, ed. L. Toulmin Smith, pt.x, pp. 94-101.

7. Smyth III, vol. 3, p. 269.

8. J. Thirsk, 'New Crops and their Diffusion: Tobacco-growing in Seventeenth century England', *Rural Change & Urban Growth 1500-1800*, ed. C.W. Chalklin and M. Havingden (1974), pp. 88-93. Hereafter cited Thirsk I. See also 'Projects for Gentlemen, Jobs for the Poor, Mutual Aid in the Vale of Tewkesbury, 1600-1630,' *Essays in Bristol and Gloucestershire History*, ed. P. McGrath and J. Cannon, *BGAS* 1976, pp. 147-169. Hereafter cited Thirsk II. See also, idem., *Economic Policy and Projects. The Development of a Consumer Society in Early Modern England*, Oxford 1978.

9. Thirsk II, p. 148.

10. Ibid. p. 149.

11. His mother was a Mary Throckmorton.

12. Dr. Thirsk (II, p. 156) draws attention to the fact that 'The parish of Winchcombe is traversed by a "Salters route" and has a "Salters Hill."' Perhaps it is worth mentioning that one of Berkeley's main streets is named 'Salter Street', while in Jumpers Lane, alongside the Berkeley Avon, stands a 'Salt House'.

13. Kingsbury I, p. 291.

14. Brown II, p. 352.

15. Thirsk II, p. 159. Tobacco 'continued as a poor man's crop in the region for another 70 years as well as spreading to twenty-two other counties.

16. Kingsbury I, p. 303.

17. Smyth I, 16; in Kingsbury III, p. 266.

18. Smyth I, 3(20); in Kingsbury III, pp. 271-4.

19. Smyth III, vol 3, p. 85.

20. Ibid, vol. 2, pp. 9-10.

21. The *Lavender* was sold in 1898 for £80, and one of the crew, Mr. Charlie Meadows, aged ninety-six, is still alive, well and talkative. He emigrated to Australia in 1978.

22. (i) 'Paid William Clement for the relief of his wife in his absence and for redemption of his tools that were pawned xiiij^s' in Kingsbury III, p. 187. (ii) 'to Humphrey Plant Carpenter and Sawyer for his three years wages beforehand to pay his debts xl^s', Ibid.

23. Smyth I, 16; in Kingsbury III, p. 266. On 2 February 1620, Tracy's indenture, granted him leave to transport 500 persons to Virginia, was 'allowed'. Kingsbury I, p. 303. 'John Peirce and his Associates' (The Pilgrim Fathers) received their grant (for Virginia) at that same court.

24. Library of Congress, Miscellaneous Records, 1606-92, pp. 72-83; printed in Kingsbury III, pp. 98-109; Bemiss, pp. 95-108.

25. M.C. Voorhis, *The Land Grant Policy of Colonial Virginia, 1607-1774*, p. 18, Ph.D. Dissertation, University of Virginia, no. 383, 1940.

26. The title 'ancient planter' was given to all planters who had arrived in Virginia prior to the departure of Sir Thomas Dale to England where he arrived in mid-June 1616.

27. Bemiss, op.cit., p. 98.

28. All these properties were negotiable, and could be bequeathed, donated, sold or transferred by the grantee.

29. They were equipped and fed by the Company who took the entire profits from their labours, but held out a promise of a land grant after seven years.

30. Each share constituted an investment of £12. 10s. 0d.

31. Here is another instance of the handicap caused by the loss of the court records of the Virginia Company prior to 28 April 1619.

32. Kingsbury III, pp. 130-134; *NYPLB*, 1899, pp. 161-4.

33. Clearwell in the Forest of Dean.

34. Yeardley later withdrew from the company giving as his excuse his heavy involvement in the Smythe Hundred which was situated between the Berkeley Hundred and Chickahominy river. The four remaining sponsors thereupon took over a quarter of the financial obligations shed by the Governor.

35. Later re-named Elizabeth City.

36. Smyth I, 3 (4); in Kingsbury III, p. 131.

37. Smyth I, 14; in Kingsbury III, pp. 248-9.

38. Smyth I, 4; in Kingsbury III, pp. 136-7.

39. It is believed that he was delayed in the Channel for some days before the 29th. His date of landing in Jamestown was 29 April. Brown II, p. 308.

40. Smyth, clearly the general secretary and accountant of the Berkeleys, appears to have possessed the reputed acquisiteness of the magpie or jackdaw, as *The Smyth of Nibley Papers* in New York Public Library and the 2000 (approx) in the Gloucestershire County Library testify.

41. Dated 3 April 1619 from Stoke (Gifford), Smyth I, 5; in Kingsbury III, p. 137.

42. Smyth I, 6; in Kingsbury III, pp. 138-9.

43. Smyth I, 7; in Kingsbury III, p. 148.

44. Smyth I, 8; in Kingsbury III, p. 151.

45. Smyth I, Ibid., footnote.

46. Smyth I, 3 (19); in Kingsbury III, pp. 260-1. The date given here for Thorpe's departure is 'February 1620'. In Smyth I, 3 (9) – Smyth's list of Berkeley's original party plus four men already in Virginia and four that went with Thorpe – is a note in Smyth's hand giving the date as 27 March 1620.

47. Manchester Papers no. 241; in Kingsbury III, p. 87.

48. Declaration printed by Thomas Snodham, 1620. Many copies of this exist, e.g., in the British Library, Bodleian, Cambridge U.L., Library of Congress, New York Public Library etc.; in Kingsbury III, p. 331.

49. in Kingsbury I, p. 212.

50. Smyth I, 3 (12); in Kingsbury III, p. 190.

51. Yeardley landed in Virginia (via the shipwreck on the Bermudas) in May 1610, and remained there until 1617. He returned as full Governor in April 1619. Yeardley was a first cousin to Richard Yerwood, one of the stepfathers of John Harvard, founder of Harvard College.

52. In Kingsbury III, pp. 178-89.

53. Smyth I, 3 (17); in Kingsbury III, pp. 193-5.

54. In March 1976 I gave a presidential address to the Bristol and Gloucestershire Archaeological Society. Some of the information on the subject, the *Berkeley Plantation in Virginia*, had been culled from certain of *The Smyth of Nibley Papers* which had been published in *NYPLB*. Subsequent discussion suggested that the name of the port near Bristol from which the Berkeley party had set sail should have been Kingrode, and not Hungrode. Several works were quoted, including Kingsbury. There are, strange to relate, ports named Hungrode and Kingrode on the Avon below Bristol. A careful check of the original document showed that Hungrode was, in this instance, the correct reading. Dr. Kingsbury lacking local knowledge, and possibly using a map of the lower Avon upon which only the larger port was recorded, was led into this error. See map.

55. (i) Charter of Ship, Smyth I, 3 (17); in Kingsbury III, pp. 193-5;
(ii) Remembrance, Smyth I, 3 (8); in Kingsbury III, pp. 195-6;
(iii) Commission, Smyth I, 3 (5); in Kingsbury III, pp. 199-201;
(iv) Agreement, Smyth I, 9 + 3 (7); in Kingsbury III, pp. 201-7;
(v) Ordinances, Smyth I, 10 + 3 (6); in Kingsbury III, pp. 207-10.

56. Smyth I, 3 (13-16); In Kingsbury III, pp. 178-89.

59. Smyth I, 3 (9); in Kingsbury III, pp. 197-9.

58. Indenture of Robert Coopy, Smyth I, 11; in Kingsbury III, pp. 210-11.

59. Letter to Yeardley, Smyth I, 3 (11); in Kingsbury III, p. 212.

60. Mayor of Bristol - Certificate, Smyth I, 3 (10); in Kingsbury III, p. 213.

61. Accounts 16 September 1619 - 16 September 1620, Smyth I, 3 (32); in Kingsbury III, pp. 214-15.

62. See appendix no. 1.

63. Smyth I, 3 (10); in Kingsbury III, p. 213. There are two other lists of this party; (i) a certified copy of those who arrived safely in Virginia (Smyth I, 3 (18); in Kingsbury III, p. 230) and (ii) an annotated copy – presumably Smyth's working copy – on which in addition were recorded the names of other settlers who had been in Virginia for some time, and also four who accompanied Thorpe in 1620. It will be needful to examine this document shortly here and more extensively later (Smyth I, 3 (9); in Kingsbury III, pp. 197-9).

64. Smyth I, 11; in Kingsbury III, pp. 210-11.

65. There is a brief endorsement at the end of the Indenture which states 'Rob. Coopy he forso[ok] the voyage — by assent.'

66. Kingsbury III, pp. 178-189.

67. Cost of transportation of goods, billetting of personnel etc.

68. Smyth I, 3 (10); in Kingsbury III, pp. 213.

69. Smyth I, 3 (9); in Kingsbury III, pp. 197-9.

70. See chapter 6 for further details relating to Singer.

71. Smyth I, 3 (36); in Kingbury III, pp. 618-19.

72. The freight space alone must have been a major problem. The *Margaret* was 'about 45 tons'. There were thirty-six settlers and the ship's crew nine, plus several tons of freight and personel possessions, meagre though these must have been.

73. Kingsbury III, pp. 94-8.

5

The Early Years

GENESIS — THE DISTANT PAST

The discovery of the New World has been described as by far the greatest event in the history of the Old.[1] The identity of the one who made this exploratory breakthrough is a matter of conjecture, with many claimants such as King Arthur, Madoc the Welshman and the Vikings vying for that honour.

Historically, however, Columbus made the discovery of the New World in October 1492, although 'Attempts from Bristol to find rumoured islands in the Atlantic go back . . . as early as 1480,'[2] while in 1497 John Cabot sailed from that port and made a landfall on the east coast of the mainland of America at a time when the Spaniards were concerned primarily with the West Indies.

Despite Cabot's feat, it has to be recorded that whereas Spain, Portugal and later, France, began colonization on the mainland of America early in the sixteenth century, it was not until 1607 that the first permanent British settlement was established at Jamestown in Virginia. There had been earlier letters patent granted to such men as Sir Humphrey Gilbert (1578) and Sir Francis Drake (1584) for genuine exploration and possible settlement, but those expeditions had failed.

It might fairly be said that the consolidation of those early attempts at permanent settlements in Virginia foundered partly because of the Armada scare and its aftermath, but principally because the private financial investments involved were totally inadequate for mounting and sustaining such projects over long periods.

THE SECOND STAGE

The revival of interest in the possibilities of colonization in Virginia began in July 1602, after the return to Exmouth of Captain Bartholomew Gosnold from a brief voyage of reconnaissance to the area of the Chesapeake Bay. His report stressed the natural bounty of the soil in Virginia, and the boundless opportunities which awaited those who possessed the foresight and courage to make the venture. In the following year Hakluyt published his *Voyages*[3] and persuaded the Mayor and Aldermen of Bristol, and many merchants of that city, to raise £1,000 to fit out two vessels to explore further the financial potential of Virginia.

In 1605 the Earl of Southampton sent out yet another expedition to study and assess the prospects for permanent settlement along the eastern seaboard of what later became known as New England. The force was commanded by Captain George Weymouth, and, with the return of that expedition, the second phase of colonization, now to be accepted as of a permanent nature, can be said to have begun.

THE VIRGINIA COMPANY – ITS CREATION

The failure of the previous 'ventures' in the New World had shown that lasting colonization was an undertaking which required great financial resources and reserves and considerable expertise in the organization and administration of large and distant projects. Thus it was that a group of businessmen and commercially minded gentry, many of whom had had experience in such enterprises as the East India Company,[4] finally petitioned for, and obtained from, the King a charter granting them 'our licence to make habitation, plantation and to deduce a colony of sundry of our people into that part of America called Virginia, and other parts and territories in America . . . lying and being all along the sea coasts between four and thirty degrees of northerly latitude from the equinoctial line and five and forty degrees of the same latitude . . .'[5]

The Virginia Company, whose first charter was dated 10 April 1606, was initially two companies centred upon London and Plymouth, with Bristol and Exeter associated with the latter. The first charter was granted in the names of Sir Thomas Gates, Sir George Sumers, Richard Hakluyt and Edward Maria Wingfield, representing the London Company, and Thomas Hannam, Ralegh Gilbert, William Parker and George Popham the grantees for the Plymouth body. The above, naturally, were merely the nominees of their respective corporations, and it is unfortunate that the complete lists of members of these early formations are not known. The London, or the first company as it was termed in that charter, were assigned the zone thirty-four to forty-two degrees, while the second or Plymouth group were granted the priveleges of exploration, trade, and colonization from thirty-eight to forty-five degrees. The conditions of settlement in the overlap areas were clearly defined with the object of preventing possible clashes of interest.

Both companies made their initial foundation in the summer of 1607, the London company establishing Jamestown on the James river and the Plymouth counterpart locating its bridgehead at Sagadahoe. The largely inexperienced colonists were faced with severe climatic conditions during the ensuing winter which, allied to rapidly dwindling food stocks, resulted in great hardships and heavy casualties. When spring came the survivors from the Plymouth foundation abandoned their settlement, and the sponsoring company, launching no fresh enterprise, effectively lost its identity.[6] The Jamestown party, which had endured similar privations and appalling loss of lives, hung on grimly, and thus established the firm base from which the British colony on both sides of the James river expanded and developed. In consequence of the differing reactions of these two initial foundations, the London or Southern Company, became virtually the sole effective representative unit of the parent body, and synonymous with the Virginia Company itself. Consequently the title 'The Virginia Company' will now be used exclusively for the London unit which expanded to fill the vacuum created by the collapse of the Plymouth body, and in so doing absorbed some of the latter's membership and resources.

FIRST FOUNDATION AND GROWTH

The government of the Virginia Company was vested in the London based Council for Virginia, appointed by the King himself, and representing both the original companies. This body included the above mentioned Sir Thomas Smythe, Sir Walter Cope, an M.P. already involved in foreign commercial enterprises, and two persons connected with Bristol, i.e., Sir Ferdinando Gorges and Thomas James.

On 19 December 1606 the first party of the Virginia Company's colonists sailed, with sealed orders, down the Thames from Blackwell, rounding the Kentish coast and on into the English Channel. That tiny fleet, comprising their flag ship, the *Susan Constant* (100 tons) commanded by Captain Christopher Newport, the *Godspeed* (forty tons) Captain Gosnold, and the *Discovery* (20 tons) Captain John Ratcliffe, there met appalling weather conditions which delayed them for six weeks. This resulted in severe sickness amongst crews and passengers,[7] and caused the colonists to consume precious rations, the loss of which became a matter of vital concern – indeed of life and death, in the following winter.

In mid February the colonists cleared the Channel, saling southward to the Fortunate Isles (Canaries) before laying course for the West Indies. During this passage westward dissension developed between the leaders, and resulted in Captain John Smith, a most experienced adventurer, being accused of mutiny and placed under arrest, a charge which Stith attributed to envy.[8] They visited a number of West Indian islands, where the plenitude of fish, fowl and game revived their spirits and strengthened their bodies. Leaving the West Indies on 20 April they had their first sight of Virginia on the 26th, and after a prolonged and careful survey they selected, on 13 May, as their permanent settlement a small peninsula, defensible against the Spanish and Indians, sixty miles up the James river, but where there was close inshore deep anchorage enabling their ships to be moored to the trees.

The sealed orders were then opened and the names of their governing council in Virginia were known. They were the three ships' Captains and Edward Maria Wingfield, Captain John Smith, John Martin and George Kendall. Wingfield was elected president. A surprise ommission from the council membership was George Percy, a brother of the Earl of Northumberland. Perhaps the London Council was influenced in its decision by the fact that he was a volunteer, and not an official of the expedition, or because the Earl was suspected by some of having been privy to the Gunpowder Plot.[9]

The following morning, 14 May 1607, the party of 104 Adventurers landed, and the birth pangs of the colony of Virginia had begun with the establishment of its first genuine settlement and capital, Jamestown. As Virginius Dabney wrote 'There were no shirkers on that first day in Jamestown, as the settlers began "in the name of God to raise a Fortress" . . . Unfortunately there was a grievous lack of leadership and planning. Wheat was sown . . . but not nearly enough . . . and the early enthusiasm soon wore off . . .'[10]

It is clear that the devastating misfortunes which befell those early Jamestown colonists resulted not entirely from the hostility of the natives, the malarial and kindred sicknesses of high summer and the severity of the winter weather, lethal though at times those were. They sprang in some measure from (a) the terms of settlement laid down by London legislation, (b) the very nature of man and (c) last but not least from the early lack of discipline and strong leadership. These human defects resulted in too little being done and too little produced. Thus the hoped for self dependance in the matter of grain, plant and root crops, fell far short of that which was required and compelled the settlers to rely upon imported food supplies. Yet to procure these their shipping space was insufficient as occasionally were their financial reserves. Hunger and actual starvation followed. This was tragically true of the winters of 1607-8 and 1609-10, the latter being known as 'the starving times' – when the population was reduced to desperate straits, and occasionally even to cannibalism itself. [11]

The Virginia Council in London slowly recognized the weaknesses of leadership and the damaging effect wrought by the lack of private incentive inherent in the initial policy. Gradually they won from their royal patron a far greater measure of company control which enabled them to introduce, in stages, a more rational plan of partnership which, finally, led on to the principle of limited private enterprise. This was achieved by means of fresh royal charters sought and obtained in 1609 and 1612. The ultimate expression of this more liberal policy, and resolution to fulfil the Company's social and religious responsibilities, came in the lengthy Company directive of 1618 known as 'The Great Charter'. [12]

CHRISTIAN MISSION AS SEEN IN THE VIRGINIA CHARTERS

Historically christianity came first to the New World with Columbus, and from that moment the Spanish church sought the salvation of the pagan peoples whom the conquistadors strove to subjugate and exploit. The methods adopted by the missionary arm of Spain were vigorous, and not infrequently harsh. There were, of course, many exceptions to this policy of forceful evangelization, as for example when in 1570 a Jesuit party, without armed support, led by a Father Segura, 'a man of unusual intellectual capabilities, devotion and courage,'[13] sailed up the James river, landed near the site of the future Jamestown, marched over land, via the area where Williamsburg was later built, to the York River. There the Spaniards established their mission station – the first known in Virginia. Success was short lived, for through the treachery of a native convert[14] the whole party less one Indian boy, were butchered to death. Thus perished the first genuine attempt in Virginia to convert the Indians to Christianity, and many years were to pass before another specific move was made to bring definite christian teaching to the natives as a people.

The Church of England is seen in operation in the New World on several occasions in the late 1570s through the reports of the chroniclers of the various exploratory expeditions, e.g., Frobisher (1578), Gilbert (1578), and Drake (1579).

The idea of 'foreign' mission, or conversion of the native Indians, however, first comes fully into the open in the charter granted to the Virginia Company by King James I on 10 April 1606. In those letters patent his majesty commended the Company's expressed intention concerning ministry amongst the colonists and a desired campaign for the conversion of the Indians to the christian religion – the Church of England variety. The relevant passage reads:

> 'We, greatly commending and graciously accepting of their desires to the furtherance of so noble a work which may, by the providence of almighty God, hereafter tend to the glory of His Divine Majesty in propagating of Christian religion to such people as yet live in darkness and miserable ignorance of the true knowledge and worship of God and may in time bring the infidels and savages living in those parts to human civility and to a settled and quiet government, do by these our letters patents graciously accept of and agree to their humble and well intended desires'.

It is patent that amongst the varied reasons which prompted Englishmen to plan and found settlements in America christian mission frequently held a place of some importance. This was clearly in the minds of those who formulated the policy of the Virginia Company. The same concern about religious observance and practice and the furthering of missionary enterprise, is seen in the 'ordinances' of the only private plantation of which considerable foundation records are extant. [15] This idealized policy was set out distinctly in the first royal charter granted to the Virginia Company, [16] and is reiterated in the later charters of 1609 and 1612, and also in 'The Great Charter' of 1618, the first and only major legislative directive issued by the Company before its effective demise in 1624.

The seriousness of the hopes expressed, and in certain instances the instructions laid down, and withal the constancy of the subject, can be fully appreciated by a study of Bemiss. [17]

On the 20 November (1606), before the London and Plymouth pioneer parties sailed, the king issued 'Articles, Instructions and Orders' for the good order and government of the two several Colonies and plantations. Soon after the opening preamble comes the royal declaration:

> 'we do especially ordain, charge and require the said Presidents and Councils and the ministers of the said several Colonies . . . that they . . . do provide that the true word and services of God and Christian faith be preached, planted and used, not only within every of the said several Colonies and plantations but also as much as they may amongst the savage people which do or shall adjoin unto or border upon them, according to the doctrine, rights and religion now professed and established within the realm of England . . .'

Later in that same document a return is made to the subject thus:

> 'furthermore, our will and pleasure is and we do hereby determine and ordain that every person and persons being our subjects of every the said colonies and plantations shall from time to time well treat those savages and heathen peoples . . . that they may be sooner drawn to

the true knowledge of God . . .'[18]

This constant reiteration of the need for religious teaching and practice amongst the colonists, and the obligation upon the Company to civilize and convert the Indians to christianity, is interesting and consistent with the religious trends. It will be seen, however, in the following section that whereas the clergy engaged by the Company to minister the Word and Sacrament in the colony were assiduous in their duties towards the settlers, there appears in these early years to be little evidence of anything even remotely approaching an active ministry to the Indian population.

It is fortunate that amongst the initial settlement party who sailed from these shores in 1606 there were two who have left behind them records and recollections of that memorable voyage to Virginia. The first, Captain Edward-Maria Wingfield, had been elected leader ('President') upon landing at Jamestown in 1607. Early in 1608 he was replaced and returned to England. In Lambeth Palace Library is a manuscript of Wingfield, not perhaps an apologia, but one which contains interesting insights into events of 1606-8.

The second chronicler was Captain John Smith. His life-story, including many of the accounts of his activities in Virginia, is largely autobiographical, and, some authorities feel, suspect; but, whether at times embellished, pirated or plagiarized, Smith gives a graphic and rare insight into life in Virginia during those early days of settlement. Where he writes of the voyage out and Hunt's magnificent example during the trying and frightening period in the English Channel, and of his continued exemplary behaviour in Jamestown and church affairs generally up to the later's untimely death in about August 1608, he reflects the same judgement as is found in the other meagre and fragmentary sources which have survived, cf. Wingfield, George Percy, brother of the Earl of Northumberland, is very scathing, by insinuation, of Smith, in his 'True Relation' which purports to record events in Virginia 'from the Time Sir Thomas Gates was shipwrecked . . . 1609, until my departure . . . 1612.' Here a little jealousy and resentment may have crept in resulting from those disastrous days of discord, disease and famine in 1607-8. On the other hand Dr. R.A. Brock, the nineteenth century historian of Virginia, wrote of Smith that he had been 'justly termed "the father of Virginia"'.[19] And it must be admitted that but for Smith's historical works our knowledge of events in Virginia during those early days of settlement would be sparse in the extreme. I propose therefore to believe Smith's accounts of the work of the church and its ministers during the early days of the colony, except where there is substantial evidence to the contrary.

On 19 December 1606, as has been said, the first party of colonists, 105 in number, left Blackwell and were held up in sight of the English coast by storms for six weeks. Perhaps understandably, unrest mounted almost to the point of mutiny. Here the Reverend Robert Hunt, the chaplain to the expedition,[20] won his spurs and gained a reputation which established him as, perhaps, the outstanding clergyman to volunteer for the hardships and loneliness of the parish priest in a distant, and at times a very hostile land, during the first thirty years of colonization. During those grim days in the English Channel, Hunt was himself desperately ill, and 'making wild vomits into the night', but nevertheless calmed the heated atmosphere and brought back a measure of normality which enabled the expedition to continue. Smith wrote that Hunt 'with the waters of patience and his godly exhortation (but chiefly by his true devoted example) quenched those flames of envy and dissension.'[21]

When the settlement had been established at Jamestown, Hunt continued to exercise a calming influence upon the colonists, 'many were the mischiefs that daily sprang from their ignorant spirits; but the good doctrine and exhortation of our preacher Maister Hunt reconciled them and caused Captain Smith to be admitted of the Council', and the next day 'all received the Communion'. Smith recorded that morning and evening prayers from the Book of Common Prayer were said every day, and that on Sundays two sermons were preached, and that every three months the Holy Communion was celebrated 'until our minister died.'

Smith also gives an account of the first church buildings in which services were held: 'When I first was in Virginia, I well remember, we did hang an awning (which is an old sail) to three or four trees to shadow us from the sun, our walls were rails of wood our seats unhewed trees, till we cut planks; our Pulpit a bar of wood nailed to two neighbouring trees; in foul weather we shifted into an old rotten tent, for we had few better . . . This was our Church till we built a homely thing like a barn set upon cratchets covered with rafts, sedge and earth; so was also the walls'. Smith added that the best of their houses were of similar construction, but that the majority were far worse.

The remaining references to Hunt and his work concern, (1) the fire which destroyed the church and many of the other buildings in Jamestown, when 'Good Master Hunt our Preacher lost all his library, and all he had (but the clothes on his back) yet none ever saw him repine at his loss.' and (2) alarms caused by Indian attacks, when he was as ready as any for defence. The date of Hunt's death is not known, but his will was proved in England on 14 July 1608.

It would appear that modified religious observances were maintained when parties of colonists went out on expeditions of exploration, to negotiate with the natives for corn or when attempting a peaceful relationship with them. It is recorded, for example, of one such body that 'Our order was daily to have Prayer with a Psalm, at which solemnitie the poor savages much wondered; our Prayers being done, a while they were busied with a consultation till they had contrived their business.'[22] Even after the death of Hunt daily prayers were continued, but naturally the celebration of Holy Communion was not possible.

1609 brought a realization to the Virginia Company that all was far from well in the colony, and that a more direct control by the parent body must be exercised. Consequently a new charter, giving the London Company more 'personal' authority, was sought and obtained from the king; and to boost morale and resolution and, it was hoped, to encourage recruitment of fresh adventurers of purse and person, Dr. William Symonds,[23] 'Lecturer at Saint Saviour in Southwark', on 25 April 1609, gave a powerful address at White Chapel 'in the presence of many, Honourable and Worshipful, the Adventurers and Planters for Virginia.' This was entered for publication at Stationers' Hall on 4 May, and is believed to have been the first sermon *published* for the encouragement of Virginia, and, as the title-page declared, was delivered 'for the Advancement of their Christian Purposes'. The printed version runs to nearly 20,000 words, and it will be seen even from the Introduction that the over-riding objective matches the theme in the Company's charters and instructions, i.e., 'To the Right Noble and Worthy Advancers of the Standard of Christ among the Gentiles, The Adventurers for the Plantation of Virginia.' The final paragraph ends thus 'Be cheerful then, and the Lord of all glory, glorify his name by your happy spreading of the Gospel, to your commendation, and his glory . . . Hallelu-iah.'

A similar exhortation, *A Good Speed to Virginia*, written by Robert Gray, was also entered for publication at Stationers' Hall in May 1609.[24] Further sermons along the same lines followed, e.g., that of Daniel Price at 'Paule Cross' on 28 May,[25] before the great new thrust to support and enlarge the colony was mounted. This expedition, made up of nine ships, carrying about 500 adventurers including Sir Thomas Gates, the Lieut. Governor designate for the colony, and fresh supplies, left England late in May.[26]

In late July a terrific storm struck and severed the fleet in the eastern Atlantic, sinking the *Catch* with all hands and wrecking the flag-ship, the *Sea Venture*, in the Bermudas, but with no loss of life. The story of the exploits of that party, and the successful building of two small ships in which, months later, they reached Virginia, is too well known to need recording. It is worthy of mention, however, that their fleet chaplain, The Revd. Richard Buck, an Oxford graduate, held prayers twice daily while on the island. He also preached two sermons on Sundays, solemnized one marriage, baptized two children (the girl – 'Bermuda' and the boy – 'Bermudas'), and buried six colonists, including the wife of Sir Thomas Gates. The father of Bermuda was a John Rolfe, and it is believed that it was he who, as a widower, married Pocahontas in 1614.

The seven surviving ships from the fleet finally arrived at Jamestown with much of their supplies badly damaged by the sea water. The lateness of the season rendered further planting useless, and the 500 settlers, old timers and new, faced a difficult winter period. Their worries and problems were exacerbated when Captain John Smith, their deposed leader of council, and, despite the calumnies poured upon him, the most able man in the colony, was badly hurt and had to return to England in October.

Back in England in December an important document was lodged at Stationers' Hall for publication.[27] The priority of intentions enumerated in it conforms to pattern in that it postulates that 'The Principal and Main Ends . . . were *first* to preach and baptize into *Christian Religion*, and by propagation of the Gospel to recover out of the arms of the Devil, a number of poor and miserable souls, wrapped up unto death, in almost *invincible ignorance*; . . .' This *'True and Sincere Declaration . . .'* had been drawn up with the approval of Lord Delaware, Sir Thomas Smythe and other members of the Council for Virginia in London, and can be assumed to have been a public affirmation of Company policy.

In the following February (1610) came yet another, and perhaps the best known, sermon of support for the Virginia project. This was delivered at the Temple Church, London, and was attended by the Council for Virginia and some of the Adventurers. The special preacher was the Reverend William Crashaw. In the address the spiritual tasks and mission were strongly stressed:

'Go forward in the strength of the Lord, and make mention of His righteousness only. Look not at the gain, the wealth, the honour, the advancement of thy house that may follow and fall upon thee; but look at those high and better ends that concern the kingdom of God. Remember thou art a general of English men, nay a general of Christian men; therefore principally look to religion. You go to commend it to the heathen; then practice it yourselves; make the name of Christ honourable, not hateful to them.'[28]

The party, in their tiny ships, left the Bermudas on 10 May 1610, and landed at Jamestown on the 23rd to find that the colonists during the winter and spring had been reduced by famine and other resulting hazards from about 500 to between fifty and sixty walking skeletons. Indeed, they had been driven to eating vermin, roots and reptiles, and even cannabalism was reported.

Upon landing Gates called the whole body to church where parson Buck conducted the service. The food supplies brought by Gates being totally inadequate to sustain the colony for more than a few weeks, it was decided to abandon the settlement and sail to Newfoundland. The situation was saved by the unexpected arrival of the Governor, Lord Delaware, with three ships of fresh colonists and supplies. The Governor at once set about re-establishing the religious life of the community. The church was rebuilt on a lavish scale, and with the Revd. Mr. Buck and clergy whom the Governor is thought to have brought with him – reference is made to 'true preachers' – a firm roster for daily prayers and Sunday sermons was re-restablished. The daily prayers were at 10 a.m. and 4 p.m. with an extra sermon on Thursdays. It appears probable that Lord Delaware was following the lines of 'A True and sincere declaration of the purpose and ends of the Plantation . . .' which had had, as stated, Lord Delaware's approval. Soon after the arrival of the Governor, Sir Thomas Gates was sent to England to report personally on the appalling events which had overtaken the colony and to outline the needs of the community if it was to survive and develop. Late in March 1611 Lord Delaware, by then a very sick man, placed Captain, the Honourable, George Percy in charge of the settlement and returned to England. He, however, retained the title 'Governor' until his death in 1618.

Early in 1611 Sir Thomas Dale, who had been fighting on the continent, was granted leave of absence by the States General and returned to England. There, in February, he married Elizabeth, a daughter of Sir Thomas Throckmorton, and so a cousin of George Thorpe. Well before the arrival of Lord Delaware in England, Dale sailed with three ships for Virginia carrying fresh settlers, livestock and food. He arrived on 10 May, replacing Percy as temporary Governor, and found that morale was bad, discipline poor and even the vital agricultural tasks, such as corn planting, had been neglected. In August Gates returned to the colony with a fleet of 'six tall ships'[29] and considerable reinforcements and supplies. The former included twenty women and the latter 100 cattle and 200 hogs.

These seasoned campaigners, Dale and Gates, worked well together and by vigour and stern discipline began to put the colony on its feet. It is interesting to note that once again the voice of George Percy was raised in vitriolic criticism of a rival's actions and behaviour. He had denigrated Captain John Smith's character in the early settlement. Now, a few years later, he poured out a tirade against his successor, Sir Thomas Dale, for his disciplinary methods. He recounted that deserters and law breakers were subject to uncivilized and brutal treatment, some were executed in a most severe manner, others broken on the wheel or shot. In other words Dale was administering 'field discipline' as practised in war conditions in the Low Countries, and, as C.E. Hatch wrote 'These were stern measures that produced results and few contemporary associates took issue.'[30] These included that old planter Sir Thomas Gates the Lieut-Governor, John Rolfe, Ralph Hamor and Sir Edwin Sandys. Hatch continued 'To them, motivated by the spirit of the time, hard conditions required stern handling.'[31] It must be repeated too that on his arrival Dale found the colony in a demoralized condition. Perhaps the judgement of later historians, such as Brock, on Smith's character and ability lies nearer the reality than that pronounced by Captain George Percy who clearly had a chip on his shoulder.

Recognizing the great disadvantages of the Jamestown site, Dale made a personal reconnaissance up river, and selected a more healthy area for a second settlement which was named Henrico after Henry, Prince of Wales. Dale with a band of 350 specially selected men rapidly built a well-fortified town which quickly became an important centre with the first hospital (eighty beds) in British America and a fair and 'handsome church'.[32] There the Rev. Alexander Whitaker, who had been brought over to Virginia by Sir Thomas Dale, built 'a fair Parsonage', which he named Rock Hall, on a 100 acre plot.[33]

Dale too, so wrote Dabney, recognized the importance of stimulating private initiative. This he achieved by assigning small plots of land to worthy settlers. They were told that they could grow crops for their own, as against the Company's benefit. The results were most satisfactory, and production increased almost immediately. 'The discredited system based on communal ownership was never permitted to return.'[34]

SUMMARY OF 1606-18 PERIOD

Looking back over the years 1606-18 it is abundantly clear that all charters or instructions issued to or by the Virginia Company of London, and all sermons, exhortations and broadsheets relating to the colonization of Virginia placed the religious element — (1) the maintaining of christian standards, (2) the observance of the recognised practices of devotion, and (3) the missionary aspect of the enterprise, i.e., the bringing of the gospel to the natives and their hoped for conversion — very high in the list of objectives presented to, and obligations placed upon, the adventurers, leaders and lesser colonial folk alike.

It is equally patent that whereas there is ample evidence that religious ceremonial and devotional practice were rigidly observed and preached by the priests and ministers who made the great venture to Virginia, the task of taking the gospel message to the pagan peoples of the colony never really got off the ground. This may seem strange, bearing in mind the prominence given to this subject in royal charters and company instructions, and the fact that by and large those clergymen who accompanied the early settlers were men of vigour, intellectual stature and deep devotion. The three outstanding clerical figures during the first twelve years of colonization were Robert Hunt, Richard Buck and Alexander Whitaker. All three were frequently referred to in reports and accounts of events in Virginia as men of deep devotion who laboured vigorously and unselfishly amongst the settlers and leaders in the colony. Their ministry, was both faithful and greatly appreciated, as has already been pointed out. On the other hand, evidence that they displayed any real concern in the task of winning over the Indians to christianity is strangely lacking. Certain possible reasons for this apparent apathy towards missionary enterprise can, of course, by suggested. It might be said that for much of the time the Indians were hostile to the white man.[35] This, however, is not a valid argument, for there were periods when the relationship between natives and settlers was far from hostile, and when trade and co-operation were possible. Even during those peaceful periods the opportunities to evangelize could hardly be said to have been taken. It is astonishingly true that the comparative peace which followed the baptism and marriage of Pocahontas to John Rolfe i.e., from c. 1614 to the 1622 massacre, was not seized upon as an auspicious moment to begin furthering the principles of 'mission' as outlined by the London authorities from time to time. Although Hunt was frequently spoken of in glowing terms and his utter devotion to and enterprise on behalf of the colonists was greatly admired there appears to be no single extant reference to him working amongst the natives nor encouraging members of his flock to honour the high sounding phrases found in that first royal charter.

Stith pointed out that a few years later 'Sir Thomas Dales, Mr. Whitaker, Minister of Bermuda-Hundred, and Mr. Rolfe, her husband, were very careful and assiduous, in instructing Pocahontas in the Christian Religion: and she, on her Part expressed an eager desire, and showed great Capacity in learning.' But this was a 'special case'. Pocahontas, the favourite daughter of the powerful Indian chief Powhatan, tricked into captivity, had married the important seasoned planter, John Rolfe – it was an example of mutual attraction under weird conditions. Her conversion was well-nigh vital from the view point of the validity of the marriage, and highly desirable for its stability. It was, furthermore, good propaganda for the Virginia Company, and in no sense could it be classified as resulting from the implementation of the Company's instructions relating to missionary enterprise. This is the clear implication behind Stith's exposé; he ended his account by reporting that Pocahontas 'was the first Christian Indian in these Parts, and perhaps the sincerest and most worthy, that has even been since.'[36]

The only other definite identification of a native convert in Virginia comes in 1622. That Indian, named Chanco or Chance, shortly before 'H hour' revealed to his master, one Richard Pace, the Indians' plans for the massacre of the settlers. Pace rowed across the James river and warned the Governor at Jamestown who was able to alert the plantations near the capital, Chanco thus saved hundreds of British lives and possibly even prevented the extinction or abandonment of the entire colony. These are the only specific references to Indian converts during the period 1607 to 1624, save for that mysterious figure referred to in the registers of St. Martin in the Fields, as 'Homo Virginiae.'[37]

Stith later made a comment on the attitudes, and in one instance an alleged statement, which indicated the mental approach of two of the very few clerical gentlemen in Virginia at that period to the task and problems involved in attempting the conversion of the Indians. It may, perhaps, help to explain the apparent apathy towards missionary work in the colony as a whole. He wrote:

'Captain Smith, with Mr. Stockham and Mr. Whitaker, two Clergymen of Note in the Colony, had even been of the opinion, that the Ways of Gentleness and Kindness would never be sufficient to bring the Indians over; and had therefore recommended that Mars and Minerva should go Hand in Hand, as well in their Conversion, as in all other Transactions and Intercourse with them. But they are too sanguinary in their Notion of the Matter. For Mr. Stockham plainly declares, that, "until the Throats of their Priests and Elders are cut, there can be no Hopes of their Conversion"'.

NOTES

1. A.L. Rowse, *The Elizabethans and America* (Trevelyan Lectures, Cambridge 1958), London, 1959, p. 1.

2. Rowse, ibid., p. 3.

3. *The Principal Navigations, Voyages and Discoveries of the English Nation.*

4. e.g., Sir Thomas Smythe, President of the East India Company, became in 1609, and remained for more than eight years, the Treasurer (Director or President) of the Virginia Company.

5. Bemiss, op.cit., p. 1.

6. 'And thus was this Plantation begun and ended in one year' – Stith, op.cit., p. 75. See also C.P. Nettels, *The Roots of American Civilization*, New York, 1963, p. 114.

7. For the suggestion that their minister, Revd. Robert Hunt, may have been a typhoid carrier, and the cause of an epidemic at Jamestown in 1607/8, see G.W. Jones, 'The First Epidemic in English America', *VMHB*, 1963, pp. 1-10.

8. W. Stith, op.cit., p. 44.

9. Stith, op.cit., p. 46.

10. Virginius Dabney, *Virginia the New Dominion*, Doubleday and Co., New York, 1971, p. 10.

11. Stith, op.cit., pp. 116-7, gives a number of instances of settlers eating Indians and Whites. One colonist, 'killed his wife, powdered her up and had eaten part of her . . .' before he was discovered and executed.

12. The history of the Royal Charters and The Great Charter may be studied in depth in *The Three Charters of The Virginia Company of London – With Seven Related Documents 1606-1621*, by S.M. Bemiss. For a detailed and comprehensive account of the background, birth and life of the Virginia Company of London, see the following standard works, Brown I and II, Stith, Brock, Sams and Campbell, all of which have been reprinted between 1964 and 1973. In addition the workings and legislation of the Company can be studied in depth in the four volumes of Susan Kingsbury's *Documents of the Virginia Company*, Washington, 1906-35.

13. S.M. Bemiss, *Ancient Adventurers*, pp. 1-3 *(The Jesuit Mission)* Garrett and Massie, Richmond, Virginia, 1964.

14. This native, taken by the Spaniards some years previously, had been baptized Don Luis de Valesco and educated in their best schools. Later he acted as an interpreter and Indian adviser to the Spanish leader General Menendez, before being seconded as guide to the Jesuit missionaries.

15. Berkeley Hundred founded 1619 – Smyth I, 3 (4); in Kingsbury III, pp. 130-4 = Indenture.

16. 10 April, 1606.

17. S.M. Bemiss, *The Three Charters [and]* . . . *Related Documents, 1606-21.*

18. *Bemiss, ibid.*

19. *Brock, op.cit., p. 14.*

20. *Alumni Cantabrigienses, sub nomine.*

21. Quoted by E. Clowes Chorley, *WMQ* series 2, vol. X, p. 197.

22. Narrative of Baghall and others in Smith's History, p. 53, quoted by Clowes Chorley, op.cit., p. 198.

23. Brown I, vol II, p. 1029, points out that, as it is believed that Symonds was Preacher at St. Saviour's by 1607, it is likely that he baptized John Harvard, the founder of Harvard College, there on 29 November 1607. An introduction to, and a precis of, the sermon is printed in Brown I, pp. 282-91.

24. Brown I, pp. 293-302.

25. Ibid., pp. 312-16.

26. Some authorities give early June as the starting date.

27. See Brown I, pp. 337-53.

28. Crashaw's Sermon, pp. 80-1, precis in Brown I, pp. 360-75.

29. Stith, p. 123.

30. C.E. Hatch, op.cit., p. 51.

31. Ibid.

32. Stith, p. 124.

33. See Stith pp. 136 and 233 for his, and also Revd. Stockham's, attitude toward the conversion of the Indians.

34. Dabney, op.cit., p. 23.

35. See Wilburn E. Washburn, 'A Moral History of Indian-White relations: Need and

Opportunity for Study', *Ethno-History*, 4, 1957, pp. 47-61, and 'The Moral and Legal Justification for Dispossing the Indians', 1972, *Seventeenth Century America*, 1972, pp. 15-32.

36. Stith, p. 136.

37. See chapter 3.

6

Terra Nova – *Berkeley, Virginia*

1. THE FIRST PHASE

Thus the first contingent of the Berkeley Company left Bristol in mid September 1619, and their great adventure, after months of preparation and considerable frustration, had begun. The American historian Dowdey claimed that the Berkeley foundation 'is the most thoroughly recorded of all plantations.'[1] Amongst *The Smyth of Nibley Papers*, which obviously prompted that statement, is a document of considerable interest, namely a log of the voyage made by that initial body of Berkeley colonists.[2] This account of thirteen closely written pages was kept by Ferdinando Yate, a brother of Gyles Yate, gent, of Uley, who was joint lord of the manor with Sir Richard Berkeley. It is endorsed 'The Voyage written by Ferdinando Yate to Virginia 1619.'

The introduction to that manuscript emphasizes the fact that Thorpe was not only a most active Adventurer, but was also one who appeared meticulous in the planning of the expedition and in the keeping of records which might further its future progress. Yate opened his log thus: 'I was wished by Mr. George Thorpe to take a note of every day's travel upon the seas;' With humility Yate added 'I have performed in a true collection although not in so good form as I could wish it were therefore I hope you will accept of it as it is'. He excused himself also for the brevity and deficiencies of his account of the actual voyage and the details of the first phase of the settlement proper before, presumably, the return of the *Margaret* bearing with it the log for Thorpe's perusal. His defence was that 'the seas were troublesome and many occasion at sea happeneth to hinder a man from his study and now we are ashore we have work enough to follow our husbandry some to clearing ground for corn and tobacco some to building houses some to plant vines and mulberry trees and all these must be seen unto . . .' Yate then gives his terms of reference for the log.

'A short note of our time spent at sea and the variety and change of wind and weather and the extremities that seamen endure and the mercy of Almighty God to support them in all distresses'.

Why did Thorpe 'wish' that log to be kept? A possible answer is that, envisaging a rapidly developing settlement in Virginia, with which there would be a regular schedule of voyages to and from the plantation, he wished to obtain details which would enable him the better to mount future voyages in the interests of the company in general and the passengers in particular.

Yate having ended his apologia then addressed the promoters 'To worshipful gentlemen of Gloucestershire George Thorpe of Wanswell esq and John Smith of Nibley esq wishing you all manner of prosperity and especially in this honourable attempt of planting in this country which I make no doubt with God's assistance, will be a benefit to your selves and posterity; a good to the commonwealth of England; and in time, a means to convert these poor faithless Indians'. It is interesting that Yate in the last sentence mentioned missionary enterprise. This theme, as has been stated, not only found prominence as an ideal – indeed an obligation – in the charters of the Virginia Company and in the instructions laid down by the Berkeley Adventurers, but, it would seem, was fully accepted and anticipated by individual members of the settlement party. This may in part, have been due to the method of personnel selection operated by the Berkeley sponsors.

The *Margaret* sailed from Bristol on the 16 September at '8 of the clock or there about'. On the 17th 'we lost sight of Lundie,' and on the 19th 'being the first sabbath day in our voyage we were becalmed as the night before'. The following day there was a 'very strong gale', and they were compelled 'to strike our topsail'.

Thus the log continued day by day. There were occasional references to being becalmed, but more often the entries told of wind and rain storms 'which did both annoy mariners and passengers' – sometimes the storms were 'very tempestuous'. It was understandable that those conditions did 'annoy' the personnel, for most of them were accommodated on the open deck with little or no protection.[3] The two worst periods were – first, on the 9 October, when 'the storm grew so extreme that we like to cut our main mast by the board' – but the wind eased and that extreme measure was avoided; second, during the 17 and 18 November conditions were critical. On the 17 they had 'great extremities of weather' which continued 'with as much extremity' on the 18th when 'about noon we struck our foretopmast thus remaining according to the pleasure of the Almighty God in the surging and overgrowing seas' when the ship's company were 'depending upon God's mercies and praying unto his majesty to lend us comfortable weather . . . and bring us to our expected port . . .' They began looking for land and sounding on 21 November, but it was not until at about 4 o'clock on the 25th that they first found bottom at sixteen fathoms. Final success came on the 28th 'being the sabbath day . . . we sounded and had land [bottom] at 11 fathom of water and about 11 a clock one went up in the main top and described land which was no small joy to the whole company . . .' That night they 'came to anchor in Chesapeake Bay . . .', their troubles, however, had not ended, for on the 29th another storm blew up and when attempting to way anchor the capstan broke down, which put us in 'great distress and so were driven to ride it out' until the next morning when the capstan was mended. That evening they anchored at 'Kecketan⁴ in a good harbour', when 'my Captain went ashore to see some of his friends and myself and his man with him thus leaving the seas . . .' The log virtually ends at this point, presumably because Yate felt that his commission had been completed with their landfall.

The next day they sailed up the James river and on the 4 December landed at Jamestown before proceeding to the Berkeley Grant, the new Berkeley Hundred. The first and perhaps the more hazardous part of their expedition was over, and when they arrived at Berkeley, remembering their perilous passage, and in accordance with the instruction given to Captain Woodleefe on 4 September, and in the spirit of the times, they presumably assembled together to thank God for His many mercies. There would have been an element of spontaneity in their thanksgiving, despite the fact of the instructions issued on 4 September.

At the end of Yate's log is a short epilogue which merits quoting in full, for it reveals the first impressions which the new country, as seen in the voyage up the James river and in the area of the new Berkeley plantation, made upon a man of some education and standing. It reads:

> 'I need not report any thing of the country you having had so good intelligence of it by so many worthy gentlemen: that I should but loose my labour to write any farther, but only this I must need say, that if I had the eloquence of Cicero or the skillful art of Apellose I could not pen neither paint a better praise of the country than the country itself deserveth. We are well settled in good land by means of the Governor of this country and the care and experience of our Captain our house is built with a store convenient'.

The next direct reference to the Berkeley settlement party is in the form of a certificate, dated Charles City on 14 December, and was sent by Sir George Yeardley to the Treasurer and Council of the Virginia Company in London.⁵ The Governor announced that the 'good ship of Bristol called the *Margaret*' had landed safely at the port of Jamestown on 4 December. Yeardley stated that the thirty-five persons of the Berkeley contingent plus Captain Woodleefe were all 'in safety and perfect health.' Why thirty-five when the certificate of the Mayor of Bristol, dated 15 September, had testified that there had been thirty-six aboard?⁶ A comparison of the two lists reveals that whereas a John Singer was included in the Mayor's document, he does not appear on that of

Yeardley. A careful scrutiny of other Smyth of Nibley Papers provides the answer.

In Smyth's annotated list of the Berkeley men sent to Virginia under Captain Woodleefe is the following entry, 'John Singer the Surgeon hath 50 s in hand towards furnishing his chest, and thirty shillings the month, beginning Monday 13. September, 1619.'[7] Again, in the consolidated bills relating to the equiping of that first expedition[8] there is an entry which reads – 'Paid to John Singer Surgeon for his chest of drugs etc . . .Ls'. A marginal note, however, records that 'he went not therefore to be repaid'. Furthermore, an account of the money spent by the Berkeley Company since Tracy's departure, and covering the period 18 September 1620 to Michaelmas 1621, contains the entry 'also Ls is still owing to us by Singer the Surgeon which is also mentioned in the last year's accompt'.[9]

Clearly Singer went on board on the 15 September 1619, and was present when the Mayor's list was compiled. Later that day or before they sailed the next morning he had had second thoughts and disembarked. There appears to be no further mention of that debt. This, in view of the chaos which followed the massacre eighteen months later, is not surprising.

Another problem is raised by the lists of the Mayor and the Governor. The name Richard Sherife appears on both, establishing that he embarked at Bristol and arrived safely and well at the Berkeley Grant on 4 December 1619. Yet one by the same name, and, as in those lists, designated 'the elder', is recorded in Smyth I, 3 (19) as sailing in the *London Merchant* with Thorpe to Virginia late in March 1620. This is confirmed in Smyth's master copy of the list of the Berkeley colonists who sailed for Virginia between September 1619 and the end of March 1620 (Smyth I, 3 (9)) where a Richard Sherife, the elder, is twice mentioned, i.e., (1) 'that went with Mr. Thorpe,' (2) 'went after with Mr. Thorpe 27 March 1620.' It would seem too great a coincidence that there should be two of that name and also termed the elder. If there had been, Smyth, being Smyth, would undoubtedly have commented on the fact. Thus the solution might well be that Sherife embarked on a ship returning to England within a week or two of landing on the Berkeley Grant on 4 December – he could hardly have waited until the *Margaret* returned in the New Year. It must have been a very cogent reason or reasons which compelled him to make three crossings of the Atlantic in seven or eight months. Perhaps it was part of a set plan, that a report on the original crossing, the Governor's reception and treatment of the Berkeley party and the early activities on the plantation should be brought back before Thorpe and his small group sailed. This might account for Smyth, while recording that Thorpe had chosen three of the five fellow passengers as servants for the company – Smyth I, 3 (19), yet naming four (including Richard Sherife the elder) as going with Thorpe on 27 March 1620, i.e., Sherife was already an active member of the company who was merely returning to duty in Virginia.

The grant of land where the Berkeley Company settled had a three-miles frontage on the wide James river and contained about 8,000 acres of meadowland and virgin forest. Before the ship was unloaded, two public buildings, a storehouse and an assembly hall for meals and worship, were erected, and primitive dwellings, averaging 25 ft. × 18 ft. × 12 ft. high and made of peeled and split logs, were built. The colonists, for such they now were, also constructed a wooden palisade for the protection of their homes and animals, and their future corn crops and gardens against possible ravages of the Indians and wild beasts such as wolves, bears and 'wild cats'. The fence, according to the sponsors' instructions, was to be seven and a half feet high, and should enclose '400 acres or more' and had to be completed 'with all convenient expedition'.

When the *Margaret* sailed for England the Berkeley people were on their own. There were, of course, other settlers in the same naked wilderness, but during the severe winter weather the opportunities for meeting many would be limited. The first task of the Berkeley party, as with all colonists, was to become self supporting, and to this end they at once planted grain and garden crops.

On 10 January 1620 Yeardley sent a letter to the Berkeley sponsors[10] from Jamestown. He began by thanking them for their letter of 9 September, in which they had enclosed a copy of their letter of the previous February enquiring whether he, the Governor, was now prepared to take up the offered fifth share in the Berkeley enterprise. They repeated the question and also commended their party under Woodleefe to his patronage.

The Governor's reply was diplomatic and delicately phrased. He first assured Throckmorton and his associates that following their request he had planted the Berkeley colonists 'in a very good and Convenient place'. He went on to explain that the selected site was choice and the allotment had been made despite possible West family opposition.[11] The Governor continued by saying that if Captain Francis West protested 'You may upon mine affirmation boldly reply that Mr. West is misinformed.' The latter appeared to have considered – incorrectly according to Yeardley – that some of the land belonged to his family.[12] Yeardley then explained that he was unable to take up the Berkeley fifth share because of heavy commitments in the Smythe Hundred. Finally he assured them of his readiness 'to assist Captain Woodleefe at all assays.'

A disappointed Smyth endorsed the letter 'of the Place assigned for our

Berkeley: and yet it is not the lord de la ware's land: And yet he refuseth to join us.' The mention of possible friction with the powerful West family[13] is interesting and must be borne in mind because of events in the post massacre period when the same Francis West figured prominently in what appears to have been an attempt to confiscate most of Thorpe's personal property on the grounds of supposed or exaggerated debts.

The next record which has relevance to the Berkeley Company – though at first sight there appears nothing to relate it to the Berkeley Plantation – is entered in the minutes of a Great and General Court of the Virginia Company on 2 February 1620.[14] There it is stated that four indentures, 'all engrossed', had been granted. One of these was 'to William Tracy esquire and his associates for Transportation of 500 Persons' This might be termed the conception of the second phase of the Berkeley Plantation. The gestation period was long and fraught with problems.

Later in the month an account was rendered to the Berkeley sponsors for supplies which were to be sent to Virginia in the *London Marchant* on which Thorpe and his party were to take passage. It was recorded that Berkeley, Thorpe and Smyth had each contributed £35 as their quarter share of the costs, and that Thorpe and Smyth had, in addition, jointly paid the £35 which Throckmorton 'should have paid save that he hath now quit the partnership and business'. It seems strange that Throckmorton should have dropped out so quickly, indeed, within a few weeks of the actual foundation. It is also surprising that Berkeley appears not to have taken up any of the additional financial burden. Perhaps only Thorpe and Smyth were in London and the defaulting of Throckmorton was sudden and the matter urgent. The goods paid for included hogsheads of white wine vinegar, oatmeal salt and 'meals', 'sallet oyle,' Aqua vitae (31 gallons), 'castile soap', 40 pairs of knitted stockings, 200 ells, of canvas (170), dowlas (13) and lockeram (17), 48 doz. buttons, 41 sorts of garden seeds, and hooks and lines.[15]

The *London Marchant* sailed on 27 March, a date established, as already mentioned, in Smyth's list of the early Berkeley settlers, amongst whom were four who 'went after with Mr. Thorpe 27 March 1620.'[16]

It is perhaps fitting, while discussing Smyth's master copy to take note of the appalling casualty rate amongst Berkeley's early settlers – something that they shared with most groups of fresh immigrants.

Smyth recorded that all four of the pioneer party were dead, as were the four that went with Thorpe. Of the large September party, one returned to England, one was drowned, twenty-four died, while two others were killed in the massacre of March 1622, as indeed was Thorpe. If the Berkeley casualties followed the normal pattern, most of those who were recorded as 'dead' would have died in the first year before they became 'seasoned'.

At an extraordinary Court of the Virginia Company held at the house of Sir Edwin Sandys on 3 April 1620, a week after Thorpe had sailed for the colony, comes the mention of his first involvement in the company's public affairs in the New World. The treasurer reported that the committee set up for the purpose had met, and, as requested, had drafted a letter to the Governor in which they mentioned that '2 very sufficient and able men' were to go to Virginia as Deputies to take charge of '2 particular governments under Sir George Yeardley, for managing and ordering 2 parts of the public land, and Tenants'. They added that the one for the college lands, with whom they had already 'dealt', was Mr. George Thorpe, 'a gentleman of his Majesty's privy chamber, and one of his Council for Virginia'. They stated finally that Thorpe had 'promised with all diligence to have exceeding care thereof'.[17] The second deputy – for the public lands – was not then named.

This declaration effectively refutes the suggestion made in the Baynham v. Smith case in 1626,[18] that Thorpe left the country secretly – the implication being that he had fled. There had been negotiations between the Virginia Company and Thorpe, and he had accepted the important office of Deputy for the college lands under the Governor. Furthermore, he had promised faithfully to fulfil his duties. The notice of this appointment also clearly establishes that it was the parent company, and not the Berkeley one, which first engaged his activities in Virginia. It would however, be ludicrous to believe, despite the lack of evidence, that Thorpe would not have arranged with his fellow sponsors of the Berkeley Company to keep a watchful eye on the plantation.

At an 'Unperfect' Court held on 8 April – again at the Treasurer's house – it was decided, in view of the reports which had come before the Council of trouble in Virginia between the Governor and two important planters, that a letter 'shallbe written to Mr. Thorpe and the Council of State and therein inclose their said Complaints that they may examine the truth thereof and upon certificate from thence they may accordingly proceed to right either part according to equity'.[19] Thorpe's appointment as manager or director of the college lands, the endowment, and the intended financial support for the grandiose Henrico educational project, demonstrated the Council's confidence in him as a man of ability and integrity. Five days later the minutes, as recorded above, evinced the Council's belief that Thorpe's judgement, social standing and general character were such that they could confidently appeal to him – as one apart from the Council in the colony – to assess the situation and report back. Furthermore, they appeared to be prepared to act upon the advice for which they were asking.

At a full meeting of the Company held on 11 May the appointments of the two deputies of the Company's lands, Thorpe and the as yet unnamed other, were confirmed, when the placing of the tenants of the Governor and his two Deputies was discussed. Thorpe's were to be places at the 'upp[er?] end of the College Land.'

On 17 May a Quarter Court was held at Mr. Ferrar's house in St. Sithes Lane. Once again the announcement of the appointment of the two Deputies was made and further details were given. The second Deputy was now named as Mr. Thomas Nuce. Thorpe who 'is already gone . . . to govern the College lands with [a] graunt of 300 Acres to be perpetually belonging to that place and 10 Tenants to be place upon the Land.' There ten would constitute the labour force deemed necessary to work the 300 acres for Thorpe and his successors in office. Later in the Court it was stated that 100 tenants had been allocated to the College lands. In view of the fact that that estate was 10,000 acres in extent and not in hand, the number was not generous. At that same Court Mr. John Berkeley, the ironmaster, was granted his indenture of land, and assent was given for the Smythe Hundred to be re-named the Southampton Hundred. Thus ended the first phase of the Berkeley Company's settlement, of which so few substantial details are known, while Thorpe's appointment as manager of the College estates received the approval of the Courts of the Virginia Company.

2. VIRGINIA MAY 1620 TO JANUARY 1621

Brief reference has already been made to the indenture granted to William Tracy on 2 February 1620,[20] in response to an application which had been received by the court on 26 January,[21] to enable him to transport 500 persons to Virginia. It was obvious that he was contemplating a substantial investment in colonization, but his 'Associates', in conformity with the common practice, were not named. However, on 15 April Tracy wrote a letter to Smyth[22] in which he suggested a possible, indeed a hoped for, federation with the Berkeley Company. He began the letter with an expression of delight at the 'good news of Virginia', and of hope that 'all our business happily to go on to God's glory and our good'. Tracy apologized for not being able to meet Smyth in Gloucester, but agreed to accept the decisions of 'my Cousin Berkeley' and Smyth. A meeting in London appeared to be in the offing when they will 'have time sufficient to determine all.' Tracy assured Smyth that 'I have at least 20 [persons] promised me the most part I am sure of'. He added that he felt that they would have more men available than they could 'carry', and that an individual's trade could well be the deciding factor in selection or deferment until 'the next going'. Tracy concluded 'do as you please with Sir William Throckmorton, I will do nothing but as you advise me'. It would appear that Throckmorton's withdrawal[23] was no surprise, indeed that Tracy's application in January for an indenture had been made with the hope, if not the understanding, that ultimately he would take over Throckmorton's place in the Berkeley syndicate. It will be remembered that Sir William headed the list of the original grantees,[24] and that only weeks later appeared to have lost some enthusiasm.[25] His final financial withdrawal from the company, however, may well, as already suggested, have resulted from the leadership decision, i.e., the appointment of Woodleefe and not 'cousin' Chester. His election later in 1620 as an umpire in the event of disputes between certain Berkeley sponsors indicates that he continued to have a general, if not a financial, interest in the project.

The second phase of the Berkeley Plantation's development can properly be said to begin on the 7 May 1620 when an indenture was drawn up transferring Sir William Throckmorton's share in the Berkeley Company to William Tracy[26] of Hayles in Gloucestershire, the brother of Sir Thomas Tracy.[27] At an early stage in this document Sir George Yeardley, the Governor of Virginia, is named as an original assignee, whereas in fact he never took up the option. The terms of this conveyance were £75 of 'lawful money of England . . . and divers other causes and considerations . . .'

On 17 May the Virginia Company issued a broadside[28] in which the high mortality rate amongst the colonists and the 'utter destruction' of some plantations were mentioned, and it was suggested that this might well be divine 'chastisement' for 'grievous transgressions.' A better attendance at divine worship and a fuller recognition of 'holy and just laws' were advocated. Guest-houses for the reception of newly arrived immigrants – fifty per house – were to be erected in the four boroughs[29] and on several of the particular plantations. These buildings were to be 16 ft. × 180 ft., and might be divided into two parts. It was laid down for the spiritual oversight of the settlers and 'to allure' the Indians to the christian faith, that every borough and particular plantation should be provided with 'a godly and learned minister'. The tenants of College, Company and Governor's lands were not forgotten. Each minister would have a hundred acres of glebe and six tenants to work his land.[30] The agricultural policies were outlined and mention was made of specialists for the labour force, e.g., vignerons and iron workers.

On that same date a Quarter Court heard read, and then confirmed and ordered, five patents to be sealed. One of these was for John Berkeley, Esq, lately of Beverstone Castle near Berkeley, the senior member of a cadet branch of the Berkeley Castle family.[31] He had been engaged to take over the hitherto ill-fated iron works at Falling Creek. Later in the proceedings the previous arrangements for the payment of the two Deputies were confirmed.

There are three letters written by Tracy (*The Smyth of Nibley Papers*, nos. 17, 18 and 19) which have only 'June 1620', as a dating. The first and last are addressed to Smyth, while the second is inscribed 'to my friend William Archerd [John Smyth's confidential clerk] or his deputy at M[r] Gill his house.'[32] Because of their common dating it is reasonable to examine them in the order in which they are recorded in the Nibley Papers and printed in Kingsbury III.

1.[33] Tracy began by expressing the hope that he would be paying Smyth £100 on the next day and £300 within ten days; some money had already changed hands. A suggestion of the transporting of some heifers in a hired Flemish 'hoye' was mentioned, as was the possibility of taking three mares which would be of 'great use'. The possibility of having too many men was again raised. Then followed requests that Smyth will obtain certain supplies for the party. These included all needful things for 'physic or surgery, for life is more dear than gold . . .', leather for linings, stockings of leather, linen and wooden goods. Tracy asked Smyth to bring his (Tracy's) indenture, and promised to pay the cost of the various items. He mentioned that Lady Dale's land in Virginia lay next to the Berkeley grant. The letter ended with the hope (and expectation) that Smyth will 'take pains and care for our business' and an assurance that he, Tracy, will display equal diligence in Virginia. Anxiety was patent in a postscript statement that he had not heard whether cousin Berkeley had yet hired a ship.

2.[34] The letter to Mr. Archard was brief and was concerned only with finance. Sums totalling £207 were detailed, and Smyth in an endorsement recorded '207[Li] payd to me by Mr. Tracy June, 1620'.

3.[35] In the third letter Tracy informed Smyth that Sir Edwin Sandys, with whom he had had a recent interview, had promised him kine at the going rate, and that Sir Edwin had also promised 'to make me of the Council' (in Virginia). Towards the end Tracy stated that he had obtained silkworms from Lady Dale who had also promised to 'lend' him some cattle.

On 1 June Smyth wrote a letter to Richard Berkeley,[36] the contents of which are of considerable significance. 'Complaint' might well be termed the key-note of this epistle; indeed, it has a suggestion of sourness. Smyth began by saying that neither Yeardley or Woodleefe were prepared to take up the fifth share of the adventure. An explanation of the resultant, complicated financial situation followed. He described one of Woodleefe's proposals as 'foolery', adding 'But of him and it, more when I wait on you in July . . . In the mean time we have a governor none of the wisest, providentest nor observantist of our directions'. This statement obviously referred to Woodleefe, the governor of the plantation, and not Yeardley the colonial governor, and it would appear possible that even at this date Smyth may have been considering a change of leadership at the plantation,[37] Perhaps he already visualized Thorpe, who had sailed for Virginia in March, as a suitable replacement for Woodleefe? The governor was further accused of the 'sale of our men taking new charge of others servants to draw to his private . . .'[38] Smyth expressed surprise that Berkeley had received no letters from Painter nor he (Smyth) from Blanchard who had 'vowed to me true and secret advertisement . . . especially touching Mr. Woodleefe and his estate, behaviour and usage of our men and other observations'. Mrs Godfrey also had not heard from her husband. Smyth concluded his complaints by saying 'I fear the old Virginian trick of surprise of letters (if not counterfeiting also is cast upon us by Mr. Woodleefe . . . only our ancient Yate none of the wisest writeth too much but of one side'. It would appear from two comments by Smyth that the *Margaret* did not sail from Virginia within the originally specified fifty days, but had been held back by Woodleefe who had 'followed the ship to the mouth of the river, as the date of his postscript, 'Hickaton, 18 March' suggests. In another paragraph he refered to '2 months needless stay in Virginia above our 50 days for no occasion of ours but to amend his weak ship . . .' Smyth then passed on to Tracy who, he said, is determined to go to Virginia and was 'making his provisions accordingly'. He referred to the loan by Sir Edwin Sandys of two kine to Tracy and to 'others and goats from Lady Dale'.[39] Mention was made of returned goods which were to be sold, and to Yate's letters which had been sent to Berkeley and forwarded unopened to Smyth. The latter said that he was returning Yate's letters to Berkeley and that in future all letters should be opened before transmission 'for no secret or private letter uncommunicated must be in [our?] partnership.'

John Pory, secretary of the council in Virginia, in a long letter dated 12 June 1620,[40] to Sir Edwin Sandys, head of the Virginia Company in London, reported on the current situation. The recent arrivals and departures of shipping to and from the colony were tabulated. The *Swan* of Barnstaple docked at James City on 15 May and left on 1 June. The *Duty* arrived 25 May and departed 11 June. On 27 May the *London Marchant* and the *Jonathan* 'came to Anchor in this port', and set sail on 7 and 9 June respectively. The specific dates of these arrivals have been included because of Pory's later comments. He was categorical in his advice on the more favourable periods during which new and unseasoned settlers should be sent. The best seasons were 'absolutely', the leaf-fall and winter, while spring and summer were both 'fatal and unprofitable to new comers'. He illustrated his belief by reporting that 'in these three last mentioned ships the people . . . came in sickly, and too late either by planting, setting, hoeing, clearing ground or buildings, to do any work of importance'. Another point which emerges from the above is the date of Thorpe's arrival in Virginia, i.e., 27 May.

Pory also stressed the importance of selecting only healthy persons for colonization, i.e., 'none but sound persons' should be sent, adding that 'tradespeople, husbandmen and true labourers' were especially welcome. He emphasized the above points of time of arrival and soundness of health by stating that 'the *Jonathan* may be a sad precedent, who lost twenty-five of your land people at sea, besides Mr. Rand, the Master, and three mariners, and some more of the passengers now dead on shore.' He advocated the use of the quicker routes to lessen the strain on passengers and to lower the death rate.

The detailed commercial analysis (including the reports on vines and other crops as well as the ironworks project) was cheering, e.g.,

1. 'Silk is a marvellous hopeful commodity . . . there being as many mulberry trees as in Persia . . .'
2. 'Vines cannot but prosper admirably well . . .'[41]
3. Hemp and flax 'are said to be the most growing things in the country.'
4. Salt is produced with ease, fish are plentiful, abundant timber is at hand, while the prospect of iron, pitch and tar is hopeful.

Towards the end of the letter Pory commented in a most eulogistic manner on Thorpe who had recently arrived. He (Thorpe) is termed 'that virtuous gentleman' and likened to an angel from Heaven. Pory concluded by saying that Thorpe's presence in Virginia would be a great advantage to the colony and that he would be an able adviser to the Council in London.[42]

The Virginia Company on 22 June 1620 issued a 'Declaration of the State . . . in Virginia' to which was attached a list of subscribers to the Company during the term of office of Sir Thomas Smythe as Treasurer.[43] Amongst the contributors were John Smith (probably the Berkeley sponsor) £37. 10s., George Thorpe Esquire £25, and Sir William Throckmorton £50.

Smyth I, 30[44] is, chronologically, the next reference relative to Thorpe or the Berkeley Plantation. It is a document describing a proposal by a chemist named Russell, and was apparently addressed to Smyth and dated by him July 1620. The opening paragraph gave reasons for the memorandum, and Russell's solution to a problem being faced in the colony followed. He stated that there were about 3,000 settlers in Virginia and that the most common complaint was the lack of a 'good drink, wine being too dear, and barely chargeable and hard to grow.' Russell estimated the daily consumption of such drink, and then in some detail described the qualities and advantages of the artificial wine he proposed to manufacture. It would be clear, drinkable at once, and would not become flat with keeping. It was a 'preservative' against certain diseases occasioned by long voyages at sea and would 'make no man drunk'.

Mr. Russell's terms were a payment of £1,000 and 'the benefit in Virginia of serving the colony at the said rate of 6^s the tun'. Smyth endorsed the document 'Agreed with some little variation with Mr. Russell . . . Sir John Brooke 2 Apl. 1621 told me, that . . . this wine was made of saxifrage, liquorice boiled in water: he had of the drink.' The date 2 April 1621, and indeed the whole document, is interesting in view of a letter which Thorpe wrote to Smyth on 19 December 1620, which will be discussed below.

There are five letters[45] written by Tracy to Smyth between 5 July and 9 August. Most are short and all were written by him during a period of obvious mental anxiety and financial stress. They tend to be somewhat repetitive, consequently it seems reasonable to run them together.

It would appear that 'cousin' Berkeley was one of the principal causes of Tracy's worry, and so perhaps this is the moment to look briefly at the man who gave his name to the Company and Plantation. It is strange that throughout the period February 1619 to the Massacre (22 March 1622) Berkeley tends to stay in the background. Smyth, Thorpe and Throckmorton all invested in the Virginia Company, and all were positive in their approach to the local project. Thorpe and Tracy, personally, played a part in Virginian affairs, the latter it is true for but a short while – he died there less than three months after his arrival. It would appear, however, that Berkeley did not invest in the parent company and, apart from his financial outlay, played a minor role in the affairs of the Berkeley Company until the massacre, by which time he and Smyth were the sole survivors of the sponsors. The only surviving letter of his as an individual is that written on 3 April 1619[46] to Smyth in which he put forward a relative, William Chester, as a suitable leader for the original Berkeley settlement party, and also suggested a fit surgeon to accompany them. Throckmorton a week later supported Berkeley's proposition,[47] which, however, did not come to fruition. There is no hint as to the reason why Chester, who had invested £12. 10s. 0d. in the Virginia Company,[48] did not lead either of the two main Berkeley settlement parties. An examination of the consolidated accounts for the equipping of the Berkeley contingents of September 1619 and September 1620 does not suggest that Richard Berkeley was very active in the promotion of that enterprise.

The first concern of Tracy, expressed on 5 July,[49] was to obtain a ship. London had been suggested as a likely port for hiring, but he, Tracy, was unable to travel up to the city, and so would leave the matter in Smyth's hands. A further worry was that Berkeley wished to limit to ten or twelve the number of men to be taken by Tracy, who, so he reported to Smyth, had arranged for some twenty to thirty persons. Additional personnel were mentioned and a suggestion made that some might follow in the spring. Tracy pleaded with Smyth to further actively their plans 'and leave us in God's hands,' in other words hasten their departure, for God would provide for their needs. Tracy identified his party as his wife, son, daughter, four maid-servants, six men, a Mr. Palet (The Revd. Robert Pawlet, their minister?) and a Mr. Gilfort, and 'for the rest as many or few as you deem necessary.' He felt that it would be highly desirable to take thirty, and added that he also wished to take ten or twelve dogs 'which would be of use'.[50] The problem of acquiring a ship continued to loom large,[51] while his wife being 'overwhelmed with grief at Bristol' increased his distress. Berkeley blamed Smyth for the troubles, stated Tracy, who pointed out that whoever was at fault he, Tracy, was the sufferer, and that whereas Berkeley had his estate at Stoke and Smyth had his at Nibley, he had 'nothing but Virginia', and yet he was compelled to stay on in shame and disgrace in England.[52] Tracy suggested Bristol as the port of embarkation, and reported that he had more than £100 with which to furnish and further the enterprise.

In the third letter Tracy pleaded once more with Smyth, for little was forthcoming from Berkeley who now limited the numbers of men to twenty. The situation was desperate, for cash was running out and if the start was delayed 'we will lose all our men . . . putting them out of work and me out of credit.' Tracy's distress continued into August, with delay and finance as the major worries. He felt that God was his principal hope, and that next came Smyth who must be God's instrument. On 9 August it appears that matters were coming to a head. Bristol was the probable port of departure, and Tracy suggested that Smyth should meet him there to finalize, if possible, their plans.

The Virginia Company on 12 July granted Tracy a commission[53] for a voyage to Virginia, though it would appear that he did not receive that information for some days. They stated that they had given leave that their ship, the *Supply* of Bristol of seventy tons, should sail when the party was ready. Tracy was nominated Captain 'to command and govern the ship, mariners and passengers.' There would be sixty-five personnel, or thereabouts, aboard and all necessary provisions. They were to sail at the first 'opportunity of wind' by the most direct route, and were not to 'interupt' any ships of this or friendly nations. If they were 'chased or encountered by any man-of-war or other sail', which threatened to 'hinder' them, Tracy, as Captain, was commanded 'with all his power and utmost endeavour to repel, resist and defend himself and our honour against the unjust force . . . And this our Command shall be his sufficient warrant.' To this document was fixed the Common Seal. This commission, with its emphasis upon speed of departure and the suggested complement of sixty-five people, added to Berkeley's apparent lack of co-operation and his insistance upon a figure of twenty or less for the Berkeley party, placed Tracy, and to a lesser degree Smyth also in a difficult position. The one really encouraging thought must have been the apparent availability of the ship, the *Supply*.

On 18 or 28 August, 1620, came a momentous document, the revocation of Captain John Woodleefe's commission[54] as 'Captain and governor' of the Berkeley Plantation and its people. This order was issued in the name of the four original sponsors of the company, namely Throckmorton, Berkeley, Thorpe and Smyth. In it were detailed Woodleefe's principal duties, as originally conceived. In addition to his obligations as Captain and governor he had been appointed their 'chief marchant and to commerce, truck and trade' both with the natives and the settlers to the best advantage of the Berkeley Company – all of which Woodleefe had 'faithfully promised to perform.' Now a different decision was taken. In the name of the original sponsors it was declared that 'for divers good causes and weighty considerations' they now 'revoked repealed disannulled and determined and made void' their commission to Woodleefe as leader and governor of the Berkeley Plantation. They decreed furthermore that whatsoever Woodleefe 'shall here after do or attempt to do by or under colour of our said commission . . . shall be done and executed in such sort manner or form' as George Thorpe and William Tracy of Hayles 'shall will limit or direct . . . and not otherwise,' until other directions were received.

It would seem probable that the suspicions concerning Woodleefe's conduct, which had been expressed by Smyth in his letter to Berkeley on the previous 1 June had been confirmed by later letters or reports, possibly, in view of Smyth's remarks in the above letter, from Blanchard and Painter, and personally from Yate, who had left Virginia on 20 March.[55] No report had been received from Thorpe on this matter, for Berkeley and Smyth in their 'commission' to Thorpe, dated 10 September, stated specifically that up to that time they had neither heard from him nor of his arrival in Virginia.[56]

On 28 August an agreement was also drawn up between Berkeley, Thorpe, Tracy and Smyth relating to the Berkeley Plantation.[57] This document began with a résumé of the 4 September 1619, agreement and the arrival of the first party under Woodleefe at the Berkeley Grant. The departure of Thorpe to Virginia in March was referred to, and the hope expressed that he had by then arrived safely 'the better by his presence to order and direct the affairs and business of the said plantation.' This latter remark is interesting. It suggests that whereas Thorpe before his departure had been nominated by a committee of the Virginia Company, subject to the approval of the full court, to take over the management of the College lands, an understanding had also been concluded that he would be concerned in some way with the ordering of the Berkeley Plantation. Such an undertaking would have been natural, but this is the only surviving indication that a specific arrangement had been negotiated.

The agreement outlined the transfer of Throckmorton's share in the Company to Tracy, who, to increase the strength and viability of the plantation, would head a party of fifty-four 'or thereabouts' who would leave Bristol in September. Thorpe and Tracy were to be the sole governors and directors of the estates 'so long as they two shall agree.' Arnold Oldisworth Esq., Revd. Robert Pawlet[58] and Captain John Woodleefe would act as umpires in any serious dispute. If a conflict of opinion or policy arose between Richard Berkeley and John Smyth in England on matters relating to the Plantation affairs or welfare, the umpires would be Sir William Throckmorton, Sir Thomas Roe and Sir Thomas Tracy 'brother of the said Wm' (Tracy).

A third document was drawn up on the same day (if it is accepted that the revocation of Woodleefe's authority was drawn up on the 28th, as suggested by the *NYPLB*, and not on the 18th). This was a commission to Thorpe and Tracy from Richard Berkeley and John Smyth to be jointly Governors of the Plantation which had been established 'to the honour of Almighty God, the enlarging of christian religion' and for the betterment of the colony and the Berkeley Company.[59] The purpose of Thorpe's presence at the plantation was restated – indeed the 'Commission' covered much of the same detail as did the 'Agreement'.

On the 31 August the charter for the *Supply* was drawn up between a William Ewins and the four sponsors.[60] It largely reflected that detailing the hire of the *Margaret*. The principal differences were that (1) the ship after it had transported the party from Bristol to Virginia would return to London and not the same port as had the *Margaret*. This is understandable in view of the implication in the Virginia Company's Commission to Tracy that the *Supply* was either theirs or under contract to them. (2) The rate of hire was to be £21 per month of thirty days – with the odd days being charged pro-rata – as against £33 per month of twenty-eight days for the smaller *Margaret*. This might be attributed to the difference in the vessels' ownership. The *Supply* must be ready to sail by 17 September, and it was agreed that if (which God forbid) the ship should be 'robbed or spoled on the sea or fresh (during the said voyage)' the ship owner or marchant laders (hirers) should each 'stand to his own loss.'

The next document to be considered is an agreement dated 1 September between the Berkeley Company sponsors and a small group of would-be settlers on the Berkeley Plantation.[61] They were to be tenants of the Company and not 'servants' in the usual style. The terms of the contract are so full and precise that it would appear reasonable for a better appreciation of this method of engagement during the early days of colonization to use extensive quotations.

The indenture was between the four sponsors and a Richard Smyth, a gardener of Wotton-under-Edge, his wife Joan, their sons Anthony and William, Robert Bisaker, a glover of the same place, his wife, Faith, and a Richard Hopkins,[62] a husbandman also of Wotton. The Berkeley Company, at its own cost, would transport them '(with God's assitance)' to Virginia and there maintain and keep them 'with convenient diet and lodging in their family there amongst their other servants from the day of landing until one convenient, and the same to be furnished with necessary impliments . . . and to allot unto them so much ground convenient and adjoining to the said house as they shall be able to clear manure order dress husband and use, either in orchards, gardens, vineyards or for tobacco, corn, maize or Indian wheat, woad, silk-grass flax or hemp, or for pasture and hay for kine and other cattle or for planting of olives, sowing or planting of cotton wool aniseed, wormseed and the like'. The house was to be sited near the great river (James) or some tributary, and 'so built and fitted for them to allow unto them convenient diet as the country can reasonably afford until one harvest be by them had and inned which is supposed will be about the feast of St. Bartholomew next,' They were to receive two cattle from those which the sponsors proposed to transport in April next. They were each also to be given within the next year three suits similar to those provided for the plantation servants.

In return the tenants promised to pay one third of their grain (English and Indian) and half of the profits of 'all other fruits cattle seeds and increase whatsoever raised taken or had from' the Company's land. Finally there shall be mutual respect and assistance between the parties. In due time the land would be patented to the tenants.

On 1 September Tracy wrote to Smyth[63] expressing his sympathy because of an illness, and wishing him a speedy recovery. It was, indeed, unfortunate that Smyth had been unable to come to Bristol where he would have seen for himself the neglect which would delay the party's departure at least a further twelve days. He referred to a 'book and 2 writings' of Smyth which he had returned. In the very long postscript Tracy sent his commendations to Mrs Smyth and others and invited them aboard at Bristol, facetiously adding that they might be compelled to eat 'shapes [ships?] maggots',[64] but promised them finer fare in Virginia (Pocahikiti – whatever 'dish' this may be!). Tracy stated that he had in his company his wife, son, daughter, four maid-servants, three married wives and two children. The problem of balance in a party and the limitations of room – labourers were vital – was aired. There were hopes that Mr. Pawlet would soon be with them.

Richard Berkeley and John Smyth on 10 September sent a commission to Thorpe[65] authorizing him to take over the government and authority from Woodleefe, if he deemed it necessary. In it reference was made to the joint commission to Thorpe and Tracy on 28 August. Thorpe was instructed, *inter alia*, to verify that Yeardley's rejection of the fifth share in the Berkeley Company was irrevocable. A certificate of the safe arrival of Tracy's group must be obtained from the Governor, while Thorpe was requested to make a careful inventory of all goods and equipment shipped to the plantation to enable a better financial statement to be drawn up. Berkeley and Smyth stated that, because of previous promises, they were sending over the wife, son and daughter of Thomas Coopy, their carpenter. This was being done with reluctance because in consequence 'three labouring men' (urgently needed) would be left behind. The future financial arrangements relating to the Coopy family were outlined.

A copy was being enclosed of the indenture issued by the Berkeley sponsors to a Richard Smyth[66] and his party, who would be 'our first tenants or undertakers to the halves in that kind.' Thorpe's advice was requested on the workability of the scheme, and he was reminded that if Richard Smyth and his group were well treated similar bodies of tenants by halves might well be attracted, for they 'covertly or openly will send over to their friends and neighbours.' Reference was made to letters from their work-force to friends, and others to the sponsors from their 'servants' requesting that 'two servants the piece [be] sent over for their own private benefit.' This demand 'seemeth somewhat strange' and was not yet 'satisfied', but Thorpe and Tracy were asked to consider the possibility and to report back. Then came perhaps the most crucial request, 'we must pray you to bend your utmost care and diligence to subsist, as much and as soon as is possible of yourselves: for these great supplies are unsupportable in longer continuance,' Thorpe was told that two books on husbandry and housewifery[67] and two on the care of silkworms and the culture of silk were being sent by a Thomas Lemis. The latter appears to be untrustworthy for Thorpe was warned to demand the books from the bearer 'otherwise you will be defrauded of them'. These books were recorded as costing six shillings in the accounts of furnishing the *Supply*.

Quantities of garden seeds were being sent and must be carefully nurtured for they represented very largely their future food stocks. Seeds of 'cotton wool' obtained in London were sent by Thomas Combe, described as Thorpe's partner. Smyth from his own nurseries was sending a great number of young apple stock, grafted with 'pippens, pearmaines and other the best apples . . . a bag of apricot damosell and other plumstones.' Great care was to be taken of these valuable items. Reference has already been made to the expectations of letters from Thorpe via Newfoundland with which this document ends.

Further trouble for the ill-fated *Supply* party was reported in a letter of 10 September from Tracy to Smyth.[68] The writer stated that the custom's official was being difficult – 'he must question our clothes which he hath notes on'. Tracy requested that papers which he must sign – presumably relating to the customs problems – should be sent by George Keen, a gentleman member of their party. Tracy revealed his distress when he said 'my wits distracted and liberty strained so I cannot be of use to you as I might.' The letter ended with a final plea that Smyth, who was staying at the White Lion, would send the necessary 'writings' that night; Tracy would then bring them on the morrow to the meeting which appeared to have been fixed. Thus the White Lion was probably in or near Bristol.

On the same date an agreement was drawn between the Berkeley sponsors and the Revd. Robert Pawlet[69] who was engaged to sail with Tracy on the *Supply* and to be chaplain, doctor and surgeon for the Berkeley Plantation. He was to 'dwell with the said George [Thorpe] and Wm. [Tracy] in their house and colony there for the better instruction of themselves and family . . .' (community). The responsibility for Pawlet's stipend was broken down as follows, Thorpe and Tracy (presumably because they would benefit from his pastoral care) would each pay £20, while the absentee sponsors, Berkeley and Smyth, would each contribute £10. At the end of the year's contract Pawlet was free, if he so wished, to return to England. If he continued as chaplain the original salary could remain or else another agreement, linked to a percentage of the sponsors 'increase and gains', might be negotiated.

The Mayor of Bristol, Thomas Parker, issued a certificate on 18 September[70] that the *Supply* 'this present xviiith day of September, 1620 were shipped from our port of Bristol for plantacon in Virginia' with a party of fifty-six under the leadership of William Tracy. On that list, which includes Tracy, are fifty-nine names. Perhaps Tracy, as leader, and the two children (perhaps very young) of Mrs. Coopy were not reckoned? A group of four letters, dated between 22 and 25 September, appear to make nonsense of the departure date on the Mayor's certificate. What in fact seems to have happened was that they left the port of Bristol on the 18th, dropped down river and for some reason anchored at 'Crocompill' (Crockhampill – see map) where they remained at least until the 25th.

The first of the above letters, dated 22nd September, was written to Tracy by his cousin Timothy Gate.[71] The contents indicated that Tracy was once more in serious trouble relating to some business transaction, during which he was 'cruelly' done by and had been arrested. Gate however was hopeful of better days, and expressed the wish that the 'sea will be more merciful unto you than your friends are here.' John Smyth endorsed the letter 'Mr. Gate's letter[72] to Mr. Wintour.' Why so, when it was obviously written to Tracy?

On the following day a John Bridges, a cousin of Tracy, probably a brother of 'cousin' Robert Bridges mentioned in Gate's letter, wrote to Smyth,[73] stating that a Mr. Thorn had told him that 'by Sir William Throckmorton and your self my cousin Tracy was set at liberty.' He asked for guidance as to the method of removing the action (obviously against Tracy) into the 'Chancery', adding that if Smyth would take the necessary steps he would bear the cost. The trouble-maker clearly was 'that base extortioner Winter.'

Tracy, on the 24th and now apparently at liberty, wrote to Smyth[74] saying that 'necessity' had compelled him to reduce the numbers in his party – they were '10 at least too many.' He named Richard Smith (sic) and his party and six others as those who will have to be left behind – for the present? Tracy expressed the hope that Smyth (Berkeley sponsor) 'may not take it ill that Richard Smyth and his people had had to be disembarked. He offered apologies for this action and added that he had promised Richard Smith £3, presumably as compensation. Richard Smyth (sic) receipted for £3 and 10s. 'for seed', while Robert Bysaker – one of Richard's party – acknowledge the receipt of £2. The considerable concern about this Richard will be considered in connection with a remark made by Thorpe in a letter to John Smyth dated 19 December 1620.[75] The second half of this present letter is full of explanation as to why it had been necessary drastically to reduce the numbers in the party – 'I have thrown out many things of my own yet is the middle and upper deck extremely pestered so that our men will not lie like men and the mariners hath not room to stir.'

The last letter from Tracy to Smyth dated 25 September, is brief and trouble-riddled.[76] The business was full of danger and uncertainty, and they sat 'still at Crockhampill or anywhere else for want of money.' He assured

Smyth that he had been careful over finance and had spent as little as possible, adding 'all I desire is to be set free with 10[li] in my purse we are ready and want nothing but wind.'

How long the vessel lay at Crockhampill through lack of wind appears not to be known. This delay may however have been fortunate, for it was during that period that the seriousness of the overcrowded conditions became obvious and the unpleasant decision to 'thin out' the party was taken. This clearly necessary step caused Smyth considerable administrative problems and some embarrassing exercises in public relations, e.g.,[77]

		s.	d.
1.	Margery Nelme was paid by way of compensation	14	4
2.	Richard Hopkins and Richard Peers – 'charges & damage for loss of work'.	7	0
3.	Old Wm. Peers in lieu of his tools which were 'shipped and carried away' while he was turned back at Crockhampill	5	0
4.	Wm Archard for Inn accommodation	2	6
5.	Richard Smyth and Robert Bysaker, as mentioned above, were paid £3. 10s. 0d. and £2. 0s. 0d. respectively, whereof 27s. was in lieu of 'pots, kettles & pans carried with other furniture into Virginia.'		

There is no log of the *Supply's* voyage, as there had been of the *Margaret*. There are, however, occasional references in various documents which reveal that it was not without incident, e.g.,

1. 'Paid upon the bill of exhange or note of Mr. Tracy and Mr. Oldisworth which they took up of Mr. Thomas Daunt in Ireland at Kingford in October 1620 driven in thither by occasion of a leak'[78] It would appear that the expedition continued to be bedevilled even after it finally left the Bristol Avon.

2. A deposit had been paid to the customs relating to the 'brode cloth' taken by the party, a charge which Smyth expected would be returned. He recorded later 'This the farmers of the customs at London, will not allow back.'[79] The amount was £5. 4s. 0d.[80]

3. Smyth, in his own hand, entered on one of his master copies of the lists of the Berkeley colonists[81] the following comments:

i   Joan Green 'went not'.

ii   John Page 'went not but stayed in Ireland'.

iii   Wm. Piffe, John Linsey and Roger Linsey all 'stayed in Ireland'.

iv   Giles Carter 'dead in England'.

This desertion – a feature which, apart from that of Singer the surgeon, is not found in the records of the first Berkeley party in September 1619 – may have resulted from the series of misfortunes and frustrations which befell the leader and vessel. The leak, so early in the admittedly hazardous voyage, could well have been the last straw, prompting the feeling that the whole expedition was ill-fated. Troubles must have continued (unrecorded) for it was 29 January before the would-be settlers arrived at the Berkeley landing stage – one of the longest voyages from England to Virginia on record.

4.   Tracy's problems at Bristol while awaiting departure for Virginia was referred to by Smyth on 24 October 1621, at a Court of the Virginia Company. He, then a Councillor of the Company, there 'moved that whereas Mr. William Tracy afore his going over to Virginia was arrested for 200^{Li} principal debt for which he put in bail . . .'[82]

The certificate of the arrival of the party at 'Berkeley', signed by Sir George Yeardley, the Governor of Virginia, and John Pory, Secretary of the Colony, was addressed, as in the case of the pioneer contingent to the Council and Company of Virginia in London. Some of the entries are puzzling. It is stated that fifty named persons had arrived at Berkeley Plantation. Amongst these were John Page, John Linsey, Roger Linsey and Joan Green all of whom, according to Smyth's marginal notes, did not complete the voyage. Furthermore, there is the name, Giles Carter, against whose entry in Smyth's list are written the words 'Dead in England'. Finally there are on the Governor's certificate several names not included on that of Mayor Parker. One of these was an Alice Heskins of whom Smyth in a marginal note wrote, 'Mr. Thorpe's letter 17. May. 1621[83] saith that Alice Heskyns was disposed of by Mr. Tracy in marriage of his daughter . . . q. [query] who is this Alice.' Could it be that the checking by the Virginian officials was intentionally a little lax, and that, as long as the specified number of colonists had arrived, verification of identity was deemed unnecessary? Again did the new members of the party join the ship at Crockhampill or Kingford? Were they officially members of the party of stowaways?

The closing comments on the Tracy expedition must relate to its provision, equipment, and costs as far as are known. These, as might be expected, approximate to those assembled for the original party. The weapons included swords and mustkets as well as body armour. Tools for building and agricultural purposes were again numerous. Food and clothing seem to have been on a generous scale, with cider and other beverages in greater quantities than in 1619. Perhaps this was the result of the report made in July 1620, by the chemist, Russell, on the scheme to produce artificial wine in an attempt to meet the greatly felt want in Virginia? The areas from which the supplies came were diverse, and the method of their transportation varied considerably. A few examples of such entries and the occasional accompanying comments or explanation must suffice. The numbers at the left side of the examples cited (which are from Smyth I, 3 (34)) indicate the pages in the *NYPL* vol. III, pp. 283-90, in which they are published.

1. *Areas of purchase*

Goods were bought in London, Stoke Gifford, 'and in the Country', at Nibley (Stoke and Nibley were both in Gloucestershire), and at St. James Fair and Bristol Fair.

2. *Transportation*

284	(i)	'2 wains from Nibley to Berkeley with 12s. spent by the plowman there, & to the cooper to head & dress them'[84]	52s.	0d.
286	(ii)	'carriage of 1,3000 weight from London part by horse [pack?] and part by wain to Bristol & weighing'	58s.	0d.
289	(iii)	'To the boatmen at Berkley for carriage of .2. tun di. [½] of peas, wheat, wheat ears malt etc to Bristol'	18s.	0d.
289	(iv)	'Paid for the passage of .20. men & women from the parts of Hayles to Bristol, and the hire of some horses diet & lodging at the horseshoe and at Mrs Lewis house and lodging of many servants as by several bills appeareth over and besides what Mr. Smyth thought indifferently fit to abate which Mr. Tracy referred to him etc'	£ 4 18s.	0d.
289	(v)	'The hire of a boat that carried Mrs Tracy & the women & children from Bristol to Crockhampill'	6s.	0d.

3. *Miscellany*

289	(i)	'paper, ink & parchment for Comissions and quadripartite Covenants & Indentures etc'[85]	4s.	10d.
	(ii)	for writing & ingrossing the .2. Comissions quadripartite covenants		

.35. pair of Indentures and divers other particulers as by the bill appeareth' £ 3 10s. 0d.

283 (iii) 'drugs & physics bought of Mr. Barton Apothecary by doctor Guisons directions for the flipp & scurvy etc' £ 4 3s 4d

'wainscott box and hay to pack the same in' 2s. 9d.

290 (iv) 'Singer the Surgeon (gone for the Apothecary of Bristol bridge) is at his return out of the Straytes to pay us' 50s. 0d.

This is of course a reference back to the 1619 accounts.

288 (v) 'To Boswell the Apothecary upon his bill for drugs and other like stuffs of him bought by Mr. Pawlet as appeareth' £11 18s. 6d.

This amount, when compared with the other costs, seems extremely high, especially so when the bill of £4 6s. 1d. for drugs and container (p. 283) is remembered. Perhaps it included surgical instruments? Pawlet, a minister, with it would seem some knowledge of medicine and surgery, could not be expected to have the full complement of 'tools of trade' needed by one who was to be officially responsible for the health of the Berkeley colonists. Pawlet does not appear amongst the *alumni* of Oxford or Cambridge, so perhaps he was a free church minister.

286 (vi) 'The copies of the council order for fishing & about tobacco and of Sir Edwin Sandis project, and of the artificial wine, to be sent over to Mr. Thorpe, paid the Secretary' 5s. 0d.

The 'Secretary' would have been that of the Virginia Company. The sending over of the Virginia Company's offi-

cial memorandum on the scheme for
making artificial wine will be discussed
shortly in relation to Thorpe's
activities.

286 (vii) 'hogshead of new cider sent to
Mr. Thorpe'
Was this already paid for by Thorpe,
or was it a present to him? In the cost
columns the entry reads 0.0.0. i.e. no
charge.

286 (viii) 'The charge of Robt. Hawford
at Bristol employed divers days buying
of provisions etc'   6s.   0d.

288 (ix) 'Paid at the horseshoe for a
chamber to stow our goods bought at
St. James Fair for .5. weeks'   20s.   0d.
There are several similar entries.

289 (x) 'charges of diet of Mr. Smyth
& part of the company at the white
lion, And for the board wages of other
part of the company for .14. days As
by accompt kept by Wllm Archard
appeareth'   £15   2s.   11d.

288 (xi) 'Paid for wages of .5. of our seamen for .3. weeks di. [½] 4s the week
dayly helping ended .17. September
saturday night'   £ 3   10s.   0d.

288 (xii) 'Paid Toby Felgate upon his
bill for the charges of himself and hire
of his horse to Bristol and carriage of
his sea cards, affairs & apparel'   £ 5   16s.   0d.
Felgate had been master of the
Margaret and was now master of the
Supply for this voyage. He presented
several other bills, e.g., diet for seven
weeks at Bristol at 6s. per week.
apparent alterations to cabins £4 9s. 6d.,
2,000 Newfoundland fish £5, barrels
of Irish beef, two trips to Nibley, etc.

After an examination of the above accounts several observations may be made. The sponsors appear to have learnt from experience, especially in relation to the health of their settlers. In 1619 50s. only seems to have been spent on medical supplies – see Singer entry. In 1620 the total expenditure was £16. 4s. 7d. They also apparently realised, prompted perhaps by Russell's report, the need for more liquor by the colonists. The comparative numbers in the two parties were – in 1619, thirty-five all male; in 1620, fifty including at least eleven women or female children and two young males of unspecified age. Despite this approximation of numbers the quantity of liquor differed considerably.

	1619	1620
Cider	6½ tuns	3 tuns
Beer	5½ tuns	21 tuns
Sack	11 gall.	60 gall.
Aqua Vitae	15 gall.	60 gall. and 1 'polle'

It is true that some of these supplies may have been intended for members of the initial party. It must be remembered however that many settlers died in the spring and early summer of 1620. The number of casualties at Berkeley are not known. All that can be said is that Smyth in Smyth I, 3(9) records that of the first party of thirty-five, one returned to England in March 1620, twenty-six were 'dead' – as were the four who had travelled out at an earlier date – and these did not include the two described as 'slain', presumably in the massacre. A number of the above thirty undoubtedly died during the early months but not all. News of at least some deaths would naturally have reached England before the departure of this second major party.

The second point which stands out is the difference in the details concerning religious observance and equipment between the first and second contingents. In the instructions of 1619 these matters were stressed on several occasions and at length, and it will be seen that the spiritual needs of the party were in some measure catered for – Thorpe bought Bibles, Prayer books and devotional literature, and even a Communion service was mentioned before they sailed. It will be seen that in relation to the 1620 group the only two references to spiritual matters come in (1) the agreement with Pawlet, where his duties as minister are very briefly outlined, (2) a short reference to the fact that the original party 'and divers other inhabitants' were 'there to the honour of Almighty God, the enlarging of christian religion and to the augmentation and renown of the general plantation in that country . . .' It might be suggested that the earlier emphasis on spiritual observances was due, at least in part, to the influence on the spot of that 'religious gentleman',

George Thorpe. The presence, however, of the Revd. Robert Pawlet with the second party may be the true explanation.

Thus on 29 January 1621, the second Berkeley contingent landed safely at their plantation. The focus must now briefly return to Thorpe and his activities during the latter part of this period.

On 28 June 1620, a General Quarter Court of the Virginia Company had its attention drawn by a communication from Sir George Yeardley, Governor of Virginia, to the need for additional Councillors of State for the colony. The Company then selected Mr. Thorpe, Mr. Nuce, Mr. Pountis, Mr. Tracy, Mr. David Middleton and Mr. Bluett to fill the vacancies.[87] It would of course be September before the relative order would reach the Governor, by which time Tracy, it was expected, would be on the point of departure for the colony. Thorpe was, they hoped, already there. Thus Thorpe now became one of the principal men in Virginia. As a Councillor of State, he would be in direct contact with the Governor, whom, of course, he already knew, and he would have the opportunity to take a hand in formulating and carrying out the policies for colonial administraction. All this would be in addition to his responsible position of Deputy for the College Lands upon which the progress of the proposed Henrico project would largely depend.

At a court on 12 July the Company's seal was applied to Tracy's commission already mentioned, and at the same court a committee, which included Smyth, considered Russell's report on the possibility of making the artificial wine referred to in part 2 of this chapter.[88]

An indenture was drawn up on 30 September between George Thorpe, Robert Oldsworth of Coln Rogers[89] and John Smyth. In view of the absence of Thorpe in Virginia it must be assumed that the details had been agreed upon before his departure. The subject of the document was the transfer of a portion of Thorpe's holdings and expected profits in the Berkeley Company to Oldisworth and Smyth, who in the future would also bear a like percentage of the financial responsibility towards the running of the whole enterprise.[90]

This complicated tripartite agreement arose through the failure of Sir George Yeardley to take up the fifth share specified in the initial charter referred to on 3 and 18 February 1619. This non-acceptance by the Governor resulted in Throckmorton, Berkeley, Thorpe and Smyth each having to take up a quarter share of the fifth allotted to Yeardley. This is clearly seen in Smyth I, 3 (13-16).

1.   Accounts 'until the departure of the ship the XVth of September 1619
    – 733^{Li} – 10^s – 5^d,

2. *Inde quinta pars* £146^{Li} – 14^s – 1^d,

3. 'so each of us doth bear for Sir George Yeardley 36 ^{Li} – 13^s – 6^d'

4. (later) 'which allowances made, Sir George Yeardley's fifth come to 148^{Li} – 17^s 7^d And so to each of us 37^{Li} 4^s 4^d ob.'[91]

Thorpe before he left for Virginia had probably expressed the desire to dispose of his quarter share of Yeardley's fifth, and this Smyth had effected. Thus for £50 to be paid by Oldisworth and Smyth, Thorpe was handing over all financial interests and responsibilities represented by his quarter share of the fifth which Yeardley had refused to take up.

Thorpe's letters are always interesting and informative, and they reveal quite clearly the personality of the man himself as will be seen when these are fully examined. One letter only comes within the time period of this chapter. The remainder, and unfortunately they are few in number, which have survived in their entirety – as against extracts preserved only in other manuscripts – will be considered in the next chapter.

On 19 December 1620, Thorpe wrote to Smyth from the Southampton Hundred in which he, Thorpe, and Thorckmorton had once held some interests.[92]

The epistle was carried, as Thorpe explained, by Thomas Partridge who had been in Virginia for some time. The latter, it will be recalled, was mentioned in two sets of Instructions of September 1619, issued to Captain Woodleefe by the four sponsors of the Berkeley Company prior to the party's departure for Virginia.

The reference in Smyth I, 3 (8) implies that Partridge was already in the colony (Kingsbury III, p. 195) while in Smyth I, 3 (6) (Kingsbury III, p. 210) he is stated to be 'now abiding in Virginia.' Woodleefe was then instructed that if Partridge joined up with the Berkeley party he was to appoint him 'bailiff of our husbandry.' Thorpe's letter, it would appear, establishes that Partridge was now at Berkeley Plantation, and the former wrote that Smyth was to question the latter on plantation affairs 'to satisfy yourself in any thing wherein I shall be wanting.' Thorpe excused any possible absentmindedness by the fact that he was at the Southampton Hundred 'in the business of examining witnesses concerning Captain Argall wherein we sit commonly till midnight and beside I did not expect that this would have departed so suddenly . . .' Argall, an ex-Deputy Governor of Virginia and one who had spent many years in the colony, was accused of malpractice mainly while in office. His case was being considered both in London and in the colony. Who the 'we' in Southampton examination were is not known, but Yeardley, as Governor of Virginia, would probably have presided unless his interests in that Hundred rendered him ineligible. Thorpe, as a Councillor of State, would have been an obvious 'possible' while his Staple Inn and Middle Temple background would have added to his suitability.

Thorpe because of the hurriedness of the letter, assured Smyth that 'I do intend God-willing to write to you and the rest of our Adventurers . . .' shortly. He added that by that time Captain Woodleefe's tobacco would be 'ready' – for transportation to England?

The next subject shows Thorpe's deep concern both for the anxiety of the sponsors in England and the physical and mental well-being of the settlers on the Berkeley Plantation. To appreciate fully the mind of Thorpe his statement must be recorded more or less *verbatim:*

> 'You will hear many strange reports both of the death of our own people and of others yet be not discouraged therein for I thank God I never had my health better in my life than I have had since my coming into this Country and . . . am persuaded that more do die here of the disease of their mind than of their body by having this country victuals over-praised . . . and by not knowing they shall drink water here although God-bethanked this country mends in plenty of victual every day . . . and we have found a way to make so good drink of Indian corn as I protest I have divers times refused to drink good strong English beer and chosen to drink that.[93]

His message was loud and clear. Smyth and the others, who had no personal experience of conditions in Virginia, were not to worry unduly. The high mortality rate – and it had been very high during the spring and early summer – was not entirely due to climatic conditions. His own health and that of others amply demonstrated that point. Then came the assurance that he had found the answer to at least one of the major causes of deep concern to the labour force, and that in itself would, he believed, raise morale and greatly reduce the death rate. It might be suggested that Smyth had written to Thorpe concerning the artificial wine experiment of Russell – he certainly had sent a copy of the Virginia Company's memorandum on the subject, as had been recorded above. That report however would only arrive with Tracy's party, i.e., 29 January 1620. Thorpe, had he heard previously from Smyth on that subject, would most certainly have made some comment. Consequently it must be assumed that the drink made from Indian corn – the first Bourbon of the New World, as it has been termed by some American historians – was a personal exercise devised by Thorpe to meet a very dangerous situation. His concern for the men under his care was matched by his ingenuity and enterprise.

Later in the letter Thorpe makes two interesting comments. Firstly, 'I find the Country to be such as that you may with a great deal of thankfulness to God of comfort to yourself resolve to place your second son here and account him as good a man of living (every way) as his elder brother only if you furnish him with a competent number of servants and with a reasonable stock of cattle . . .' What did Thorpe mean? The accepted genealogical table of John Smyth – as printed in his *Lives of the Berkeleys* – gives John, the eldest son, as born 8 September 1611, and the second, Thomas, as baptized 27 December 1613. That would make them respectively nine and seven at the time of Thorpe's letter – hardly an age for solo settlement. Smyth, according to the above table, married twice. The first wife, Grace, whom he married at North Nibley on 5 October 1597, was buried there 11 November 1609. No children of that marriage are recorded. The agreement, already detailed,[94] between the company and Richard Smyth and family to transport them as tenants at halves to Virginia, and the subsequent correspondence between Tracy and John Smyth, may have considerable bearing upon this problem. It will be recalled that Tracy wrote to Smyth saying that he had been compelled by pressure of numbers to leave ten persons behind. His profuse apologies appear to have been concerned principally with the omission of Richard's party — presumably the inclusion of the children would have necessitated the exclusion of two working adults. Tracy expressed the hope that John Smyth would 'not take it ill but give them content and send them after the by the next [party] . . . I pray you consider the necessity and do not believe me cross or forget [ful of] our respect to you . . .' (1) Might Smyth have married at an early age, had two sons and become a widower before 1596/7? (2) Might Smyth have had two step-sons through his first wife? (3) Might Smyth have had two illegitimate sons before he married in 1597? (4) Might Thorpe have used the title 'son' for nephew or cousin? I think not, for Thorpe would hardly have been so awry in his nomenclature. From the above it appears just possible that Richard was one of the two sons referred to by Thorpe in his letter of 19 December 1620 — Smyth I, 33.

The second point of interest lies in Thorpe's request to Smyth – 'I beseach you Sir be careful of my poor wife and children [who were of a similar age to Smyth's] unto whom I have written to come over hither. I pray further her in what you may. I will send her by the next [ship] a note of what is fit for her to bring for her journey . . .' This was fifteen months before Thorpe's death in the massacre, but nothing is known of any move on the part of Mrs Thorpe and her young family to emigrate, neither have either of the letters mentioned by Thorpe survived.

Nothing further is known of Thorpe between 19 December 1620, and 29 January 1621. From the sparse reference to him made by the Virginia Council in London and the Colonial Secretary in Virginia, it is clear that he was held in high esteem by the leading personalities in England's great experiment in colonization. Furthermore, his employment in the colony as Deputy of the College Lands, Councillor of State, head of the Berkeley Plantation – to say nothing of his appointment on the Argall court, all within six months of landing – shows that he had already established himself as a principal figure in the colony.

NOTES

1. C.D. Dowdey, op.cit., p. 29.

2. Smyth I, 13; in Kingsbury III, pp. 109-14; and *NYPLB*, March 1897, pp. 68-72.

3. The replicas at Jamestown of the three ships which made the memorable crossing in 1607 will illustrate the appalling conditions under which the emigrants lived for weeks on end, come rain, snow and tempest.

4. Now Hampton.

5. Smyth I, 3 (18); in Kingsbury III, p. 230.

6. Smyth I, 3 (10); in Kingsbury, III, p. 213.

7. Smyth I, 3 (9); in Kingsbury III, pp. 197-9.

8. Smyth I, 3 (13-16); in Kingsbury III, pp. 178-89.

9. Smyth I, 3 (35); in Kingsbury III, pp. 402-4.

10. Smyth I, 14; in Kingsbury III, pp. 248-9.

11. The De la Ware family – Captain Francis West was Lord De la Ware's brother.

12. The Berkeley Grant was (and is today) between Shirley Hundred and the West (now called Westover) Plantation.

13. Lord Delaware was Governor of Virginia, 1609-18.

14. Kingsbury I, p. 303.

15. Smyth I, 3 (19); in Kingsbury III, p. 260-1.

16. Smyth I, 3 (9); in Kingsbury III, p. 197-9.

17. Kingsbury I, p. 332.

18. P.R.O. Court of Chancery Records, C 24 – C 243, p. 4.

19. Kingsbury I, pp. 336-7.

20. Kingsbury I, p. 303.

21. Kingsbury I, p. 296.

22. Smyth I, 16; in Kingsbury III, p. 266; also N.Y.P.L.B., Vol III, p. 248.

23. Smyth I, 3 (19); in Kingsbury III, p. 260-1.

24. Smyth I, 4; in Kingsbury III, pp. 136-7. Throckmorton heads the signatures, while Thorpe clearly composed or wrote the letter.

25. Smyth I, 6; in Kingsbury III, pp. 138-9.

26. Smyth I, 3 (20); in Kingsbury III, pp. 271-4; also in *NYPLB* Vol III, pp. 248-250.

27. Smyth I, 3 (25); in Kingsbury III, p. 379.

28. Kingsbury III, pp. 275-80.

29. Ibid., p. 276. James City, Henrico, Charles City and Kicowton (Elizabeth City after that date – 17 May). In the guesthouses there were to be twenty-five bedsteads on each (side?). Measurements = 6 ft. × 4 ft. and 2 ft. off the ground. Board petitions between beds, windows for wholesome air and five chimneys for each building were specified.

30. Ibid., p. 277.

31. Kingsbury I, p. 347.

32. I have followed the *NYPLB* reading. Kingsbury III has Hill. I have found in two important instances, where I have obtained photographic copies of the original text, that the *NYPLB* had the correct reading.

33. Smyth I, 17; in Kingsbury III, pp. 289-90; also in *NYPLB* vol III, pp. 251-2.
34. Smyth I, 18; in Kingsbury III, p. 291; also in *NYPLB*, vol III, p. 252.

35. Smyth I, 19; in Kingsbury III, p. 291; also in *NYPLB*, vol III, p. 253.

36. Smyth I, 15; in Kingsbury III, pp. 292-4; also in *NYPLB*, vol. III, pp. 250-1.

37. Woodleefe is specifically termed 'Captain and governor' in his commission issued by the Berkeley sponsors on 4 September, 1619 – see Smyth I, 3 (5), in Kingsbury III, pp. 199-201.
38. It will be recalled that the 'Agreement' between the sponsors and Woodleefe, also dated 4 September 1619 (Smyth I, 9 and 3 (7), in Kingsbury III, pp. 201-7) laid down in Item 6 that 'John Woodleefe hereby covenanteth . . . That none of such men or servants as he hath or shall have . . . shall be settled or placed or abide' at any other site except the Berkeley grant, unless ten miles distant. Furthermore Woodleefe 'will not have directly or indirectly' interests or government in any other Plantation or concern, and that his 'Best endeavours' shall be directed towards the Berkeley Plantation, and it alone.

39. Reference will be made to these and similar 'loans' in the chapter on the effects on Thorpe's estate in Virginia after the massacre.

40. Ferrar Papers; in Kingsbury III, pp. 300-5.

41. Vines can be seen 'with a body as big as a man's leg, as tall, and upright as the mast of a ship.'

42 . The full quotation will be found in chapter 10, 'The Verdict of History'.

43. Sir Thomas headed the Virginia Company from its inception until he stepped down on 28 April 1619 to be succeeded by Sir Edwin Sandys.

44. Kingsbury III, pp. 365-7; also in *NYPLB*, vol. III, pp. 255-6.

45. 5 July, Smyth I, 20; in Kingsbury III, pp. 367-8; also in *NYPLB*, vol. III, p. 253.
    14 July, Smyth I, 21; in Kingsbury III, pp. 369-70; also in *NYPLB* vol. III, pp. 253-4.
    14 July, Smyth I, 22; in Kingsbury III, p. 370; also in *NYPLB*, vol III, p. 254.
    2 August, Smyth I, 23; in Kingsbury III, p. 373; also in *NYPLB*, vol III, p. 256.
    9 August, Smyth I, 24; in Kingsbury III, pp. 373-4; also in *NYPLB*, vol. III, p. 257.

46. Smyth I, 5; in Kingsbury III, pp. 137-8.

47. Smyth I, 6; in Kingsbury III, pp. 138-9.

48. Kingsbury III, p. 322.

49. Smyth I, 20; in Kingsbury III, pp. 367-8.

50. Ibid., p. 368.

51. Tracy had, obviously, not yet received his commission from the Virginia Company (see below) in which this problem was settled.

52. Smyth I, 21, etc. From the above it would appear that Tracy had sold his estates at Hayles to finance his expedition.

53. Smyth I, 3 (22); in Kingsbury III, pp. 368-9; also in *NYPLB*, vol. III, pp. 254-5.

54. Smyth I, 3 (23); in Kingsbury III, pp. 374-5; also in *NYPLB*, vol. III, pp. 257-8.

55. Smyth in his marginal notes on his master copy of the list of the Berkeley settlers stated that Yate 'returned 20.Mtij.1620. . .[1]. Smyth I, 3 (9); in Kingsbury III, p. 197.

56. Smyth I, 3 (26); in Kingsbury III, p. 400; also in *NYPLB*, vol. III, p. 280.

57. Smyth I, 3 (25); in Kingsbury III, pp. 376-9; also in *NYPLB*, vol. III, pp. 276-8.

58. Members of Tracy's party for Virginia.

59. Smyth I, 3 (24); in Kingsbury III, pp. 379-81.

60. Smyth I, 3 (29); in Kingsbury III, pp. 381-4.

61. Smyth I, 3 (27); in Kingsbury III, pp. 393-4.

62. It is interesting to speculate whether Richard Hopkins was related to John Hopkins of the *Mayflower*, who also came from Wotton. See *Hopkins of the Mayflower, Portrait of a Dissenter*, by Assistant Professor Margaret Hodges of the University of Pittsburg, published by Farrar, Straus and Giroux, New York, 1972.

63. Smyth I, 25; in Kingsbury III, p. 395; also in *NYPLB*, vol. III, p. 278.

64. If this was intended as humour, it is the only such example in any of Tracy's letters. Perhaps it was deliberately inserted to emphasize the material affects of the over long delay.

65. Smyth I, 3 (26); in Kingsbury III, pp. 397-400; also in *NYPLB*, vol. III, pp. 278-80.

66. See p. 144.

67. It is suggested (*NYPLB*), vol. III, p. 280) that these books, named as 'Markhams and Goovges,' may have been (i) either Garvase Markham's *English Husbandman*, London, 1613-15, in three parts, or his *Cheap and Good Husbandry*, 1614. or his *The English Housewife*, the second book of his *Country Contentments*, 1611. (ii) The *Foure Bookes of Husbandrie*, London, 1577, translated by Barnaby Googe from Conrad Heresbach's work on husbandry. A 1614 edition of this work was edited by Markham.

68. Smyth I, 26; in Kingsbury III, p. 401.

69. Smyth I, 2 (28); in Kingsbury III, pp. 401-2.

70. Smyth I, 3 (30); in Kingsbury III, pp. 405-6.

71. Smyth I, 45; also in Kingsbury III, p. 409; also in *NYPLB*, vol. III, p. 281.

72. Gate mentioned in this letter that he went to Cleeve and then on to Beckford to visit a Mr. Wakeman where he 'took all his part of tobacco assigned under hand and seal before Witnesses with Wakeman's consent. my brother upon my knowledge was content to take 2,000 pound of his tobacco.'
    Gate was vicar of Cleeve and his wife owned land at Bishops Cleeve which figured in the tobacco growing experiment in that area in 1619. Considerable light has been thrown upon that experiment and these cousins of Tracy (Gate and Bridges) by Dr. J. Thirsk in Thirsk I, pages 147-69, especially 152-3 and 164. See also chapter 4 of this study.

73. Smyth I, 29; in Kingsbury III, p. 410; also in *NYPLB*, vol. III, pp. 281-2.

74. Smyth I, 27; in Kingsbury III, pp. 410-11; also in *NYPLB*, vol. III, p. 282.

75. Smyth I, 33; in Kingsbury III, pp. 417-8; also in *NYPLB*, vol III, pp. 292-3.

76. Smyth I, 28; in Kingsbury III, pp. 411-2; also in *NYPLB*, vol III, pp. 282-3.

77. See entries in Smyth I, 3 (35); in Kingsbury III, pp. 402-4.

78. Smyth I, 3 (35); in Kingsbury III, p. 403. The sum paid was £10.

79. Smyth I, 3 (34), in Kingsbury III, p. 393.

80. Smyth I, 3 (35); in Kingsbury III, p. 404.

81. Smyth I, 3 (31); in Kingsbury III, pp. 396-7.

82. This statement by Smyth (Kingsbury I, p. 535) is intentionally included in a shortened form to establish the reason for Tracy's arrest. The real purpose of Smyth's communication had relevance to an event which will be discussed later when the full text will be considered.

83. This letter is not known to have survived. Another letter written on that same date, which also has been lost, is referred to in a sermon preached by Revd. Patrick Copland on 18 April 1622, to which later reference will be made.

84. The cooper was employed to deal with '4 pipes . . . 2 hogsheads . . . and 2 lesser casks' mentioned in other entries.

85. These would be the various documents issued between 28 August and 15 September 1620, see above.

86. Smyth I, 3 (24); in Kingsbury III, p. 380.

87. Kingsbury I, p. 379.

88. Ibid., pp. 403-4.

89. A relation of Arnold Oldisworth of Tracy's party.

90. Smyth I, 12; in Kingsbury III, pp. 412-15.

91. Kingsbury III, pp. 188-9.

92. Smyth I, 33; in Kingsbury III, pp. 417-8.

93. Smyth I, 33; in Kingsbury III, pp. 417-8.

94. Smyth I, 3 (27); in Kingsbury III, p. 393-4. See also Smyth I, 27 for the letter of apology.

7

Virginia, 29 January 1621 to 21 March 1622

On 29 January 1621 the *Supply* landed Tracy and his company upon the Berkeley Plantation and a new era began. The party included several married ladies, i.e., Mrs. Tracy, Mrs. Coopy, Mrs. Finch and Mrs. Rolles[1], and a number of single females, some of whom soon became wives. Tracy's daughter, Joyce, married Captain Nathaniel Powell, a seasoned Adventurer and a member of the Council in Virginia. Frances Grevill married 'Mr de la War' – a relation of the late Lord Delaware, Governor of Virginia, 1610-19. In addition Isabell Gifford was married to Adam Reymer (who does not appear on either of the two main Berkeley lists) while still at sea — presumably by the Revd. Robert Pawlet, minister designate to the Berkeley Plantation. There is, in addition, that obscure reference by Smyth to Alice Heskins who had been 'disposed of by Mr. Tracy in marriage of his daughter . . .' Had Alice become a bride or a servant? There were, over and above Tracy's son and daughter, a few young people who were emigrating with their parents, i.e., the son and daughter of Mrs. Coopy, a daughter of Mrs. Finch and two sons of John Howlet. Here then was the nucleus of a 'community', such as had been envisaged from the time of the initial grant, for that charter had been issued for the specific purpose of locating not only a plantation – which could be sited and maintained by an all male body of settlers, but also a town and hundred. It was to be a type of an estate or habitancy based upon the medieval town and manor whose name it bore, a foundation which would, it was hoped, reflect the form and character of the parent body.

For Thorpe, Tracy's arrival marked a stage in the development of the settlement, in as much as it brought another sponsor of the company who would now share with Thorpe the responsibility of the daily detail and long term planning of the affairs of the plantation. For Thorpe, if he had confidence in Tracy, this was no doubt most welcome, especially so in view of Thorpe's colonial, as well as his Berkeley, commitments.

Even before the arrival of the Tracy party there is clear evidence of Thorpe's involvement in colonial affairs in several directions. He was Governor of the Berkeley Hundred – an obligation now shared with Tracy, Deputy of the college lands of 10,000 acres with a responsibility for a building project, and Councillor of State for the colony.

Fortunately several letters or reports from the Colonial Council to the governing body in England, and also letters from Thorpe himself, all covering the period January to July 1621, have survived. These illustrate his ability, activity and his many interests, while at the same time his enthusiastic and caring nature can be seen. The confidence placed in him, and the esteem in which he was held, by leaders both in England and in the colony, are also patent.

On 21 January 1621, the Governor and Council in Virginia sent to the Earl of Southampton and the Council of the Virginia Company in London a letter[2] requesting them to forward to the King a strongly worded protest concerning the 'late Proclamation against the importation of tobacco.' The protesting instrument began 'To the King's most excellent Majesty. The humble Petition of the distressed Colony in Virginia Showing that whereas it pleased your Majesty that now many years since, out of your Religious desire to spread the Gospel of Christ, and Princely Ambition to enlarge your own Dominions . . .', and ends with a final plea, indeed almost an ultimatum, 'either to revoke that Proclamation, and to restore us to our ancient liberty, or otherwise to send for us all home; and not to suffer the Heathen to triumph over us and to say Where is now their God? So shall we all (as we already are in duty bound) pray for your Majesty's long life and happy reign.' Thorpe signed immediately after the Governor, and six others councillors followed suit.

On 8 March the King forbade the Virginia Company to hold lotteries, a move which spelt financial disaster for the whole settlement project. This royal decree caused great bitterness of feelings and at a court held on 12th April John Smyth of Nibley, now a member of Council, moved, 'That for so much as ye lotteries were now suspended, which hitherto had continued the real and substantial food, by which Virginia hath been nourished; That instead thereof, She might now be preserved by divulging fame and good report, as she and her worthy Undertakers did well deserve . . .'[3] The long speech which followed advocated far greater publicity for the Company and its policies, and proposed that a factual history of the colonization of Virginia be written. The Council fully endorsed the motion. Unfortunately, Captain John Smith undertook the task. Had John Smyth of Nibley been allowed to write that history, later generations might have had a better, and more detailed account, one indeed which would have given a clear and true picture of that hard but interesting period of early colonial development. Smyth's printed works, e.g., *The Lives of the Berkeleys*, and *Gloucestershire Men and*

Armour, and his manuscript histories, e.g., *Tetbury Hundred* and *Bosham Hundred*, demonstrate the tragic loss, historically, sustained by this country and the United States through the medium of the wrong pen.

The *Supply* left Virginia for England early in April, 1621, carrying a cargo of tobacco, of which 2,000 lbs were credited to Mr. Thorpe, Captain Powell, Mr. Baine and Mr. Basse, on behalf of their respective plantations. In addition the following sent tobacco on their own account, Mr. Basse (1,500 lbs), Mr. Thorpe (600), Captain Martin (400), Mr. John Sabine (400) and Mr. Richard Godfree (200). The *Supply* also carried six passengers who paid £6 per head. They were Mr. Basse, Captain Martin 'and his man', Mr. Yate (probably the log keeper of the first Berkeley settlement party), Mr. Nicholas Cambe and Mr. John Sabine. The freight rates were 3*d*. per lb for the tobacco, so with 5,100 lbs aboard and six passengers at £6 each the gross income for the return voyage was £99 15*s*. 0*d*. The sum, presumably, went to the Berkeley Company to help off-set their hire of the *Supply* which was at the rate of £21 per month of thirty days. The amount of tobacco sent by Thorpe is interesting, for it suggests that he had been industrious during his nine months in the colony on behalf of the College lands project of which he was director. His share of the first figure (2,000 lbs) would represent the produce of the College lands, while the 600 lbs that of the 300 acres estate granted to him by virtue of his office. This seems to be borne-out by remarks in Thorpe's letters of May and June 1621 to officials of the Virginia Company in London. Captain Powell was, probably, either Captain William Powell, who will be mentioned in chapter 8, or Captain Nathaniel Powell who married William Tracy's daughter, Joyce. Both Powells were seasoned colonists. Brown, op.cit., stated that the *Supply* also carried letters from Tracy and Thorpe to their associates – presumably the Berkeley sponsors. Unfortunately, none of these letters has survived. This is especially sad in the case of Tracy, who might well have given his reactions to life in Virginia, the land to which he had long been attracted, and where he hoped he would be able to build up a new life for himself, his family, and his followers from Hayles. He might also have recorded his appreciation of the plantation and its potential. All that has been lost, for Smyth noted on his master list of the Berkeley colonists that Tracy died on 8 April 1621,[6] thus giving him little opportunity to write further letters. Perhaps Tracy's letters mentioned above would have contained indications of some illness from which he was suffering, and which a few days later caused his death. Confirmation of Tracy's tragically early demise is contained in a series of depositions made at the Court of Common Please on 17 November 1621, 'in Mr. Wallers office.'[7] All attestors swore on oath that they were certain that Tracy had died in April of that year. All five depositions are of considerable interest for the information they give, over and above the death of Tracy. Consequently two of the shorter ones, nos. 4 and 1, will follow at this point, and all five and the postscript will be included in the appendices. The postscript, deposition no. 6 in fact, stated that there were other depositions, including that of Mr. Thomas Tracy – William's son presumably, and George Keen, probably one of Tracy's party, described as a Gent, and of whom Smyth on his master copy wrote 'Returned to England', though no date was given.

Deposition 4

'John Ward of Ratcliffe aforesaid mariner deposeth that he continued in the land of Virginia from January until May last And that in April last he was in the Town of Barkly where Mr. Tracy dwelt and died (as it then was said) and that he was in the house of Captain Powell there who married the daughter of the said Mr. Tracy by whom as also by the son and daughter of the said Mr. Tracy and by many other credible persons there he did fully hear and understand of the death of the said Mr. Tracy whereof he is in conscience most assured.'

Deposition 1

'John Mennye of Sandwich in the county of Kent Gent aged 23 years or thereabouts maketh oath that in June last past he this deponent was in the house of Mr. William Tracy in the Town called Barkly in the Hundred of Shurly in the land of Virginia at which time the widow of the said Mrs. Tracy did keep her chamber as a mourner, and also deposeth that he was much conversant in the company of his son with whom he did lodge together as bedfellows for divers nights namely a fortnight or thereabouts by all which mean and divers others he is in his conscience assured and persuaded that the said Mr. William Tracy is dead.'

The minutes of the court meetings of the Virginia Company during the first half of the year (1621) contain interesting entries relating to the Berkeley Company and the Berkeley family.

1.   On 30 April Mr. John Smyth appears to have acquired three shares in the Company.[6]

2.   At the next meeting (2 May) Mr. Oldisworth, who had come over with Mr. William Tracy's party, was, on Smyth's recommendation, elected to serve on the Council in Virginia, of which body Thorpe, Tracy and Pawlet were already members. This was an extraordinarily large number for a single plantation.

3.   Mr. John Berkeley (often erroneously termed 'Sir John'), who had some years previously sold the family estate of Beverstone Castle, figures in the minutes of several meetings of this period in which is described the progress of the negotiations relating to the transportation of himself, his son, Maurice, and his trained personnel who were to complete and run the ironworks at Falling Creek.[7]

On 3 May the Governor of Virginia and the Council of State issued a 'Warrant'[8] which stressed, even under peaceful conditions, the obvious value of cattle to the individual settler and to the colony in general. At the same time it enables a better appreciation to be formed of the reason for the considerable litigation over the ownership of cattle and agricultural produce which followed upon the tragic events of 22nd March 1622, cases which continued for some years in the colonial courts. On this occasion the controversy involved the 'custody' of seventeen head of cattle which had been left by Captain John Martin, on his departure for England, in the charge of Lieutenant Saunders, but of which a 'Mr. John Bargrave of Patricksbourne in Kent' disputed ownership. The Council, 'being persuaded of the integrity and honesty of Lieut: Edmund Saunders,' consigned to him the care of the cattle until Captain Martin returned, or the disagreement between him and Bargrave had been settled. Five signed the warrant, i.e., The Governor (Yeardley), George Thorpe, Nathaniel Powell (who married Tracy's daughter, Joyce) Thomas Nuce, and the Colonial Secretary, John Pory. Thus Thorpe had become involved in a quasi-legal inquiry, less formal no doubt than that occasioned by the Argall case of the previous December, but locally at least of statutory importance.

On 9 May 1621 Thorpe wrote from James City, on behalf of himself and Pory, the secretary of the Council in Virginia, to Sir Edwin Sandys, the Treasurer of the Company, thus:

'For answer of Your letter touching that letter of Captain Powell against Sir George Yeardley [the Governor]. You may be pleased to understand, that before the receipt of the same letter Captain Powell had reconciled himself unto Sir George in pledge of which reconciliation they had both received the Sacrament. Sir George was therefore unwilling that the matter should be any way revived; but rather desirous that it might be forever buried. Notwithstanding we can by no means perceive that if we should enter into the examination thereof, that Captain Powell can justify any material part thereof, yet if you shall be pleased to give us any further directions therein we shall ever be ready to enter into the particular examination thereof. Concerning Captain Maddison's petition you shall here inclosed receive the depositions of the then servants of Captain Maddison and others, which (as we think) will give you large satisfaction what no cause at all Captain Maddison had to complain. So remaining ever ready to receive your further command we rest.'[9]

On the 15 May Thorpe wrote two letters, one to Sir Edwin Sandys and the other to John Ferrar.

George Thorpe to Sir Edwin Sandys

1621 May 15. James City. 'Honourable Sir, Unto whom although I owe very much and am willing to pay something, yet so slender hath been the harvest of our labbours, that I can scarce find out what to offer, in so much as I doubt [not] God is displeased with us, that we do not as we ought to do, take his service along with us by our serious endeavours of converting the heathen that live round about us and are daily conversant amongst us, and yet there is scarce any man amongst us that doth so much as afford them a good thought in his heart, and most men with their mouths give them nothing but maledictions and bitter execrations, being thereunto falsely carried with a violent mispersuasion (grown upon them I know [not?] how) that these poor people have done unto us all the wrong and injury that the malice of the devil or man can afford, whereas in my poor understanding if there by wrong on any side, it is on ours who are not so charitable to them as christians ought to be, they being (especially the better sort of them) of a peaceable and virtuous disposition,[10] only they are a little craving and that in a niggardly fashion for they will commonly part with nothing they have whatsoever is given them, they begin more and more to affect English fashions, and will be much allured to affect us by gifts if the Company would be pleased to send something in matter of apparel and household stuff to be bestowed upon them, I mean the Kings. I am so persuaded it would make a good entrance into their affections, they being as I think first to be dealt with by the book of the world as being nearest to their sense. I think likewise that the company shall do well to make some public declaration of their intent and desire of the conversion of this people, and there withal a testification of their love and hearty affection towards them, to be sent hither and published, thereby to mollify the minds of our people.

You will perceive by our letters in what a poor taking we are in for your Iron works, yet I have furnished them with a mason of my own, that hath built many iron furnaces in England, and I hope shall perform this here whereunto my help and often presence shall not be wanting. The whole people have begun to plant vines this year, and for my own part I have planted for the College near ten thousand and do intend God willing every year to set more than double that number. The silkworm seed is all perished saving a very small quantity sent me in the *Supply* of Bristol of which the Governor hath taken great care, and I hope we shall bring it to perfection, and do intend to save it all for seed.

In the matter of our Government here we are many times perplexed sometimes for lack of legal officers, and sometimes for want of books. I would therefore entreat you to send us the new book of the *Abridgement of Statues* and Stamford's *Pleas of the Crown* and Mr. West's *Precedents* and what other law books you shall think fit, and if you please likewise to send us Gerard's *Herball*, thereby to make comparison of the simples of the country.

By reason of the Spaniards behaviour towards Captain Chester, we have some reason to doubt we may also hear of them in this place. I pray therefore be a means we may have some pikes sent us, which weapon the manner of our peoples fighting with the natives hath worn quite out of use but if [we?] shall have to do with the Spaniard we must fight with him in his trenches which he that can do wih a pike is a better soldier that I. So with my prayer to the Almighty for your health and happiness I rest.'[11]

(Postscript) 'If you chance to hear me ill spoken of by any that come from hence I pray you judge charitably till you be better informed, for I thank God I have the testimony of a good conscience that I have done no man wrong, only do I desire to bring drunkeness and some other sins out of fashion and if I live I doubt not but I shall do it.'

Thorpe's report on the slow development of the iron-works project, and his statement that he, although having no direct responsibility for that enterprise, had lent them a skilled mason, and that his 'help and presence' would not be lacking, indicates his deep concern in yet another facet of colonial progress. The mason, presumably, came either from amongst the Berkeley men or else was one who had been sent from England to engage in the building programme for Henrico College. Thorpe's obvious unease over the Virginian 'defence of the realm', and his request for weapons with which to fight off the

Spaniards, should they appear, suggests, even if it does not indicate, his considerable influence, if not authority, in the colony.

The postscript shows clearly that already Thorpe's attitude towards the natives was being resented by some settlers, whose feelings, indeed insensibility towards, and treatment of, them were, at times at least, obviously unchristian and undesirable. This clash of personality and approach between the humanitarian and missionary-minded Thorpe and the sweating and oftentimes tough colonists has been paralleled in many other parts of the world during the expansion period of the British Empire throughout the seventeen to nineteenth centuries, as indeed have the attempts of the former to stamp out the bad habits, practices and immorality which not infrequently went hand in hand with the colonization of undeveloped countries in those early days.

The closing statement of the postscript is interesting and revealing. Thorpe stated that he desired to bring drunkeness and certain other sins 'out of fashion', adding 'if I live I doubt not but I shall do it.' Thorpe is writing of conditions throughout the colony in general, and not of the Berkeley Plantation, and yet he claims that if he is spared 'I shall do it'. Here is the declaration of a good and Godly man who is so certain of his own authoritative position in the colony that he can confidently forecast success in that campaign. That this was no boast of an arrogant man will be clearly seen in the massive 'Instructions' issued by London on 24 July of that year.

On the same day (15 May) Thorpe wrote also to John Ferrar giving a somewhat more restricted report on progress on the College estate, and the more crying needs of the tenants on the Company's lands, and indeed of the settlers in general.[12]

'I thank you for your kind letters and do with all my heart wish that the success of your business here were answerable to your virtuous intendiment and great cost, and do hope that God will so bless our future labours as to make them answerable to your good beginnings. We have this year commanded all the people here to set vines, which at first they were very unwilling, but are now better persuaded of it, and have performed it cheerfully. I have set for the college near ten thousand and for myself three thousand. Our silkworm seed is all perished at sea, except a very small quantity sent me by the *Supply* of Bristol by an unknown friend, whom I would gladly thank if I did know, because it is all we have that came to life, and I hope it will do very well. I intend God willing to save them all for seed being not above 5 or 6 c. [5 or 600]. The country will be generally in great distress for all manner of apparel against winter, many men wanting already wherewith to cover their servants nakedness. I beseech you therefore be mindful of us in that kind. There is one thing more, that if you do not give us speedy remedy in, will undo us all, and that is the want of lines to sweat our tobacco on, of which I wrote to you by the *Temperance*, and do now again remember because the crop of this year will, as it were, utterly perish without that supply. The people here are driven to sift their meal in sifters made of leather burned full of holes with a hot iron, which is so wide that the bran and all of the maize goes through, which I am persuaded makes their bread very unwholesome, and is a great cause of their fluxes. I would entreat you therefore that some hair sieves may be sent for a trial.

You shall receive by this ship a rundlet of earth of two sorts which I think doth hold alum or coporis [copperas?] I pray you let there be trial made of it. I found it as I travelled to see the country . . . The cooper of the *Bona-Nova* seems willing to bring over for habitation some of his trade. I pray you favour him in procuring his passage they being necessary men.'

These letters, especially that to Sandys, reveal the nature of the man, for they portray one of a strong christian conviction, who had been shocked by the attitude and behaviour of the generality of the settlers towards the Indians, and especially so in view of the God-given, and company-ordered, task of converting and civilizing them. To this failure he at least partly attributed the lack of greater progress in the colony. Indeed his verbal castigation of the colonists was considerable, and, if but partly justified, disclosed a situation which alone would make understandable the Indian attack of 22 March 1622.

The Company's injunction relating to the need to experiment with new crops, e.g., vines, silk culture etc.,[13] had finally been accepted by the whole colony, for Thorpe reported that they 'have begun to plant vines', adding that 'near 10,000' had been set for the college, and that he hoped to double that number in succeeding years. In his letter to Ferrar, which followed similar lines, he stated that he had planted 3,000 vines for himself. These statements, added to evidence of the bills of lading for the *Supply* in the previous month, attest to Thorpe's energy and agricultural involvement.

The lack at times of 'legal officers' and books of reference on that subject and his request for specific titles, both on law and herbs, emphasize Thorpe's wide interests, and that he was playing a considerable part in the affairs of the colony in general.

There is another letter to John Ferrar, also amongst the Ferrar Papers in Magdalene College, Cambridge, over which there is some doubt as to its date and provenance.[14] If it were dated 15 May, as has been suggested, it would mean that Thorpe wrote two letters to John Ferrar on the 15 May 1621, on totally differing subjects. I believe however that this second letter should be dated somewhat earlier. The contents of the two epistles have nothing in common, Thorpe's tone differs markedly, and there is no trace of any cross-reference in either letter. Let the letter speak for itself. Thorpe wrote:

'You shall do well if you from henceforth cause all the people to be sent hither to be searched by some skilful and honest physician and chirurgeon to the intent you may be certified concerning the health and soundness of their bodies for I do assure you that those few boys assigned to my oversight there were two that were so diseased with old ulcers in their legs (one of them confessed he hath had [them?] seven years that I do despair of their ability to work, and of the life of one of them, one other that is broken bellied [ruptured?], a fourth that is maimed in one of his hands and a fifth that is so diseased in his whole body he hath not been able to help himself ever since I had him which with the care of a search might have been avoided, besides many others both men and boys that have died in this country of incurable maladies that they brought with them.'[15]

The first piece of evidence concerning the date comes from the letter itself. This is numbered clearly 1019. The other Thorpe letters in this Ferrar group are numbered as follows

8 May 1621	no. 1020	draft of letter no.1021
9 May 1621	no. 1021	letter to Sandys
15 May 1621	no. 1022	letter to Ferrar
15 May 1621	no. 1023	letter to Sandys
27 June 1621	no. 1024	letter to Sandys yet to be dealt with.

The opening sentence, indeed line, seems to place this letter of reprimand early in Thorpe's term of office – 'You shall do well if from henceforth . . .' Thorpe had been in Virginia since the previous May – nearly a whole year if the 15 May 1621 dating is accepted. Does not the 'henceforth' suggest that Thorpe is referring to an initial labour force for the College lands? Furthermore this report is clearly being made soon after their arrival, and indicates the shock Thorpe received on inspecting the new arrivals. A possible alternative, if a May date but not the fifteenth be accepted, is that the letter was written a few days after Thorpe had arrived in the colony to take up his post as Deputy for the College land, a public reminder that there was, now, someone in Virginia who fully represented the college lands. This supposition however is hardly tenable, for though negotiations between the Virginia Company and Thorpe on the appointment of Deputy had taken place before the latter had embarked for the colony on 27 March 1620, the verification and sealing of the commission only occurred on 28 June 1620. Thorpe would hardly have written so strongly unless he was in possession of his commission, and firmly installed in his office. Nevertheless, it might be arguable that Thorpe, with his forthright nature, and confidence in his standing in the council chambers of the London Company, might have written such a letter upon first inspecting the limited work force allotted to the college lands. He would be saying in fact: 'I am now here and in charge of the college enterprise, and if that project is to succeed then the manpower must, physically, be up to their task.'

I would suggest that the letter was written soon after the arrival of a fresh batch of workers, perhaps the first contingent of such following Thorpe's official take over as Deputy of the College lands.

If the 1621 is original, but the 15th May in a 'later hand' is an error, then the exact date is a more open question. Thorpe's commission was sealed 28 June 1620. Assuming some days for its preparation for transmission, and a further ten to sixteen weeks to allow for the availability of a ship and the variability of the duration of the voyage, Thorpe could have received the document at any time from about October, but remembering that the New Year then began on 25 March, and that Thorpe's next known letter was dated 8th of May, 1621, the letter in question was, probably, written between 25 March and 7 May 1621.

Clearly too Thorpe's criticism of the London authorities' lack of care in their selection of candidates is not confined to those allocated to Thorpe and the College lands, for Thorpe added, 'besides many others both men and boys who have died in this country of incurable maladies that they brought with them.'

It would appear appropriate now to mention one other appointment in Virginia, which has been attributed to Thorpe. Dr. Kingsbury, when commenting on the Ferrar Papers (vol. I, p. 61) said: 'The last group of these papers comprise thirty–five letters, all but one or two of which were written by planters or adventurers, resident in the colony, to Sir Edwin Sandys. Of these, five came from Governor Yeardley, ten from either John Pory or George Thorpe, secretaries to the colony at different times.' Despite considerable research, I have discovered no confirmation that the office of Secretary of State in Virginia was held by Thorpe. However, were this so, it would account for the fact that almost all of Thorpe's letters which have survived were written to officials of the Virginia Company in London, i.e., Sir Edwin Sandys and John Ferrar. It might also explain the authoritative tone of some of his declarations, and his candid censure, on occasion, of those who were indeed his employers.

Reference must now be made to a letter from Sir George Yeardley, who had been Governor of Virginia since 1618, to Sir Edwin Sandys, reminding the latter that the Council in London would soon need to appoint a fresh Governor for the colony. This document, which is amongst the Ferrar Papers, has been reproduced by Dr. Kingsbury in vol. III, pp. 122-9. In a footnote Dr. Kingsbury maintained that this undated letter was in reality a bringing together of parts of three letters written over quite a considerable period of time. The central section of this composition is, presumably, not earlier than January 1621. Three times in that document Yeardley commends Thorpe to Sandys and the Council as the most suitable person to succeed him as Governor of Virginia.

1. Kingsbury III, p. 123. Thorpe is 'one upon whose shoulders the government of this whole Colony would most fitly sit.'

2. p. 124. Thorpe 'assuredly will be the most fit man to be Governor of Virginia . . .'

3. pp. 124-5. 'to give Your furtherance for this gent Captain Thorpe to be chosen and established Governor of Virginia in my stead.'[16]

Despite this powerfully worded 'advice' from Yeardley, the man on the spot and one who had spent most of the years from 1610-21 in Virginia, and presumably knew the local conditions better than those who had never set foot in the colony, the council appointed Sir Francis Wyatt,[17] who had married the niece of Sir Edwin Sandys, to succeed Sir George Yeardley when his three year term of office should end on 18 November 1621.

On 27 June Thorpe wrote to Sir Edwin Sandys.

'Noble Sir, I am not a little glad that after so much opposition the business of Virginia doth stand upon so equal feet that you were able to make so near a friend so worthy governor thereof, unto whom at his arrival, if my advice or service may be of use, I shall much rejoice seeing. I can never forget how much my obligation unto you is, God hath all this year hitherunto extraordinarily blessed us with health and now of late also after a great drought with the hope of a plentiful harvest of all kinds, whose holy name be blessed. I am within these ten days going to Abochanchano who hath divers times sent for me as he saith out of a desire he hath to be further informed of some things by me offered unto him at our last meeting. I pray God give me success according to my intention.'[18]

Thorpe in all probability knew that his name had been put forward for nomination to the office of Governor, but the opening sentence shows no sign of disappointment, indeed, welcomes the appointment of Sir Francis Wyatt. Then after reporting on the prospects of a good harvest – despite 'a great drought', Thorpe announces that he will be visiting the Indian chief Abochanchano for discussions in ten days time. This clearly was not the first visit, for the chief 'had divers times sent for me.' The purpose of the visit undoubtedly was secular, but it would have been surprising had not religion entered into the conversations. Thus, once again, Thorpe demonstrated his strength of character, his loyalty to the Company and his missionary fervour.

On 25 July the Treasurer and Company sent instructions to the 'Governor and Council' in Virginia (Kingsbury III, pp. 485-90). Three times in that letter Thorpe is addressed:

1. 'And to you Mr. Thorpe we will freely confess, that both your letters and endeavours are most acceptable to us: the entering upon those staple commodities of wine and silk, we greatly commend; and assure you it is the Company's care to reward your merits; which debts they will discharge, . . .'

2. 'We are in hope to send to the college tenants a very sufficient minister. We desire you, Mr. Thorpe, that a house may be ready for him, and good provision to entertain him: and the like course be held in all plantations.'

3. 'We desire you, Mr. Thorpe, and Mr. Newce [deputy for the company lands], to be careful of the present [Blank] and that the moiety be equally divided and returned to the Company: for the stock of the Company is utterly exhausted.'

Here can be seen the crippling effects of the King's policy on tobacco and his ban on the lotteries, which John Smyth described in Council (12 April 1621 – Kingsbury III, p. 451) as the 'real and substantive food, by which Virginia hath been nourished.' This grim financial situation was, no doubt, the main reason why little was heard of any building programme for the Henrico project.

NOTES

1. Possibly there were two Mrs. Rolles.

2. Manchester Papers, no. 290; in Kingsbury III, pp. 424-5.

3. Kingsbury I, pp. 451-2.

4. Smyth I, 3 (31); in Kingsbury II, p. 396.

5. Copies of these – on the two sides of a sheet – may be seen in Smyth II, Vol. 5, p. 65.

6. Kingsbury I, p. 460.

7. Kingsbury I, p. 475 – 76 and 483. Berkeley also became a member of the Virginia Council.

8. P.R.O. State Papers, C.O. James I., vol. III, no. 36, III; also in Kingsbury III, p. 444. See also postscript to chapter 9.

9. Ferrar Papers, pencil no. 1021; in Kingsbury III, p. 445. No. 1020 in the Ferrar Papers, is a rough draft of this letter, but dated 8 May 1621.

10. This judgement is strongly supported by no lss an authority than Dr. Wilcomb E. Washburn of the Smithsonian Institution, both in his contribution to *Seventeenth-Century America* (pp. 15-32 (especially 18-23) and also in 'A Moral History of Indian-White Relations: Needs and Opportunities for Study' – *Ethnic History*, 4 (1957), pp. 47-61.

11. Ferrar Papers, pencil no. 1023; in Kingsbury III, pp. 446-7. It is endorsed on the back by Nicholas Ferrar 'From Mr. Thorpe 16 May 1621 by the B. N. [*Bona Nova*] to Sir E. Sandys.'

12. Ferrar Papers, pencil no. 1022; in Kingsbury III, pp. 448-9.

13. See Kingsbury III, pp. 279 and 474.

14. The College Assistant Librarian, on 17 May 1979, wrote: 'I have examined the Ferrar letter no. 1019 which is badly damaged. There is definitely no place of origin mentioned. The date 1621 appears next to a torn off part and 15 May is written further down in a modern hand.' In a letter of 10 July 1979, the Assistant Librarian gave further details, which combined with the previous letter, have a considerable bearing upon the problem. (i) The date on letter no. 1019 is contemporary with the letter. (ii) The 1020, dated 8 May 1621 'is a draft of a letter dated 9 May 1621 and which is numbered 1021 was written by George Thorpe and John Pory to Sir Edwin Sandys.', i.e., the letter discussed above. Thus it would appear that the known Thorpe material in the Ferrar Papers has been placed in one block, i.e., 1019 to 1024, and, presumably, when assembled these letters were numbered in what was believed to have been their correct chronological order – the firm dates on 1020 to 1024 indicate this. The inference therefore must be that letter no. 1019 was written prior to

8 May 1621. Letter no. 1018 is dated 1623, and has no relevance to Thorpe or to the Berkeley Company.

15. Ferrar Papers (pencil no. 1019).

16. The full text of these strong recommendations will be found in chapter 10, 'The Verdict of History.'

17. His wife was a daughter of Sir Samuel Sandys the oldest son of Archbishop Sandys, and her mother was a Culpeper. Sir Francis was Governor of Virginia, 18 November 1621 – May 1626, and again from November 1639 – February 1642.

18. Kingsbury III, p. 462.

8

The Massacre – 22 March 1622

On 22 March 1622, the Indians staged a well co-ordinated attack upon the English settlers in Virginia. An unknown number of the colonists – perhaps between 350 and 400 – died that day. That there were so many survivors was due to the action of one man, and he an Indian. That fateful Friday naturally aroused powerful feelings on both sides of the Atlantic, and still today is at the heart of many discussions and literary works on seventeenth-century Anglo-Indian relations. This chapter sets out to examine the events of that day and the principal reasons which led up to that dramatic moment in the colony's history.

The term massacre has been used almost universally for the Indian attack upon the settlers that twenty-second of March 1622. However, from time to time, a lone voice has passed other judgments. Pory, the Colonial Secretary of Virginia in 1619-21, for example, appears to have considered that onslaught as the revolt of a subject people attempting to regain a freedom and independence of thought and action which they had lost, or appeared in grave danger of losing. This point of view has a present-day champion in Dr. J.F. Fausz, of St. Mary's College of Maryland, U.S.A. Dr. Fausz has made an extensive study over many years of the Tidewater area of Virginia during the early period of British settlement. His master's thesis in 1972 (*Settlement on the James River Basin, 1607-1642*) at the College of William and Mary, Williamsburg, was a general survey of the development of early colonization in Virginia. There followed in 1977 his massive doctoral dissertation entitled *The Powhatan Uprising of 1622: A Historical Study of Ethnocentrism and Cultural Conflict.* Here Dr. Fausz forcefully challenged the word 'massacre', so long in common use, declaring that that bloody assault upon the colonists must be viewed rather as an 'uprising' of a people attempting to regain, before it was too late, their land, dignity and culture which appeared to be slipping from them for ever. In the 1979 winter issue of *Virginia Cavalcade* Dr. Fausz in an article 'George Thorpe, Nemattanew, and the Powhatan Uprising of 1622,' once more maintained his thesis on the nomenclature of the event of 22 March 1622.

In 1967 I began researching into the Berkeley Company and George Thorpe's place in the early history of Virginia, and in 1972[1] described him as the first missionary martyr of the Church of England in the New World. Although I am not in full accord with Dr. Fausz in all his beliefs, I agree completely with his theory that the conflict of ideologies was a major factor in the decision of Opechancanough to mount the attach upon the settlers. In view of our considerable common interest in Thorpe and a great measure of unanimity on the reason behind, and the timing of, the Indian attack upon the settlers in 1622, I shall quote on several occasions from Dr. Fausz's 1979 article, and also from his doctoral dissertation.

Nevertheless, and despite my concurrence with Dr. Fausz on his designation of the events of 22 March 1622, I have for convenience sake used the conventional and more generally accepted term 'massacre' throughout this study.

THE BACKGROUND

'The settlement of America had its origins in the unsettlement of Europe', so said Lewis Mumford, to which might be added 'and so began a conflict of ideologies which, supported by fear or personal deprivation, erupted from time to time into open conflict between native and newcomer for more than two and a half centuries.' All this started in 1607 when more than one hundred pioneers set foot upon the soil of Virginia with a view to establishing a new home in the New World, At first, the disturbance by the white man, and his, at times, aggressive and insolent attitude and occupation of land, were by far the principal causes of the fear and hostility of the Indian.[2]

There were of course periods of peace between the two parties when intercourse and trade brought benefit to both sides. Furthermore, it must be remembered that basically the Indians were an hospitable people, and that on more than one occasion, when the white settlers were in desperate straits through famine, aid from the natives helped to preserve the badly threatened colony.[3]

From 1609/10, when the Indians witnessed the arrival of 150 fresh colonists and their policy of settlement expansion, open hostilities became inevitable. The principal Indian figure of the Tidewater area from the first landing at Jamestown was Powhatan.

He had inherited the suzerainty of six tribes of the central region, which included the Powhatan and Pamunkey peoples, and gradually by conquest achieved a confederacy of some thirty tribes, representing perhaps some

8,000 people, over which his sovereignty was exercised in varying degrees. His influence and position were recognized by the settlement leaders by whom he was frequently referred to as 'Emperor' or the 'Mighty Powhatan'. In the fighting which resulted from the 1610 developments, he was faced by Sir Thomas Dale, at first Marshall of Virginia and then deputy Governor, a soldier who had distinguished himself in the Low Countries. Dale considered Powhatan an able foe, and one who was shrewd and guileful also during periods of peace.

The most prominent Indian war-chief under Powhatan was an eccentric extrovert named Nemattanew, who in the Anglo-Powhatan campaign acquired a considerable reputation both as a leader and because of his ostentatious 'battle uniform'. This comprised an outer layer of feathers with swan's wings attached to his back, which, not unnaturally, gained for him the nickname 'Jack of the Feathers'. His outstanding bravery and his consistent survival unscathed under fire appeared to substantiate the native belief in his invulnerability against British bullets.

Despite the cunning of Powhatan and the heroic leadership of Nemattanew the primitive weapons were no match for the firearms and armour of Dale's forces. The humiliation of defeat and the capture and marriage of his favourite daughter, Pocahontas, to John Rolfe, already mentioned, compelled Powhatan to sign a treaty of friendship with the British.

Nancy O. Lurie maintains that the marriage of Pocahontas had not the influence upon her father's decision that is generally accepted. Her thesis is that the 'chieftain's interest in the marriage was not entirely paternal', rather that Powhatan felt that his alignment with the colonists would 'help to solidify Powhatan's power and prestige amongst the confederated tribes.'[4] Others feel that Powhatan's spirit was broken and that he was even now beginning to hand over his position and power to his half brothers who finally succeeded him, the one in title (Opitchapan) and the other (Opechancanough) in leadership, when he died in 1618. Opechancanough, like Powhatan in his prime, was an able ruler and bitterly anti-white, fearing for the future of his people both physically and culturally. Soon after his assumption of the reins of government by peaceful usurpation from his brother, Opechancanough witnessed his fears rapidly materializing. The colony was firmly established and from 1618/19, because of changes in Company policy and the introduction of 'Particular' plantations which were being founded on the best lands along and near the James river, expansion on a massive scale appeared certain. Furthermore, the projected foundation of a college for the education of Indian youth coupled with a drive for the taking in of Indian children into English homes, and later the proposed housing of native families in various

British settlements presented the very real threat that his people would be steadily weaned from the traditions, cultures and religion of their ancestors.

i. Town

When Dale first arrived in Virginia in 1611, he brought with him instructions to build a new town, to be named Henrico, in honour of Henry, Prince of Wales, some miles up the James river from Jamestown. The site finally selected, highly defensible, was a peninsula with the river flowing on three sides. It is now an island, known as Farrar's Island, and is near to Richmond. the present capital of Virginia. The area promised well agriculturally. It was during the reconnaissance for, and building of, Henrico that Dale and Nemattanew first clashed in skirmishes. The town was well planned with five watch towers, three streets of 'well framed houses', a church, store houses and, most surprising of all, a hospital for 80 patients. Alexander Whitaker, who came to Virginia with Dale, was the first minister.[5] However, Henrico did not, as was anticipated, replace Jamestown as capital of the colony, indeed, by 1616 it had become a place of little significance.

ii. College

Henrico College was scheduled to be the initial stage of an educational programme of considerable ambition for the colony of Virginia, and represented the first major attempt at the civilization and conversion of the Indian. The Virginia Company discussed the project at length and finally issued orders that 10,000 acres of land should be set aside for its site and maintenance. In the more distant future was the intention of building an University, probably on or near the same site, where the white children would attend and for which the Henrico scholars would be prepared. In addition, and as a result of private enterprise, yet a third seminary – known as the East India School for the children of settlers – was projected. Henrico College and University were so interrelated in the appeals and in peoples' minds that they will be discussed together, while the third project, for a school, will be considered separately.

Education from the days of the first charter had been considered the most hopeful, practical method of civilizing and converting the Indians. Sir Thomas Gates in 1609 had been instructed to take a number of Indian children and to bring them up in the English way of life. Tracts published soon afterwards, e.g., *New Life in Virginia* and *Good News from Virginia* supported this same policy. All these instructions and pleas led to nothing. In 1616, however, came the first practical move for the education of the Indian youth when, on 26 February 1616, King James wrote to the Archbishop of Canterbury asking that collections should be made in churches four times in the next two years for the erection 'of some churches and schools for the education of the children of the barbarians . . .' Two days later the Archbishop sent out a letter on those lines.[6] The response appears to have been disappointing, and the project faded. It will be remembered, however, that later that year Sir Thomas Dale, on his return to England, took with him a number of young Indians to be educated, one of whom at least, Thorpe's servant, was both educated and baptized.[7]

On the 18 November 1618, the Virginia Company issued 'Instructions' to Sir George Yeardley, Governor-Elect of Virginia, by reason 'of a special Grant and licence from his Majesty', that a 'college for the training up of the children of those infidels in true religion moral virtue and civility' should be built. They then ordained that a 'convenient place be chosen and set out for the planting of a university at the said Henrico in time to come and that in the mean time preparation be made for the building of the said college for the children of the infidels . . .'[8] Ten thousand acres were to be set aside for this twofold project.

At a Court of 26 May 1619 it was announced that as a result of the King's letters to several bishops the sum of £1,500 had been subscribed, and because of the feelings of the subscribers it was directed that action should be taken. It was then decided that fifty men should be sent to work the college lands and another fifty for certain company lands.[9] On 14 June the Court set up a committee to deal with the affairs of the proposed college, and the latter made their first report on the 24 June. The principal points were:

1. A minister was to be engaged at £40 a year, plus fifty acres of land.

2. The majority of the men to be sent for the college and public lands were to be unmarried.

3. The college contingent were to include bricklayers, brickmakers, carpenters, husbandmen, potters, smiths and turners.

Later Captain William Weldon was appointed to command the fifty college tenants, who, incidentally, were to be 'well furnished and armed'[10]

Their ship, the *Bona Nova* (of John Ferrar) landed at Jamestown on 4 November, and within a week thirty of Weldon's men were hired out to 'old planters'. Thus started a controversy which continued for weeks and finally resulted in Weldon's replacement and the appointment of Thorpe in his place.[11]

Little information has survived relating to the progress of the Henrico College project. The Company had said that the fifty tenants at halves who went out with Weldon should include a variety of trades necessary for the erection of buildings and cultivation of the land. It was the latter task which appears to have been given the first priority. The labour force, three-fifths of which were hired out upon arrival, would seem to have been not fully employed until Thorpe took over from Weldon. The date of Thorpe's assumption of power is uncertain but must have been in the autumn of 1620 when his commission had come through and the authorities in the colony had been informed. This was early enough for the land to have been prepared and 10,000 vines planted,[12] and other crops considered. It will be remembered that Thorpe also reported that he had planted 3,000 vines on his own account, and in reply to his letters the Company declared their satisfaction with the progress and had every intention of rewarding him. These 3,000 vines would have been planted on the 300 acres allotted to him on the Henrico estates. Had they been on the Berkeley Plantation they would have had no relevance to the Company, and would not have been mentioned by Thorpe. Perhaps too some of the tobacco, a quick growing crop, which was mentioned in connection with Thorpe,[13] may also have come from the Henrico lands, for he would have been anxious to present the Company with some early return for their investment. All this activity must have caused Opechancanough considerable anxiety.

EAST INDIA SCHOOL

The third scholastic establishment had its conception and early planning as a result of private enterprise. Sir Thomas Dale died in command of the East India fleet on 19 August 1619, and was succeeded by Captain Martin Pring whose ship, the *Royal George*, returned to England in 1621. Rounding the Cape of Good Hope they encountered British ships sailing east who gave them good news of Virginia, and presumably of the various appeals for churches and educational projects, The chaplain of the *Royal George*, the Revd. Patrick Copland, ('whom Dale had interested in Virginia while they were serving together in the East Indies'),[14] thereupon made a collection from passengers and crew for the building of a church or school in Virginia. This amounted to £70. 8s. 6d.

On landing in England early in October Copland informed the Virginia Company of this contribution. The Company's Quarter court were notified of the benefaction and appointed a committee 'to treat with Mr. Copland about it.' They advocated that Copland should be admitted as a free member of the Company.[15] At the Committee meeting held on 31 October, Mr. Copland spoke and said that though the sum was small he believed he could persuade the East India Company ('whom he meant to solicit') to make further gifts. The committee felt that the greater need was for a school rather than a church, and that of the four cities, Charles City promised to be the most suitable site. Finally they recommended that the school should be named the East India School in appreciation of the benefactors.[16] A further £30 was given by an anonymous donor.

At a court on 19 November, 'hope' was expressed that contributions towards the maintenance of the school master would be forthcoming from 'each man that sends his children', when the school was opened.[17] The Quarter Court of 21 November confirmed the proposals of the committee, and made their own recommendations

1.   There should be a schoolmaster and usher for the school

2.   Not less than 1,000 acres should be set aside at Charles City for the proposed school with an overseer and five others, who were to be of the status of apprentices, to work the estate.

3.   Copland, because of what he had already done, and because he 'had further also written to divers Factories in the East Indies to stir them up to like charitable contributions towards this pious work' should be granted '3 shares old Adventure' (300 acres) as a free gift and admitted a free member.[18]

The Virginia Council in London on 5 December wrote to the Governor and Council in the colony informing them of these developments,[19] beginning 'There is one thing . . . not great in itself but of great good hope . . .' Then followed the full account of the events and decisions. Later in the letter came an interesting list of cargo being shipped to Virginia by the vessel bearing this epistle and also a second ship named the *Discovery*. The items included 'divers sorts of seeds, and fruit trees, as also Pigeons, Peacocks, Maistives (mastiffs?) and Beehives . . .' Why peafowl? In view of the mastiffs, perhaps they were considered good alarm birds like guineafowl?

A Mr. Dilke was appointed by the Company as usher.[20] Later he expressed the wish to resign his post, and on 10 April his wish was granted and the Company made him an *ex gratia* payment of £3.[21] Light may be thrown upon the ready acceptance of Dilkes' wish to resign in a letter written to the Governor and Council of Virginia on 10 June 1622. They notified them that they were sending 'along one Leonard Hudson a carpenter with his wife and five of our apprentices for the erection of the East India School, the monies would not reach unto the sending of an Usher as was first intended; . . .' They went on to say that they 'thought good to give the colony the choice of the

Schoolmaster; or Usher, if so be there be any there fit for the place.'[22] Hudson and party sailed on the *Furtherance* in May or June,[23] and arrived in Virginia to find the colony slowly endeavouring to recover itself from the Indian onslaught. The East India School project died, but no doubt Hudson and his team found full employment in the rebuilding programme which by that time must have already begun.

SIR THOMAS DALE – A MILITANT CHRISTIAN

A remarkable collection of testimonies to Dale's religious nature is found in Ralph Hamor's *A True Discourse of the Present State of Virginia*.[24] Hamor, an educated man,[25] came to Virginia with Sir Thomas Gates (via the wrecking on the Bermudas) in 1610, and remained there until 1614, when he returned to England. There in 1615 his *True Discourse* was published by William Welby, by whom it was issued in two printings.

The *Discourse* is of considerable importance for it gives a balanced, contemporary first-hand account of colonial affairs at a time when Gates and Dale were attempting in those difficult years to place the colony on a better footing by means of private ownership, discipline and sensible administration. It contains probably the clearest and most unbiased account of Pocahontas' capture, retention (as an insurance) and marriage, and also three letters of consequence and illumination. These were written by Sir Thomas Dale, John Rolfe and the Revd. Alexander Whitaker. Captain John Smith, incidentally, incorporated many passages of the *Discourse* in his *General Historie* (1624).

The first of the three letters preserved by Hamor was written by Dale to a friend, Richard Mocket, a London cleric, whom he addressed as 'Most Reverend Sir'. The contents were varied, and revealed a man of God burdened with heavy responsibility, conscious of the magnitude of his tasks, and seeking spiritual help that he might fulfil what he believed to be his mission: 'Ye have given me encouragement to persevere in this religious warfare . . . from him in whose vineyard I labour, whose Church with greedy appetite I desire to erect.' Dale gave a long and detailed account of events in Virginia, and of Anglo-Indian relations. He described his contacts with Powhatan whose 'daughter I caused to be carefully instructed in Christian religion, who after she had made some good progress therein, renounced publicly her country, [and] idolatry, openly confessing her Christian faith . . .', adding that her marriage to an English gentlemen of good understanding was 'another knot to bind this peace together.' Dale clearly faced a personal spiritual crisis. His three years of service had been completed. Should he, however, return home? Dale laid bare his mind and soul to his friend at the end of this long letter thus: 'Now Sir, you see my condition, you and all worthy men may judge, whether it would not be grief to see those fair hopes frostbitten and those fresh budding plants to wither, which had I returned, had assuredly followed: for here is no one that the people would have to govern them, but myself . . .' He said that he had been strongly pressed by friends to return home, but 'I knew not upon whom to confer the care of this business in my absence . . . These things have animated me to stay . . . rather than see God's glory diminished, my King and Country dishonoured, and these poor people, I have charge of ruined . . . Remember me, and the cause I have in hand, in your daily meditations . . .'

Dale remained a further two years until relieved by a Deputy Governor, by which time Virginia, through Dale's able leadership and influence with the natives, had taken, at least in material matters, large strides towards permanence and profitability. Dale's reputation as a military man of God rests, however, not so much upon his own utterances, as upon the observations of men of education and action who served under him during those dark, dismal and dangerous days which followed the 'Starving Times' of 1609-10.

The two other letters preserved by Hamor in his *Discourse*, both present Dale as an able soldier, a wise councellor and a deeply religious man.

The Revd. Alexander Whitaker, one of the three outstanding ministers in Virginia during the lifetime of the Virginia Company, wrote thus to his friend, the Revd. Doctor William Gouge, the minister of Black Friars, London, in June 1614: 'The colony here is much better. Sir Thomas Dale our religious and valiant Governor, hath now brought that to pass, which never before could be effected.' Later, when reporting on the conversion of Pocahontas, Whitaker commented that this was something for which 'Sir Thomas Dale had laboured a long time to ground her in.' Hamor also warned Gouge that, despite 'the virtuous deeds of this worthy Knight' he had been slandered and 'much debased by the letters which some wicked men have written from hence, and especially by one C.L. if you hear any condemn this worthy Knight . . . you may upon my word boldly reprove them.' C.L. has not been identified, but it is likely that one of those 'wicked men' was George Percy, who had stigmatized his leader, Captain John Smith, in 1607/8, and had tried also to damage the reputation of Sir Thomas Dale, who had replaced him as acting Governor in 1611, by accusing him of scandalous and defamatory conduct.

The third letter preserved by Hamor was written by John Rolfe, a seasoned and successful adventurer, who had experienced the shipwrecking and marooning on the Bermudas, where, it is believed, his first wife died. The letter, written by such a man to the colonial Governor, is strange. Rolfe, clearly, was in a mental turmoil. He had married Pocahontas, the only such legal Anglo-Indian union to that date, and now appeared worried on the score of public opinion. Rolfe explained his motives in pursuing the goal of mixed marriage, and sought to justify his actions by declaring that what he had done was 'for the glory of God, for my own salvation, and for the converting to the true knowledge of God and Jesus Christ, an unbelieving creature, namely Pocahontas.' The whole letter reads like a confession, for at the start he declared 'I freely subject myself to your grave and mature judgement, deliberation, approbation and determination, assuring myself of your zealous admonitions, and godly comforts, either persuading me to desist, or encouraging to persist therein . . .' Later Rolfe termed Dale '(most noble Sir) the patron and father of us in this country . . .' He ended by 'beseeching Almighty God to rain down upon you, such plenitude of his heavenly graces, as your heart can wish and desire.' It was a remarkable letter by any standard, written as it was by a tough colonist to the effective Governor of Virginia, a man of great military reputation, a rigid disciplinarian, and indeed the strong man of the colony, and not to a priestly confessor and spiritual counsellor. Why did Rolfe not write to Whitaker, the good and Godly priest who had lived in the colony since 1611, and was highly respected? No answer can be given to that question, but the tenor of the letter indicated that Dale, a leader of considerable worldly experience, was also a man of deep spirituality and human understanding.

Another clear and significant testimony to Dale's religious nature is given by Hamor himself, a man who was named in the second royal charter, and had spent four years, 1610-14, in Virginia, During part of that time he had been secretary of the colony, and so was in a position to give an authoritative opinion on one who had served during that period as Marshal of Virginia, and, later, as acting Governor. Professor Rowse edited Hamor's *Discourse* in 1957, using a copy of the first issue. To that publication Dr. Richard B. Harwell, Director of Publications at the Virginia State Library, added a 'Prefatory Note'. In that 'Note' Harwell quoted, and commented upon, the single variation of text found in the second issue of the *Discourse*, omitted, possibly by accident, from the first printing. Those few lines form a brief appreciation of Dale, and an outline of religious observances in the colony during Hamor's time of residence in Virginia. They read:

'Sir Thomas Dale (with whom I am) is a man of great knowledge in Divinity, and of a good conscience in all his doings: both which be rare in a martial man. Every Sabbath day we preach in the forenoon, and catechize in the afternoon. Every Saturday night I exercise in Sir Thomas Dale's house. Our Church affairs be consulted on by the Minister, and four of the most religious men. Once every month we have a Communion, and once a year a solemn Fast . . .'

In both texts Hamor commented on the fact that Dale had unselfishly extended his period of service in the colony:

'It is not for nothing Sir Thomas Dale, so nobly without respect to his living, to his Lady here in England, past the prefixed time of his resolved return, yet remaineth there; I am sure if he pleased he might return with as much honour as any man thence, I say not more.'

Taking all the evidence into consideration, it can be said that the influence of Dale, both personal and through the agency of his Indian proteges, would appear to have been the decisive factor, indeed the only known factor, in awakening or engendering the humanitarian and missionary zeal displayed by Thorpe during his last years.

THORPE ARRIVES

The advent of Thorpe – when his nature, vigour and missionary mindedness became evident to Opechancanough – must have caused the gravest apprehension. Here was a man whose very existence, because of his office, and more particularly in view of his personal feelings and fervour, represented a most serious threat to the Indian way of life and cultural heritage. The education and inevitable – indeed declared – attempt at indoctrination of the future Indian scholars in the projected Henrico College would present the supreme challenge to native tradition and religon. This sudden new danger, coupled with the rapidly expanding activities of the white colonists, confronted the native leaders with the threat of total — and permanent – subjugation within an ever decreasing area, or migration, and the prospect of the possible extinction of their primeval tribal practices and religion. By 1621 the situation, as Opechancanough saw it, had deteriorated so badly that immediate action was called for before the trend became irreversible. It was at that time, Dr. Fausz maintains, that Nemattanew was sent for.

The first scheme devised by Opechancanough took the form of a massive Indian gathering, ostensibly to honour Powhatan with post-funeral rites – possibly with the thought of a sudden assault upon the colonists. This plan was aborted, and Yeardley believed that nothing sinister was intended. Later, it is claimed, Opechancanough approached a chief of the Eastern shore (not part of the Confederacy) to obtain from him a supply of a poison, peculiar to that region, which would somehow or other be administered to the colonists. The chief refused to co-operate.[26] It was possibly at that time that Sir Francis Wyatt took over the office of Governor from Sir George Yeardley.[27]

Soon after assuming office, and in reply to a letter sent by the Virginia Council in London, Sir Francis Wyatt and his Council wrote to London a report on the situation. The exact date of that epistle is not known. Dr. Kingsbury suggests January 1622.[28] The report stated that 'Whereas Sir Francis Wyatt finding the country at his arrival in very great amity and confidence with the natives, and being desirous by all means to continue and enlarge the same as a thing very necessary at the beginning of his Government did and with the advice and consent of the Council, send Capt. Thorpe with a message and a present . . . to the two Kings.'[29] Then followed a long account of Thorpe's report.

1. The King was delighted to renew the treaties with the new Governor.

2. Opechancanough appeared to favour hosting certain White families in Indian settlements and allowing Indian families to reside with the Whites.

3. His response in the discussions on religion was most hopeful.

4. They talked on astronomy and Thorpe reported that the Great Bear was so called in both languages.

5. Opechancanough 'then in the midst of hunting' proposed a further conference on his return. They were to meet at 'Pomucke', i.e. Opechancanough's main residence.

This was clearly both a stalling operation and also an attempt by Opechancanough to ingratiate himself and his people with the colonists, and throw the settlers off their guard by his show of friendliness and co-operation in every way.

Perhaps at this point reference should be made to the English type house that was built by Thorpe for Opechancanough. An examination of the background to this strange action, makes it explicable.

1. Campbell recorded that Powhatan, in the early days of settlement, invited Captain John Smith and 'requested that he would send men to build him a house . . .' Smith despatched a party of Englishmen and four Dutchmen to do so. Campbell added that 'Powhatan's Chimney', looked 'like a chimney of one of those Dutch houses described by Irving.' It was built of stone and measured eighteen and a half feet high, ten and a half feet at base and 'has a double flue'. He concluded his account by saying that 'There is no other such chimney in all that region.'[30]

2. Yeardley was instructed by the Virginia Company to humour Opechancanough to maintain the peace and to win his favour.[31]

3. Thorpe 'also built the King a handsome house, after the English fashion, in which he took such pleasure, especially in the lock and key, that

he would lock and unlock his door, a hundred times a day.'[32] It would appear that this action must have had the sanction of Yeardley, who later claimed that he had put up some of the money for this work.[33]

Events from the commencement of Wyatt's Governorship are, chronologically, uncertain. One of these, the death of Nemattanew, has been placed as early as 1621 and as late as two weeks prior to the massacre; the details too vary in the telling. The basic facts are that Jack of the Feather persuaded a trader named Morgan to go with him, in the interest of business, to Pamunkey. Some days later the chief returned to Morgan's house wearing the trader's hat. Two of the latter's servants on being told that their master was dead, and suspecting the worst, seized Nemattanew and made off with him to Thorpe at Berkeley, presumably the nearest magistrate.[34] On the way, perhaps attempting to escape, the Indian was shot. Realizing that the end was near Nemattanew requested his captors to bury him amongst the whites, so that his people would not know of his death, clearly an attempt to preserve their belief in his invulnerability against the colonists' bullets.

Opechancanough, on hearing of the death, at once swore vengeance,[35] but quickly recovered himself and simulated indifference, the better to maintain the semblance of great friendliness towards the settlers. This façade was vital to Opechancanough if his scheme for the sudden attack on, and annihilation of, the colonists, obviously even then under consideration, was to have any hope of success.

On the night before the Indian attack an event occurred which saved hundreds of lives and in all probability the colony itself. A native convert, Chanco, one of the three up to that time whose names we know,[36] that evening received a visit from his brother who gave him the chief's command to kill the colonist, Richard Pace, in whose house he was living, saying that he intended killing another Englishman named Perry.[37] Chanco, on his brother's departure, because of his master's kindness, woke him and told him the details of the Indian plot. Stith reports that Pace at once informed Captain William Powell, obviously a near neighbour, secured his own house and rowed across the James river to alert the Governor in James Town. Neighbouring plantations were warned, and the capital, the most populated settlement, stood to.

The next morning ostensibly friendly Indians entered all plantations which had not been informed, bearing gifts and goods for sale, and in some instances sat down to a meal with the occupiers.[38] Then suddenly with a co-ordination of timing, so it is reported, that spoke of orders from a central authority, they set upon the colonists with weapons of all kinds, many snatched from their hosts. They by-passed centres of real resistance, such as

James Town, but wrought havoc where surprise was achieved and little defence had been possible.

The losses on the isolated and unprepared plantations were heavy. The settlers had received no warning, were unsuspecting and, because of the recent extremely friendly attitude of the natives, were totally unprepared defensively for the Indians' sudden *volte-face*.[39] Many were killed before they realized what was happening, others attempted to beat off the attackers with inadequate weapons, while the more fortunate were able to snatch up their guns or swords and barricade their houses, thus offering an effective resistance. In most cases where this happened the Indians withdrew to seek less organized defence. The heaviest recorded casualties were at Martin's Hundred where seventy-eight were officially stated to have been killed, but it is generally believed that the figure was higher, perhaps reaching one hundred. More than fifty were said to have died at Bennet's Plantation,[40] while at Falling Creek, where John Berkeley was ironmaster, twenty seven, including Berkeley, two women and two young children, were murdered.[41] Maurice Berkeley, the son of John, and two children are known to have survived. The latter are said to have run away and hidden in the woods, while Maurice may well have been at Jamestown on business. At the College Lands seventeen are known to have died, and at Weynoack 'of Sir George Yeardley his people' twenty-one were killed. Captain Nathaniel Powell, his wife, Joyce (née Tracy, and great with child) and ten others were killed in their plantation, which was named Powle Brooke.[42]

The situation at Berkeley Plantation, though ill documented, is interesting. The plantations of Berkeley and Westover, both with extensive water-frontage, march together, and their mansion houses today, (presumably on the original sites) are only about a mile apart. Both were sizeable plantations and too far from Jamestown to have received any warning, yet their losses were comparatively light. Only six died at Westover,[43] and eleven at Berkeley, one of whom, Thorpe, might well not have been killed had not his trust in the natives been so great. All this might suggest a quickness of reaction on both plantations, and that perhaps the Westover people were alerted by noise, including gunfire no doubt, which they would have heard from nearby Berkeley, if that plantation had been attacked first. It was reported generally that when the natives faced determined resistance they passed on to the next house or plantation. Thus it would appear that the Indians encountered considerable resistance at Berkeley, and that the majority of those killed on that plantation probably were those caught in the open, possibly in the fields, or in the case of the Rowles family, where Richard, his wife and child died, surprised in their house. The fact that the Berkeley cattle were later taken to Shirley Plantation, a few miles away, suggests that the Berkeley Company members successfully fought off the attackers, suffered eleven casualties, but prevented the Indians killing or driving off at least some of the Berkeley animals.

The official Berkeley casualty list is as follows: 'Captain George Thorpe, Esq.', John Rowles, Richard Rowles and his wife and child, Giles Wilkins, Giles Bradway, Richard Fereby, Thomas Thorpe, Robert Jordan and Edward Painter. Thomas Thorpe and Edward Painter were members of Woodleefe's party, while all the Rowles (if John – who appears on no list of Berkeley settlers – is a mistake for Benedict), Wilkins, Bradway (Broadway) and Fereby (Ferriby) came out with Tracy. Jordan appears on no known list of Berkeley colonists, and may have been recruited in Virginia. The identity of Thomas Thorpe who sailed with Woodleefe is not certain, but it is possible that he was Thomas, the son of John and Rebecca Thorpe, who was baptized in St. Martin's in the Field on 23 June 1598 – see chapter 3.

In the Virginia Company's official account of the massacre special mention is made of George Thorpe's death, which, in retrospect, can be seen as, probably, the major factor in the subsequent rapid decline in the Berkeley Company's fortune. On the morning of the massacre he appears to have been out and about when he was 'warned by his man (who perceived some treachery intended to them by these hellhounds) to look to himself . . .' The servant then 'ran away . . . and so saved his own life;'[44] Thorpe 'was so void of all suspicion . . .' that he refused to follow the advice and advanced to talk and reason with the Indians. They immediately assaulted and killed their most staunch friend and champion; furthermore they savagely mutilated his body.[45]

It has been suggested, because his body was badly mutilated, that George Thorpe was a primary target for the Indians – a marked man, by virtue of the religious and cultural threat he represented.[46] Certainly Opechancanough would have considered that his elimination was essential. I do not agree, however, that the hideous mutilation of his body resulted from the same specific cause, except in so far as he was a very prominent member of the Virginia Council of State,[47] and so symbolized to the Indians the 'white peril' which threatened their very lives and livelihood.

Thus Thorpe died, a man whom Fausz linked, yet contrasted sharply, with that able but eccentric Indian war-chief, Jack of the Feather. Dr. Fausz wrote thus of them – 'George Thorpe and Nemattanew – became martyrs to the long-festering cultural hatreds between the English and the Indians. The story of their inter-related lives, and intense personalities, has suffered from obscurity ever since they played key roles in the larger drama that unfolded in

Virginia . . . [they] epitomized, respectively the ideological extremes of active Christian proselytizer and hostile pagan defender of the Indian values, and as culture heroes, they provided a personal dimension to the larger Anglo-Powhatan struggle.'[48]

POSTSCRIPT

It is suggested in two American publications[49] that Thorpe survived the massacre and signed a warrant on the 3rd May, 1622. These statements are based on a misreading of the original document in the Public Record Office.[50] The Research Department of the P.R.O. have confirmed that the correct date is 1621, and not 1622.

NOTES

1. *Gloucester Journal*, 22 May 1972.

2. Fausz wrote (*Cavalcade*, p. 111) 'The seeds of that conflict were planted in 1607 when aggressive, arrogant Englishmen, bestirred by a christian mission to dominate and convert the heathen, arrived in Virginia seeking to impose their culture and religion on the equally proud, aggressive and arrogant Powhatan . . .' I cannot accept this statement in its entirety, for there is little solid evidence of vigorous evangelization during the first few years. It was as though the settlers, despite their royal charters' instructions, were following the advice of Richard Hakluyt, that solid settlement should precede active missionary endeavour, for it is clear that at first it was the conduct of the colonist, the disturbance of tribal lands and fear for the future which were the main initial reasons for the frequent hostilities by the Indians. This is borne out in a letter written by Sir Walter Cope, to Lord Salisbury in 1607, quoted by A.T. Vaughan, in which the writer, basing his information upon Captain Newport's statements, said that the Indians 'used our men well until they found they began to plan and fortify. Then they fell to skirmishing and killed 3 of our people.'
'*Expulsion of the Salvages - English Policy and the Virginia Massacre*', *WMQ*, series III, January, 1978, p. 63.

3. There are numerous allusions in the early narratives to the food, e.g., corn, fish, fowl and fur, supplied by the Indians. Wilcomb E. Washburn summed up the situation thus: 'The English knew well enough how important was Indian food: the early accounts are filled with references to the "Indian fields" along the rivers of Virginia, and little else but native produce sustained the whites in the early days of settlement.' ('The Moral and Legal Justification for dispossessing the Indians', in *Seventeenth Century America Essays in Colonial History*, p. 23). Dr. Washburn pointed out that the natives were hunters, agriculturists and fishermen.
See also H.U. Faulkner, *American Economic History*, New York, 1943.

4. N.O. Lurie, 'Indian Cultural Adjustment to European Civilization,' in *Seventeenth-Century America, Essays in Colonial History*, op.cit., 1959, p. 48.

5. Stith, p. 124.

6. Peter Walne, 'The Collections for Henrico College, 1616-1618,' *VMHB*, vol. 80 (1972), pp. 258-266.

7. Above chapter 3.

8. Kingsbury III, p. 102.

9. Kingsbury I, pp. 220-1.

10. Kingsbury III, p. 148.

11. Weldon gave as his reason for hiring out much of his labour force the fact that the

provisions provided for the party were insufficient, and the men had to be 'farmed' out to survive. The company replied that these provisions were available if requested.

12. Thorpe's letters to (i) Sir Edwin Sandys, and (ii) John Ferrar, both dated 15 May 1621.

13. Smyth I, 35; in Kingsbury III, pp. 435-6; Brown II, pp. 414-5.

14. Brown II, p. 442. It is strange how, through the tangled web of events relating to Virginia, the name Dale, a distinguished soldier, appears again and again as a christianizing influence in the colony, e.g., building Henrico, instructing Pocahontas in the christian faith, bringing young Indians to England to be educated (and in one case at least he was baptized), and now, vicariously, helping to found a free school. See pp. 185-8 of this chapter for a fuller appreciation of Dale. The term 'free' indicated in Virginia at that time a school that taught Latin. See S.M. Ames, *Reading, Writing and Arithmetic in Virginia, 1607-99*, no. 15, Williamsburg, 1957.

15. Kingsbury I, p. 532.

16. Kingsbury I, p. 539-40.

17. Kingsbury I, p. 550.

18. Kingsbury I, pp. 558-9.

19. Kingsbury III, pp. 530-34. MS Records of Virginia Company III, pt. II, pp. 21-21A.; Brown II, p. 443 added that two other ships – the *Hart* and *Roe-buck* – homeward bound from the East also 'gave towards the building of the aforesaid Free-school in Virginia the sum of £66. 13s. 6d.'

20. Kingsbury I, p. 616.

21. Kingsbury I, p. 629.

22. Kingsbury III, p. 650.

23. Brown II, p. 474 gives the sailing date as June, but a printed Broadside (Kingsbury III, p. 639,) (copies in New York Public Library and the Society of Antiquities) which tablulates a number of sailings states that the *Furtherance* left in May. Could the Broadside refer to its leaving the Port of London, while Brown refers to Plymouth or some other south coast port of call?

24. Reproduced in 1957, from the first London edition of 1615, with an introduction by A.L. Rowse. This work was printed by the Virginia State Library, as no. 3 of its Library Publications.

25. He probably attended Merchant Taylors School and Brasenose College, Oxford.

26. The nearest date for this attempt is the 'last summer,' i.e., 1621, contained in the official

account of the massacre by Edward Waterhouse – Kingsbury III, p. 556.

27. 18th November, 1621.

28. Kingsbury III, pp. 581-8; MS. Records Virginia Company III, pt II, pp. 1-2a.

29. Ibid, pp. 583-4.

30. Charles Campbell, pp. 65-8.

31. Stith, p. 172.

32. Stith, p. 211.

33. Smyth I, 43. This will be discussed in the following chapter.

34. Craven, *Southern Colonies in the Seventeenth Century*, p. 167.

35. Campbell, p. 160; Fausz, *Cavalcade*, p. 117.

36. The other two are Pocahontas and Georgius Thorpe.

37. Kingsbury III, p. 555, where the respective positions of Pace and Perry are made clear.

38. Kingsbury III, p. 551; Campbell, p. 161.

39. 'Yea in some places [the natives] sat down at breakfast with our people at their tables, whom immediately with their own tools and weapons either laid down, or standing in their houses, they basely and barbarously murdered, not sparing either age or sex, man woman or child . . . they also slew many of our people then at their several works and husbandmen in the fields . . .' Kingsbury III, p. 551.

40. Kingsbury III, p. 571.

41. Two of these, John Howlet and one of his sons, had come over with the second main Berkeley party. Kingsbury III, p. 567. Perhaps Howlet was the builder of furnaces whom Thorpe said he had lent to the ironworks project?

42. Kingsbury III, pp. 555 and 569.

43. Kingsbury III, p. 567. This figure includes the casualties on the properties of the three West brothers.

44. Kingsbury III, p. 553. It is not known whether the 'man' was white or a native. Perhaps like 'Georgius Thorp' he was an Indian, maybe too, as with Georgius, he was a convert to the christian faith. Was this a case, similar to that of Chanco, of the faithful servant warning his loved master of Opechancanough's plan of a sudden assault upon the colonists?

45. Kingsbury III, p. 553. 'They not only wilfully murdered him, but cruelly and felly, out of devilish malice, did so many barbarous despites and foul scorns after to his dead corpse as are unbefitting to be heard by any civil ear.'

46. J. F. Fausz, Ph.D. Dissertation, William and Mary College, Williamsburg, Virginia.

47. The body of Captain Nathaniel Powell, an 'Ancient Adventurer' and a Councillor of State, was also badly savaged and his head, it is said, hacked off and taken away.

48. Dr. Fausz, *Virginia Cavalcade*, op.cit., p. 111.

49. Professor R.B. Davis, *Intellectual Life in the Colonial South, 1585-1763*, University of Tennesse, Knoxville, 1978, p. 332. The Revd. Dr. G.J. Cleaveland, *The Alumni Gazette*, College of William and Mary, March, 1970, p. 8.

50. State Papers Colonial, vol. 3, no. 36, III.

9

Aftermath of the Massacre

'The Indian massacre of 22nd March 1622,' so wrote Professor Robert C. Johnson of Temple University, Philadelphia, 'was one of the few events in the early history of Virginia that received widespread attention in England.'[1] The news of that catastrophe reached England during the first week in July and spread rapidly by conversation, correspondence and through the medium of the printing press.

One of the earliest of these private comments was made by a law student in London. This young man, Simonds D'Ewes, on the 7 July (1622) wrote in his diary that

'From Virginia we had exceeding bad news for the inhuman wretches we had given peace to thus long, conspired together: one hour gave beginning to their butchery, an Indian boy told the Englishmen of it, those that were secure were slain chiefly in St. Martins Hundred to the full number of two hundred 29 of all sorts. Then they burnt some houses & villages & spoiled most of the plantation & corn thereabouts: tis likely but for the former boy more had been slain.'[2] On August 28 D'Ewes recorded in his diary that he 'was partaker of an exact discourse of the massacre . . . which happened the 22 of March', adding that as he hoped to obtain further and more detailed information, 'I defer to speak of it.'[3]

On 12 July another London student, William Wynn, wrote to his father, Sir John Wynn, of the disaster thus:

'In Virginia, the savages have by a wile come (as they were wont) to traffic into our English houses, and with our own weapons slew 329 of our men, whereupon tis thought that Council will resolve upon a war against these barbarous villains: I may not omit how a gentlewoman seeing the barbares approach her house took a musket but without shot therein and her maids with shovels with which they marched through the barbares Companies, they not daring to approach them.'[4]

A third example is dated 13 July when in a letter to Sir Dudley Carelton, then in the Low Countries, John Chamberlain wrote:

'Another [ship] likewise is come from Virginia with ill news that the savages have by surprise slain about 350 of our people there one and another. It was by their own supine negligence that lived as careless and securely there as if they had been in England, in scattered and straggling houses far asunder, whereby they were so easily subject to the surprise of those naked people, who besides other spoil and booty have possessed themselves of arms and weapons, but the best is they have no skill to use them. Among them that are lost is one Captain Barclay [John Berkeley] and Captain Thorpe whom I was well acquainted withal and had been a pensioner: the disgrace and shame is as much as the loss, for no other nation would have been so grossly overtaken.'[5]

Several interesting points emerge from these independant accounts. The first that meets the eye is the gradual increase in the number of reported casualties. On the seventh – only a day or two after the first news of the massacre had reached London – the figure quoted was 229, five days later this had risen to 329 while on the following day the total dead is put at 350. This was almost exactly the official figure finally put out by the Virginia Company. It is believed, however, as was stated above,[6] that the actual number killed was in excess of 350, but that for propaganda purposes, i.e., that would-be settlers might not be too much discouraged, the lower, perhaps much lower, figure of 347 was finally officially adopted.

Secondly there is the sense of shame that such a disaster should have been allowed to take place. It was indeed a stain upon the nation's honour and good name that ignorant 'naked savages' should have been allowed the opportunity to inflict such damaging losses upon a vigorous and civilized nation. The reaction was natural; someone must be at fault, and so, to soften the blow, and to salvage some little of the nation's prestige and to southe the wound a scapegoat must be found. The result was that those in England firmly placed the blame upon the administration in the colony, in that they had been too kind to the natives in receiving them into their homes, and had not observed the elementary precautions for defence. The Governor and his council, in their reply,[7] indignantly pointed out that the company should 'consider what instructions you have formerly given us, to win the Indians to us by kind entertaining them in our houses, and if it were possible to cohabit with us, and how impossible it is for any watch and ward to secure us against secret enemies that live promiscuously amongst us, and are harboured in our bosoms, all histories and your own discourse may sufficiently inform you.'[8] They also pointed out that when the troubles in 1621 arose, i.e., when the poisoning of settlers was feared and the Powhatan assembly was held for the post-funeral rites and reburial of the bones of Powhatan (Stith, p. 209), the then Governor, Sir George Yeardley, 'Himself in person went to every plantation and took a general muster of all the men and their arms, gave straight charge that watch and ward should be kept every where.' They continued by pointing out that with no proof of evil intent, the obviously friendly attitude of the natives, and the pressure of their own labours, the ordinary settlers believed it unnecessary, indeed impossible, especially on the smaller and more isolated plantations, to continue to maintain over a long period a high degree of watch and ward.[9] They reported, too, perhaps in an attempt to pour oil on troubled water, or maybe in self defence, that 'We have anticipated your desires by setting upon the Indians in all places . . . we have slain divers, burnt their towns, destroyed their weirs and corn.' They added that Yeardley had recently taken from the natives 1,000 bushels of corn and that a further 3,000 had been obtained 'by trade or force.'[10]

The first published account of the massacre was written by Edward Waterhouse,[11] a member of the Virginia Company, early in August, and was addressed to the Company. He gave as his reasons for embarking upon this task the fact that rumours were rife, tales were exaggerated and misreported often unintentionally, but sometimes from hostility towards the Virginia Company. Waterhouse clearly feared that these wild and unfavourable stories might affect adversely the company's whole settlement future. He said too that his findings were based upon the accounts given by relations of eye witnesses, letters sent by the Governor (Sir Francis Wyatt), Sir George Yeardley, and 'other Gentleman of quality and of the Council in that Colony, read openly in your Courts'. Supposedly they were trustworthy.

After a brief resume of the Company's achievements in Virginia and of the economy and immigration figures for the years 1619-21, Waterhouse proceeded to give the background of the massacre, the perfidy of the Indians and the too trusting attitude of the settlers. The co-ordination and suddenness of the attack, he went on, was only matched by the fiendish savagery of their assault and the barbaric treatment of the dead.

Waterhouse wrote with deep feeling of the contributions made by certain leaders in the colony (some of whom were close friends) towards its material and spiritual development. The one selected for particular praise was Thorpe whom he, obviously, greatly admired. Having paid a lavish tribute to those men, living and dead, he stressed that the preservation of the colony as a viable unit was due to the friendliness of Chanco, without whose warning 'the slaughter had been universal.' Waterhouse passed on to analyse the colony's situation, and put forward what might be termed a fresh colonial policy for the consideration of the London Council and a revised strategy for the colony. Indeed, it appears almost to savour of hypocrisy, for he said that the Indians failed to appreciate that the massacre 'must needs be for the good of the plantation after, and the loss of this blood to make the body more healthful, as by these reasons may be manifest.' Then follow several arguments supporting this theory.

1. A betrayal of trust never goes unpunished.
2. In the past Council and colonists had, even to their own disadvantage, been fair, considerate and generous towards the natives. The massacre by

'cutting the knot' of friendship, now gave the company the 'right of war' to invade, destroy and occupy. The colonists, with a clear conscience, could 'enjoy their [Indian] cultivated places . . . the fruits of others labours . . . their cleared grounds . . . situated in the fruitfulest places . . . shall be inhabited by us,' He added that hitherto the settlers themselves had had to grub up the woods and clear the ground.

3. The Indians having been driven out, the indiscriminate killing of wild life, deer, turkey, wildfowl and fish, very important food commodities, would cease and be replaced by a rational culling system. The settlers' own livestock, in particular swine and goats, which in the past had been heavily poached, would now be safe.

4. The colonists would now be justified in not only hounding and killing the Indians, but also in following the Spanish example of *Divide et impera*[12a] by encouraging quarrels and enmity between the tribes, and not only those involved in the massacre. The advice of Tacitus, *Ita dum singuli pugnant universi vincuntur*[12c] is also quoted in support of the policy.

5. The Indians, no longer friends, can now be 'compelled to servitude and drudgery, and supply the room of men that labour.' They could be employed on the plantations and in the mines, while some could be sent as slave labour to the Sumers Isles.

6. The colonists had learned a bitter lesson, and in future would be on their guard. Waterhouse summed up this section, and indeed the previous five, by quoting the French proverb 'Ill luck is good for something.' Dr. Washburn succinctly put it thus, 'The Virginia massacre of 1622 . . . provided the English with the "bloody shirt" needed to justify hostilities against the natives whenever convenient.'

7. This is a catalogue of the material advantages for the colony which would result outside Virginia. The settlers would receive sympathy from others, the King would contribute 'munitions and arms' from the Tower for use in the colony, and a 'large supply of men and other necessaries' would shortly be sent to support and extend the settlement.

A long review followed, concluding with an appeal for support from the whole nation. This read, 'Lastly, it is to be wished, that every good patriot will take these things seriously . . . and consider how deeply the prosecution of the noble enterprise concerneth the honour of his Majesty and the whole nation, the propagation of Christian Religion, the enlargement, strength, and safety of his Majesty's dominions, the real augmenting of his revenues, the employment of his subjects idle at home . . .' This long harangue concluded with the reminder that all can contribute in differing ways, by 'purse . . . person . . . favour . . . counsel . . . prayers . . .'

The second publication relating to the massacre also appeared in 1622, probably in September, and took the form of a long poem by Christopher Brooke, entitled 'A Poem on the Late Massacre in Virginia. With Particular mention of those men of note that suffered in that disaster.' Here again Thorpe is given pride of place.[13] Brooke, a lawyer by profession, was a poet of some distinction. Amongst his close friends he numbered John Donne, William Browne, Michael Drayton and Ben Jonson. Brooke became an active member of the Virginia Company in 1609, and as a member of Parliament was one of the leading spokesmen for the Company in the House.[14] Brooke thus was deeply shocked by the massacre, and doubly so when he learned that two of his friends, Nathaniel Powell and George Thorpe had been killed. The poem occupies nineteen pages, the latter half of which is an oration honouring the leaders in the colony.

EFFECTS IN VIRGINIA

All three major enterprises in Virginia in which Berkeley or Thorpe played an important part were destroyed by the massacre. In two instances the end came quickly, i.e. Henrico College and the Iron works at Falling Creek, while, in the case of the Plantation, its life under the aegis of the Berkeley Company was more protracted. It must be remembered, however, that it never really died, indeed within a hundred years or so it became one of the leading plantations in the new world – not in size, it is true, but a centre of social and political activities.[15]

i. Henrico

The ambitious and idealistic educational dream of Henrico virtually died with the massacre, although theoretically it remained alive as a possibility for several years. The causes of its demise were many and interwoven.

Understandably surviving settlers, new arrivals and the people in England were reluctant to subscribe fresh money for the re-establishment of a college to educate and convert members of tribes who so recently had tortured and murdered hundreds of their relations and friends. The policy instead was now to make war, to kill and to spoil, activated no doubt by thoughts of revenge, and as an insurance for the future. The Company's own troubles, both internal and external, were such that though they considered the possibility of revival, events, including the withdrawal of their charter in 1624, made this impossible. Finally Virginia was made a crown colony in

1624 and the King, Charles I, became so involved in home affairs, that a project like Henrico, in a foreign field, faded away.[16]

ii. Falling Creek

The havoc at the Falling Creek works was exceptional. Berkeley and most of his labour force were killed,[17] and the works, tools and machinery were wrecked beyond salvage. The death of John Berkeley also brought tragedy in another sphere. He is reported to have discovered a 'lead deposit and made use of it to furnish other settlers with bullets and shot.' The secret of its location died with him, although William Bird (a subsequent owner of Falling Creek) in a letter dated 20 may 1684, mentioned testing lead ore, but gave no indication of the location.[18]

iii. Berkeley Town and Hundred

For the Berkeley Plantation the massacre signalled the beginning of the end of its association with its Gloucestershire dominated patronage and leadership. Following upon the heavy losses, personnel and material, resulting from the Indian assault, the Governor of the colony and the remaining members of the Council of State (six died that day) decided to concentrate surviving settlers and their stock from the outlying plantations at suitable and defensible ones. Berkeley was deemed unsafe and its people and cattle were moved to Jordans Journey.[19] They were under the command of Thomas Kemis, Gent, who had succeeded to the leadership of the plantation on the death of Thorpe. The date of their move is not known.

There is no official list of survivors, but Smyth writing on 1 August 1622, about a month after the first news of the massacre had reached England, gave a list of thirteen (maybe fourteen) that 'remaineth to us as servants in Virginia'.[20] They were: Thomas Kemis, Thomas Baugh, Richard Milton, John Gibbs, Thomas Shipway, Alexander Bradway, William Clement, Richard Sheriffe (the younger), Thomas Molton and George Heale, the drummer. The women who survived were Frances the daughter of William Finch, Elizabeth Webb (who had married in Virginia) and Elizabeth the daughter of Thomas Coopy. There is reference to 'with mother of new married to –' – a further survivor? There is a marginal note 'dead' along side the name of Kemis on Smyth's list, but that death occurred later.

Of the ten men, three, Clement, Sheriffe and Molton, were survivors of the 1619 party, while the remaining seven had sailed with Tracy, provided that Shipway can be identified with Sheepy[21] of the disembarkation list. Clement and Molton were described earlier by Smyth[21] as cooks and gardeners, while young Sheriffe was a Cooper. Unfortunately, there is no record of the occupation of the members of Tracy's party except that little George Hale was the drummer, and certain others were designated 'Gent'. This occupational record of the four suggests that Berkeley 'Town' was not overrun. The two cooks, cooper and drummer would operate normally in the inhabited area, while at least three, if not four, women survived and only one, Mrs. Rowles (plus her husband and child), appear on the list of eleven who were murdered. It is known that Thorpe, one of the eleven, was killed in the open, so it may well be that the majority of the 'slain' were, as suggested earlier, also caught in the open on the plantation and there died.

Smyth concluded his 1 August list with the statement that four fresh settlers 'went over in the *Furtherance* in June 1622 . . . before the news of the massacre was heard of . . .' These were George Pelton, Richard Willis, Clement Melton and Richard Buttry. A John Burdely who 'bore his own charges', went over during August 1622 in the *Margaret and John*. Against the name Willis is the marginal note 'dead'.

In July 1623 a 'List of Subscribers and Subscriptions for Relief of the Colony' was issued.[22] The introductory paragraph declared that the relief would not only be for the colony in general, but also for 'our particular friends', and concluded with the statement that the authorities 'purpose' to send that relief 'this present Summer 1623.' Eighteen people subscribed, and the amounts ranged from £20 to £400. Number 12 (Smyth) reads – 'I John Smyth will supply my servants now living in Virginia in Berkeley hundred and such others as this next August I send over to increase them to the sum (at least) of 100^{li}' (£100). Two points arise in that declaration. (i) As late as July 1623 Smyth was not aware that the Berkeley settlers had been moved from their plantation. (ii) There appears to be no extant list of 'such others as this next August I sent over'. There is, however, a most interesting and relevant deposition quoted in the minutes of the General Court in Virginia on 3 January 1625.[23] It reads thus:

'Sargent Holland sworn and examined sayeth that there are planted at Sherley hundred for Barkley hundred Company these men as followeth

Sargeant Gabriell Holland	John Taylor	William Gillman
Richard Firmely	Charles Partridge	. . . Prisman
William Clement	Mr. Hamden	. . . Bullman
Richard Sheriffe	Theophilus Beastone	Nicholas Pierse
Thomas Moultone	Thomas Peck	. . . Croser
Edward Purquite		

The deposition concluded with the statement that 'For whom [= those named above] duties were to be paid by Capt. Thorpe to Mr. Sandys minister[24] which whether they were paid or not this examinant knoweth not.'

Of those sixteen, nine are names not found in the extant lists amongst the Smyth of Nibley Papers and probably were those whom Smyth had promised to send. The remaining seven are interesting, for they show that Smyth's list of survivors on the Berkeley Plantation, compiled on 1 August 1622, was far from complete. Of the seven 'old hands' Clement, Moultone and the younger Sherife were included in Smyth's list of August. What of the remainder? Charles Partridge had sailed with Thorpe on 27 March 1620, Sgt. Gabriel Holland had come with Tracy's party, Mr. Hamden was probably the John Homleden, Gent, who embarked with Tracy, but who (according to Smyth[25]) was 'disposed of' by Tracy. He, now that Tracy was dead, and the plantation under-strength, had probably returned to the 'fold'. In addition Richard Firmely might be identified with Richard Fereby (sometimes Feriby) of Tracy's party. What of John Taylor? Is it he who came over with the first major party, but of whom Smyth, in a marginal note wrote 'dead'? There are some instances of men, and women, too, who were reported dead or who, having been captured by the Indians, had been presumed dead, but who, later, were found to be alive and well. This may well have happened in the case of Taylor.

From the above deposition it would appear that the Berkeley Plantation people had been moved from Jordan's Journey to the Shirley Plantation before the sitting of the Court on 3 January 1625. This would have been a simple operation, for Shirley is only a few miles up river from Berkeley. Not all, however, seem to have transferred, for at the Court two weeks later (17 January) is the following minute – 'It is ordered that Richard Milton [one of the survivors of the massacre who came over with Tracy] shall live at Shirley and look unto the cattle of Barkley hundred for which he shall be allowed fifty pound weight of tobacco and the milk of the said kine. Provided that he carefully look unto them.'[26]

As has been seen Smyth sent support to the Berkeley community. This however was meagre. Furthermore, the situation facing the Berkeley people was made even worse by the loss of their three leaders and men of influence in the colony.[27] This grievous handicap was greatly aggravated by an event which signalled the end of an era. The massacre, the Virginia Company's 'continued failure to pay cash dividents, and the hostility of the Crown to Sir Edwin Sandys,'[28] one of the powerful figureheads of the Company, were no doubt, the reasons why the Company's charter was revoked on 24 May 1624, whereupon Virginia was created a royal colony and its people came under the control of the Crown. It soon became obvious that Smyth was finding it difficult at a distance to deal with the increasing problems facing the Berkeley settlers. Thorpe and Tracy, his co-sponsors and men of influence, who might have saved the day, were dead, while most of the other men of standing within the Berkeley Company who had made the voyage to Berkeley Plantation were either dead or had returned to England. Those who remained found it difficult to withstand the powerful vested interests which were now developing under the new regime, some of whom were none too honest if reports received by Smyth bear any relation to the truth. This is clearly seen in Smyth I, 40-2, which, apart from the occasional quotation, have received little attention. Consequently those three items, two letters from Virginia and one seeking fresh sponsors in England, will be quoted *verbatim*, and, largely speak for themselves.

EFFECT UPON PERSONAL ESTATES AND PROPERTY

The effect upon the colonial estates and properties of those who perished in that bloody attack upon the settlers on 22 March 1622, was, in some instances, very considerable. This may well be judged by various records of the subsequent enquiries and litigation which have survived. Indeed, the death of a single person in Virginia, even during peaceful conditions, raised not insignificant problems for their families and dependants back in England. The affidavits relating to William Tracy, to which reference had already been made, testify to the trouble involved, despite the fact that Tracy's wife, son and daughter were all at that time alive and still in Virginia. An earlier example occurred as a result of the death by drowning of the Revd. Alexander Whitaker in 1617. It is recorded that in 1618 his sister arrived in the colony to make 'enquiry after the goods of her deceased brother, but found that he left little of value . . .'[29] This, in view of his many years in Virginia and his obvious standing, is surprising. Indeed, the matter appears even more suspicious when Whitaker's will, proved on 4 August 1617, is examined.[30]

A proven case of the dishonest appropriation of the goods of a deceased person occurred between January and April, 1623. A John Robinson and his son and heir were sailing to Virginia. The father, who was carrying with him £200 worth of valuables and servants, was advised to make his will. He replied, 'If I die my son and heir is here aboard with me, to whom I leave my whole estate.' Robinson died, and the ship's master, Mr. Douglas, took the Robinsons' chests and trunks and the 'father's whole estate' against the son's wishes. Furthermore he 'intendeth to dipose of the father's estate and servants 'at his own pleasure', neither would he allow the son 'any means to live upon here'. The son's plea was allowed by the Governor, and a Mr. Ganey, a relation of the son, was granted letters of administration on his behalf.[31] Had the lad not been on board and on disembarkation been able to appeal to the Governor at Jamestown no doubt that property would have been lost.

Judging by the case of certain personnel connected with the Berkeley Plantation who died in the massacre of 22nd March, it might appear that the estates and effects of the deceased were occasionally looked upon as there for the 'milking', to be disposed of by the authorities in a manner 'advantageous' to the colony's economy. The first example which stands out is that of Captain Nathaniel Powell who married Tracy's daughter, Joyce, between February and April 1621. Nathaniel and Joyce, great with child (it would have been their first),[32] were both killed at their estate, 'Powell Brooke', near the mouth of the Appomattox River on that fateful Friday. Their names appear in the official casualty list. Yet four years later, on 21 July 1626, Nathaniel's brother, Thomas Powell, on behalf of himself and his 'poor brothers and sisters' appealed to the Privy Council for the restoration of their brother's estate which was of 'a good value.'[33] Brother Thomas had earlier taken out letters of administration in London. Despite this, the Governor and Council of Virginia had certified that the estate had been in the hands of a William Powell, who was no relation, and that since his death it had been occupied by a Mr. Blany who had married William Powell's widow. The Powell family in their plea to the Privy Council stated that their previous request on the subject, made in 1624, had been ignored; hence this fresh appeal. Perhaps the authorities in Virginia, when the re-establishing of the abandoned plantations began, were anxious that these should become viable as soon as possible, thus aiding the economic recovery of the colony, and had handed the estate over to a surviving colonist irrespective of actual ownership. That is a charitable explanation. But, in view of the fate of Thorpe's estate, others might be nearer the truth.

There are in *The Smyth of Nibley Papers* in New York Public Library, two manuscripts, i.e., nos. 43 and 44, which have a considerable relevance to the second half of this chapter. No. 43 is an inventory of the effects of George Thorpe in Virginia, while no. 44 is a letter from William Thorpe, the son and heir of George, enquiring about his father's effects. Both are set out here *verbatim*. The inventory is necessary as a prelude to discussion of the proceedings of the Virginia courts in which claims were made against Thorpe's estate. It provides a backcloth for that litigation. It will be noticed that both in the inventory and in the court claims the value of items is expressed in pounds of tobacco. This is not very helpful unless the price of tobacco at that specific time is known. Melvin Herndon in his monograph, *Tobacco in Colonial Virginia*, Williamsburg, 1957, pointed out that the price of tobacco varied from about 10s. per pound at the commencement of the tobacco growing period in Virginia to 1d. in 1630. In this table of average prices for the years under review, i.e., 1622-5, it varied between 3s. and 2. 4d.

The Inventory – Smyth I, No. 43
(Original spelling has been retained)

An Inventorie of all and singular the goods and effectes of Captayne George Thorpe Esquire deceased, valued and prised the 10th day of Aprill Anno 1634 by Samuell Sharpe, Richard Biggs and Thomas Palmer as followeth, vizt.

	lb tobacco
Imprimis a wrought velvett cloake lyne with plush	0100
Item an old bl: silke grogram sute	0050
Item an old bl: cloth cloake lyne with velvett	0050
Item an old bl: satten suite	0030
Item a stuff wastcoate	0008
Item 4 paire of old silke stockings	0020
Item one paire of old enameld spurres	0000½
Item one/paire of bl: silke garters	0003
Item 3 dosen of old silke poynts	0001
Item a knott of bandstrings	0000½
Item 2 paire of old lynnen stockings	0000½
Item 2 pa' of gloves	0004
Item one truncke	0005
Item a walnutt chest with locke and key	0008
Item a bl: satten suite	0040
Item an old bl: silke grogram dublett & old satten hose	0010
Item a very old ash col: satten suite	0020
Item 4 paire of sheetes	0026
Item 5 very old shirtes	0005
Item 2 cupboard clothes	0005
Item 2 pillow beares	0002
Item sixe handkerchirs	0001
Item an old wrought night capp	0003
Item an old quilt capp & 2 old holland capps	0001
Item 2 towells	0001
Item 2 books & a small remnant of calico	0016
Item a pa' of worne shooes galloshes & pantaples	0005
Item 33 fallinge bands	0004
Item 8½ yards of course holland	0016
Item a paire of gold waights	0001

Item a paire of fine old sheets & a pillowbeare	0008
Item 33 course napkins	0012
Item 3 course table cloathes	0012
Item 3 old holland capps 2 kerchers a neck cloath & two napkins	002
Item 16 pa' of diaper napkins, a table cloath. a cupbord cloath & a towell	040
Item a fallinge band & a candlesticke	000¼
Item 2 pie plates, 2 deepe dishes & a voyder	008
Item 6 small platters & 2 sawcers	006
Item 2 pa' of swasse compasses, 23 wooden trenchers, a small lookinge glasse, 6 litle pursline dishes, a pa' of sisers, 2 pewter porringers, with a few white fish hookes and lynes and a torne trunke past use	005
Item one trunke marked AC	003
Item 2 small remnants of broad cloath	028
Item one old bl: cloath cloake garded	020
Item an old bl: stuffe cloake	015
Item an old bl: taffatie cloake	012
Item an old broad cloth cloake lyned with stuff	016
Item a velvett jerkin laced, said to be Mr. Owldswoth ('s)	008
Item a pa' of old satten hose	006
Item a pa' of old grogram hose	020
Item a suite of very old bl: cloath	008
Item 2 very old shamways dubletts	008
Item a trunke marked with T very old	
Item a pa' of trunke hose quite out of fashion	010
Item a pa' of blew silke stockins	006
Item 4 very old satten dubletts	030
Item 2 pa' of very old satten hose	020
Item 2 old grogram clokes not ded worne	040
Item a taffatie skairfe	005
Item an old bl: cloath cloake turnd & lyned with velvett	025
Item a cloth cloake lyned with plush	060
Item a pa' of worsted stockins & a pa' of wrought hangers & 3 pa' of white gloves	004
Item an old case of bottles	004
Item a great chest	006
Item a pa' of russett bootes	004
Item 2 litle old sea compasses, 3 peeces of copper & a box of beads	002
Item a greene carpett	012
Item a peece of foxe furr	001
Item a bla: feather, a hammer & an anvil	002
Item 2 swords	010
Item 3 sheets & a blankett	012
Item 3 old feather bedds, 2 boulsters, a quilt & 2 ruggs	150
Item 3 pillowes & 2 pillowbeares	002
Item 3 pa' of old sheets & 2 old tapestry hangings	023
Item five coverlitts	020
Item a coverlitt of fox skinn & one of ?rabones	005
Item a pa' of old curtaines	003

Item a copper still, old	003
Item 4000 of 5d nayles	006
Item 2 sugger loufs	005
Item a brasse bakeinge pan with a hole in the side	002
Item great brasse pott	015
Item a litle iron pott	002
Item a mohaire gowne	020
Item all the plate, rings & seales, the plate wayinge 43 oz⅛ valued & prised	150
Sum totalis	1323¾

Other goods not valued nor prised

Item the collers of Barkley to the Governor
Item an iron bound trunke full only of wrightings and papers not to be prised
Item a case of botles cont. 14 botles, the which Capt. Mathewes doth challenge to be his
Item a small runlettof Rosasolus and 3 runs. of Virginia, which were drunke out amonge the people that fetcht downe his goods.
Item a quadrant not prised
Item a box with some spices spent upon Barkeley people
Item a great chest & a barrell of tooles with divers lose [loose] hookes
Item a guilt boule, a silver cupp, 5 silver spoones, a case with a knife & a guilt spoone a paire of knives with guilt handles

Sir George Yeardlie and the priasers doe desire to be recompenced for theire paines, he in preservinge and keeping the goods, they in comminge and spending of theire tyme in praisinge the goods. Moreover Sir George doth require 400 lb. of tobacco which he paid for Captain Thorpe to those that built Opachankenses house.

Samuell Sharpe
The marke of Richard Biggs R.B.
The marke of Thomas Palmer T.P.

Vera copia   Ben Harryson   Clic. Con.
[Clerk of the Council]

It is not until the minutes of the Council and General Courts of Colonial Virginia, between 1622-32, are examined that the uncertainty relating to the true ownership of the properties of deceased persons, and the situation concerning their alleged commercial transactions, undertaken in the immediate pre-massacre period, can be appreciated. It must be remembered that in those early days of settlement, and, amongst a small community, borrowing, exchange, and purchasing must have been carried out in a more informal manner, and with far less documentation than under normal circumstances. Nevertheless, sharp practice undoubtedly there must have been. Thorpe's alleged debts figure frequently in the courts of 1623-5. I doubt whether all these were genuinely his. Some probably related to the Berkeley Company or the College, while others appeared even fraudulent.

At the court held on 7 March 1624 there are two entries relating to alleged debts of George Thorpe. (i) Sir George Yeardley said that 'Capt Jon West and Lieutenant Gibbs did testify before him under their hands that there was owing by Capt. Thorpe or Berkeley Company 8 barrels of Corn to Capt Nath. West.' (ii) 'Thorpe indebted to Mr. Blany 417^{li} tob.' Later at that court it was ordered that 'the goods of Capt Thorpe shall pay this debt unless it shall further appear that the Company of Berkeley Hundred [had] the corn they to satisfy it or if they had it premiscuously they to be paid by Capt Thorpe.' It is interesting to note that the claimants were (i) a West brother and (ii) Mr. Blany. Captain Francis West had caused trouble for the Berkeley Company at the original settlement by claiming part of their grant, but had lost his appeal.[34] Blany, a merchant, was the illegal occupant of the late Captain Nathaniel Powell's estate. Sitting on the bench that day, with five others, was Dr. John Pott who succeeded Captain Francis West as Governor in 1629, and himself was superseded by Sir John Harvey in March, 1630. In the following July Pott was tried and convicted of cattle stealing. This was the first trial by jury in Virginia.[35]

On 28 June the Court (on which both Pott and Captain Francis West with three others were sitting) ordered that Thorpe's 'goods' or Berkeley officials 'shall pay seven barrels of good Indian Corn unto Mrs Frances West widow . . . or . . . other valuable consideration.'[36] Two Berkeley settlers, John Gibbs (not Lieut. J. Gibbs) and Richard Milton, gave witness. The former said that he had heard Thorpe say, about a fortnight before his death, that he owed Mr. Dade seven barrels of corn, but he only knew of the delivery of two. Milton merely said that he knew that Thorpe had borrowed two barrels.

The minutes of the court held on 13 December tabulated the 'Debts due from George Thorpe late of Barkley deceased or Barkley Hundred.

To Mr Abraham Percy marchant	30^{li} of To[bacco]
More due to Mr Abraham Percy	205^{li} of Toba
Thomas Haris £25 of lawful money of England	
Mr Treasure demanded for 2 duty boys[37] 15^{li} at 18 pence a pound	
To Mr Marmaduke Rayner	175^{li} of Tobacco
To Mr Smith	30 bushel of Corn
To Mr Edward Blany	417^{li} Tobacco
To Capt Francis West	seven barrels of Corn
To Mr David Sandys [relation of the Treasurer] for Ministers Dues	35^{li} Tobacco
To Robert Fisher for 5 weeks	

work about Apochankeno his house	90^{li} of Tobacco
To Sir George Yeardley	310^{li} Tobac
To Mr Buck[38]	241^{li} [Tobacco][1]

The Court of 8 February 1625 made a fresh table of 'Debts Demanded from Capt Thorpe Deceased in Tobacco as hereafter.' The total came to 1571 lbs of tobacco. However, after each debt, follows the entry 'he is to rebate' so many pounds.

The total of the rebate is 189 lbs, which if taken from 1571 gives the figure 1382.[39] In Smyth I, 43, Thorpe's total estate, less a few items 'not valued nor prised', was estimated at 1323¾ lbs of tobacco. Thus the court was ordering the liquidation of Thorpe's entire estate to repay the supposed debts. I will make no detailed comment on this table and its claims at this point, except to say that two of the major items seem to be palpably dishonest, as would appear from Smyth I, 43, which will be considered at the end of this chapter. It is also interesting that all suggestion that the Berkeley Company might take responsibility for some of the debts has been dropped. Perhaps here, as in the case of the Powell estate, expediency triumphed, i.e, the Governor and his colleagues on the bench deemed that a plantation was part of the life blood of the colony, and must if possible be kept viable. Powell died, and his plantation in its entirely was given to a stranger, despite the claims lodged by the next of kin. Thorpe died the same day, but he had no plantation. Was his estate therefore looked upon, in some measure at least, as food for the colony's economy? Over 400 lbs value, at the very least, would seem to have been a debt chargeable directly to the Governor's office, and not to Thorpe.

At the next monthly Court, 7 March 1625, a further claim was made against Thorpe's estate – three years after his death. this, however, may well have resulted from the discovery of a letter[40] being found during the clearing up of Thorpe's property following the February order for its liquidation. The order ran – 'It is ordered that the heifer which my Lady Dale by her letter did give to Capt Thorpe, shall be consigned over to the Lady Dale's overseer, in satisfaction of six barrels of corn, due from the said Capt Thorpe to my Lady Dale being lent by Mr. Colfer her overseer, which Charles Hamer her overseer now accepteth of in court'[41]

The claim calls for considerable comment.

1. Lady Dale was closely connected with the Berkeley Company, for she was a Throckmorton, while her mother was a Berkeley of Stoke Gifford. Thus she was a cousin of Thorpe, Sir William Throckmorton, Richard Berkeley and William Tracy – four out of the five sponsors of the Berkeley

Company.

2.   Tracy in a letter to John Smyth, while preparing for his departure to Virginia, wrote that Lady Dale had given him silkworms 'and she promiseth to lend me kine'

3.   There is no indication of the year in which Lady Dale's letter was written.

4.   Lady Dale's patent was ratified 11 June 1621, when the Governor was directed 'to allot the place . . . if it be not already planted'

5.   Three overseers of Lady Dale's plantation are identified. (i) Watkins mentioned in the letter, and to whom the epistle must be shown because the heifer had already been given. (ii) Colfer and Hamer 'her overseer now' in the Court evidence. Thus a long lapse of time is suggested.

On 16 October the subject of cattle was again raised. This time, however, two cows are mentioned, and more details are given in a deposition of a John Taylor, aged about thirty-seven, and taken on 23 June 1625. The 'Interorgatories . . . ministered' to Taylor were:

1.   Did Thorpe have 'in his possession' cattle belonging to Lady Dale?

2.   Did Sir George Yeardley lend two cows of Lady Dale to Thorpe, and what were their names and markings?

3.   When did the transaction take place?

4.   Did Taylor know the names of any who might have been 'present or privy' to the delivery of the two cows or any other animals by Yeardley?

5.   Did Yeardley, or any other person, posses any of the Dale cattle?

In the replies the cattle are referred to as 'cows belonging to Sir Thomas Dale', who had died 9 August 1619. This suggests that Sir Thomas Dale's estate in Virginia had been maintained after his departure in 1616, and that the patent of June 1621, granted to Lady Dale, was confirmatory, thus accounting for the words 'if it be not already planted.' Taylor's replies ran thus:

1.   '. . . Thorpe came unto him and demanded which were two of the best cows belonging to Sir Thomas Dale bidding of him to appoint him out two of the best cows for he was to have them' This was done and the cattle were delivered to Thorpe 'about six days after, but by whose order he knoweth not'. Watkins was the overseer, and promised him (Taylor) a 'reward to have the care of the cattle.'

2.   To the best of his knowledge Yeardley had not given the order for this delivery, and he thought it must have been Watkins whom he had seen talking to Thorpe.

3.   The time was 'about the time of our Lord 1620'.

4. The cows were named Bellowman and Morgan, and had Sir Thomas Dale's markings on the horns.

5. Yeardley never spoke to Mr. Taylor, or to his knowledge to any other, 'for the delivery of any cattle' belonging to Lady Dale.

This was as much as Taylor could 'say' to the questionnaire produced by Hamer 'in the behalf of the Lady Dale.'

CONCLUSIONS

Firstly, it is undisputable that Thorpe had at least two cattle from the Dale herd, and that the transaction took place in or about 1620 can be assumed from Taylor's evidence. Secondly, it is clear from the above letter of Lady Dale that Thorpe had written to her on the subject of the fulfilling of a promise made earlier to someone concerning cattle. Furthermore, Tracy's letter of June, 1620,[42] confirms that Lady Dale had in 1620 promised to *lend him* kine for his Berkeley foundation.

Tracy died less than two and a half months after landing in Virginia. Thus the assumption must be that Thorpe, either on behalf of Tracy, or after the latter's death, when he, Thorpe, became the sole governor of the plantation, had written to Lady Dale reminding her of her promise. Consequently it can be fairly presumed that the cattle were the responsibility and property of the Berkeley Plantation, and not of Thorpe personally.

FURTHER INSIGHTS INTO THE MASSACRE'S AFFECTS IN VIRGINIA UPON THORPE'S ESTATE AND UPON HIS FAMILY

Amongst the Smyth of Nibley Papers in New York Public Library are two documents which concern closely, George Thorpe and his family, and which display an astonishing lack of sympathy and understanding towards his next of kin by high officials in the colony.

MS. no. 43, the inventory on pages 208-10, is surprising in its date and contents. It is calendared 10 April 1634, that is twelve years after the massacre had occurred. This in itself calls for comment, for four months later Thorpe's eldest son and heir, William, wrote a letter to a Mr. Taylor, who clearly was soon to sail for Virginia, requesting him to make certain enquiries relating to his father's death and his estate.[43] So concise and pertinent are those questions that the whole letter must be recorded. It reads as follows:

'Mr Taylor, I pray, inquire for these particulars when you arrive in Virginia.

When Mr. George Thorpe my father late of Wanswell in the County of Gloucestershire died in that country.

Item: What goods and chattels he had at the time of his death in that place and the particulars of them if they may be gotten and to whose hands they came unto and in whose hands they now are.

Item: What servants he had that escaped the massacre and where they live

Item: Whether any inventory were taken of Mr Thorpe's goods and to procure a copy thereof and what course must be taken for the procuring thereof

Item: What lands he had at or near Barkley Town and the content of them and how they may be received by his heir

Bristol 14th
of August 1634

Your loving friend
Wm. Thorpe, Son
and heir of George Thorpe.'

It seems extraordinary, even taking into consideration the chaotic conditions which must for a time have prvailed in the colony following the massacre and the subsequent dissolution of the Virginia Company by royal command in 1624, that so many years should have been allowed to elapse before Thorpe's estate was catalogued and the details passed to his family.

The blame for this inordinate delay – if delay there was – must surely be shared between the surviving sponsors or partners of the Berkeley Plantation i.e., John Smyth of Nibley and Richard Berkeley of Stoke Gifford, and the Governor and officials of the colony in Virginia. Margaret Thorpe's letter to Smyth, dated 30 June 1622,[44] revealed a woman financially embarrassed and, consequently, mentally distressed. She had written to her husband concern-some transaction, and was hoping to hear from him 'ere long', but some thing was wrong, and she needed a loan. Did she suspect that she would not hear? The news of the massacre only reached England during the first week in July. Even so Smyth and Berkeley, by the end of the month must have had some idea of the extent of the losses and destruction on the Berkeley Plantation,[45] when humanity, if not *nobless oblige*, should have prompted considerable activities. By the following July some support for the surviving and new colonists had been centrally organized. In this enterprise Smyth, as stated above, played a small part. No evidence survives, however, to indicate any interest in, or action relating to, the estates of Thorpe or others of the Berkeley Plantation who had died in the massacre. The Governor of Virginia and his Council of State, of which Thorpe had been a prominent member, would appear to have been equally culpable in not contacting Thorpe's family in Berkeley.

The inventory, when it was finally drawn up, had its items computed in terms of the value of a pound of tobacco. It is surprising to note, when the catalogue is closely scrutinized, that the list of Thorpe's effects is made up almost entirely of old clothes and bed linen, with six trunks or chests, one of which is described as 'very old' and another as 'past use', and numerous napkins and dishes. Plate, weighing 43⅛ ozs, and rings and seals were valued at 150 lbs, while '3 old feather beds, 2 boulsters, a quilt and 2 rugs' were priced at the same figure. In view of the fact that garments, bedclothes and table linen are recorded in considerable quantities – and some of the garments were of high quality, even if old, it must be assumed that Thorpe's house survived the massacre intact, thus supporting the earlier suggestion that the members of his household remained indoors and successfully defended themselves. There are, however, surprising omissions in the inventory. Thorpe was an educated man who had been used to the niceties of life in England, and for nearly two years had been a prominent person in Virginia. Why then, apart from the old beds and chests, is there no mention of furniture, e.g., tables (table linen is recorded), bookshelves, cupboards etc, books (only two are listed), and the knick-knacks which one would have expected to find in the home of a gentleman of his background, character and standing? Probably the answer can be suggested in one of the entries included under the heading of 'other goods not valued or prised'. This reads 'a small runlet[46] of Rosasolus[47] and 3 runs of Virginia, which were drunk out amonge the people that fetched down his goods.' The consumption of about seventy gallons seems a little excessive even if the operation took place in the hot weather! The 'appropriation' of furniture etc probably occurred either during the time when the Berkeley personnel were temporarily settled at Shirley, or else when the inventory and storage were being undertaken. Possibly the small amount of silver, rings and seals that remained bore initials, coats-of-arms or crests, and thus would have been identifiable, and, in so small a community, 'too hot' to steal.

The concluding statement of the inventory runs thus: 'Sir George Yeardley and the praisers do desire to be recompensed for their pains, he in preserving and keeping the goods, they in coming and spending of their time in praising the goods. Moreover Sir George doth require 400 lbs of tobacco which he paid for Captain Thorpe to those that built Opachankenses house.' This entry is blatantly dishonest in at least one instance, and maybe in two.

In the Virginia Court minutes of 13 December 1624, a table of Thorpe's alleged debts is recorded – see above. Entry no. 9 states 'To Robert Fisher for 5 weeks work about Apochankeno his house . . 90^{li}', no. 10 reads 'To Sir George Yeardley . . . 310^{li}'. Thus here we have the 400^{li} claimed by Yeardley. In the minutes of 8 February 1625, however, Fisher (here termed a Pole) and Yeardley are ordered to 'rebate' 11^{li} and 37^{li} respectively of their claims.

Yeardley was present at the two courts, both on the bench and as a plaintiff, so he knew the full details. Here in the latest claim he was putting forward the original figure of 400, instead of the ordered revised one of 352.

The second charge of possible dishonesty against Yeardley, rests on the nature of the claim for work relating to the building of the house for the Indian Chief. Many historians from Thorpe's contemporary, Captain John Smith, onwards record that Thorpe had built a house for the Indian Chief and that the latter had been greatly intrigued by it. It is abundantly clear, however, that Thorpe was a recognised liaison officer to the Indians on behalf of the Governor and the Council both to ratify treaties of peace and to attempt the implementation of the official policies of both the King and the Virginia Company to win over the natives to the christian faith. Thus the inference surely must be that the cost of the erection of that European type house, built specially for the mighty chief or king, was to have been borne by company funds controlled by the Governor, Sir George Yeardley, and the Council, of which Thorpe was a member, and accounted as expenditure necessary first to help ensure the safety of the colony – bearing in mind past hostilities – and, secondly, to encourage the conversion of the Indians through their great leader. For this there was the precedent already mentioned when, ten or twelve years earlier, Captain John Smith, the then President (before the title Governor was used) also built a European type house for Powhatan, Opechancanough's predecessor, to ensure his continuing friendship.

It is indeed strange that this claim in Smyth I, 43, should be dated 1634, for by that time (1) Captain Francis West, who with his brothers owned the Westover and Shirley Plantations which flanked the Berkeley estate, and who had been present at many of those early courts, and had been Governor of Virginia, from November 1627 to March 1629, was probably dead, for he is not mentioned after February 1633, and the family tradition is that he was drowned.[48] (2) Dr. Pott who, as has been stated, had been replaced as Governor in 1630 and four months later was convicted of cattle stealing, and had lost his standing.[49] (3) Sir Francis Wyatt, Governor at the time of the massacre, was in 1634, it is believed, little concerned with Company affairs. (4) Finally, and most puzzling of all, Sir George Yeardley himself had died in November 1627 while in office,[50] when he was succeeded as Governor by Captain Francis West.

Re-examining this manuscript it is confirmed that the introductory paragraph stated that the inventory was compiled on '10th day of April Anno 1634.' Attention has already been drawn to the fact that at a court held on 7 March 1623 Yeardley had been ordered to appoint men to price Thorpe's goods and to prepare an inventory for the court. That inventory, seemingly, is dated eleven years later. Furthermore, it must be pointed out that in the concluding paragraph of that catalogue Yeardley is referred to on three occasions in the present tense – (1) 'Sir George Yeardley and the praisers *do desire* to be recompenced for their pains, (2) he in *preserving and keeping* the goods (3) Moreover Sir George *doth require* 400 lb of tobacco which he paid for Captain Thorpe to those that built Opahankenses house.' Thus the dating for the inventory (April 1634) and the use of the present tense for Yeardley's activities, when, supposedly, he had died seven years earlier, are not really reconcilable.

MS. 43 however concludes with the statement that it is a copy made by the clerk to the Council. The full declaration runs:

Vera copia   Ben Harryson   Clic. Con.

The obvious solution surely must be that the clerk made a mistake when transcribing the true copy, and recorded 1634 instead of 1624 in the opening paragraph of his copy. This suggestion, however, attractive though it is, and though it may well be true, poses that equally difficult problem, to which reference has already been made, namely why had not Thorpe's family been informed of the details of his death and the extent, value and location of his estate and goods? That this had not taken place is clear from William Thorpe's letter of August 1634.

Again it raises the question of Yeardley's claim for the value of 400 lbs of tobacco out of Thorpe's estate. That expenditure the Colonial Treasurer, surely, should have authorized and borne, both on the score of the safety of, and commerce in, the colony, and to further the declared religious policies of King and Council? If, however, the building of that house for 'King' Opechancanough was indeed the brainchild and enterprise of Thorpe, and Thorpe alone, and had no connection whatsoever with the Company's softening up strategy, then it is a most remarkable example of Thorpe's generosity, self-sacrifice and missionary fervour.

Thus either Sir George Yeardley was being thoroughly dishonest in attempting to 'milk' the estate of a murdered member of his old Council of State for his own benefit, or to bolster the finances of the colony[51] (and his past friendship with, and obvious admiration for, Thorpe in the earlier years would seem to rule that out), or else here is demonstrated in a clear and practical manner the devotion and depth of feeling which Thorpe must have possessed towards the natives, and the intensity of his desire to win the Indians over to the cause of Christ, and thus to ensure the prospect of their eternal salvation.

If the spirit of '*de mortuis nil nisi bonum*' is followed, and Yeardley's claim is accepted as both honest and fully justified, then clearly Professor F.W. Craven is correct in attributing the beginnings of missionary enterprise to George Thorpe when he wrote of 'ideas which were to govern missionary effort from the day of George Thorpe to that of Eleazer Wheelock.'[52] Furthermore, it is also patent that here in the person of Thorpe is one who fully justified the title 'Martyr', given to him by Edward Waterhouse in his official account of the massacre and its effect upon the colony for the Virginia Company, and echoed by others such as Christopher Brooke.

With that judgement I fully concur, and accept that on the 22 March 1622 at the Berkeley Plantation in Virginia there died, in the person of George Thorpe, the first missionary martyr of the Church of England in the New World.

Requiescat in pace

NOTES

1. *VMHB*, vol. 72, p. 259.

2. British Library, Harleian MS.481, f.14r. – Simonds D'Ewes, 'A Diarian Discourse, or Ephemeritian Narration.'

3. Ibid., f.16v.

4. National Library of Wales, Wynn Papers no. 1027. William was admitted to Grays Inn 6 August 1621. His interest in Virginia was understandable, for an older brother, Captain Owen Wynne, who succeeded to the baronetcy on the death of the oldest brother in 1649, had been a member of the Virginia Company since 1612, when he subscribed £37. 10s. 0d., and paid £50. A Captain Peter Wynne, possibly of the same family, was a member of the initial settlement party at Jamestown in 1607, and played a not inconspicuous part in those early days. He died in Virginia in 1609. Sir Thomas Gates, wrecked on the Bermudas and not knowing of Wynne's death, appointed him as his Lieutenant Governor of Virginia, Brown I, p. 1055.

5. The letters of John Chamberlain, p. 446, edited Norman E. McClure, Philadelphia 1939.

6. Brown II, p. 466, where figures in excess of 400 are quoted. This figure is also mentioned in Colonial Papers, 1574-1660 (America and West Indies) p. 32 (July 29).

7. Kingsbury IV, pp. 9ff.

8. Kingsbury IV, p. 10.

9. Letter dated 20 January 1623, from the Council in Virginia to the Virginia Company in London. Library of Congress, MS. Records of Virginia Company, III, pt. II., pp. 4-5a; in Kingsbury IV, pp. 9-10.

10. Fuller details of the retaliatory actions of the colonists, their attempts at times to trade with certain tribes, and ultimately the achieving of a modified (and intermittent) *modus vivendi* will be found in many standard American works, e.g., Brock, Brown, Campbell, Kingsbury, Sams and Stith, and also in such unpublished disertations as those of Fausz and Rutman, for which see Bibliography.

11. 'A Declaration of the State of the Colony and Affairs in Virginia; With a Relation of the Barbarous Massacre in the time of peace & League, treacherously executed by the Native Infidels upon the English, the 22 of March last. Published by Authority and Imprinted at London by G. Eld, for Robert Mylburne, and are to be sold at his shop, at the great South door of Pauls,' 1622. Printed in full in Kingsbury III, pp. 541-80.

12. Fully translated (a) divide and rule, (b) Thus as long as they fight separately they [the tribes] will be defeated as a whole.

13. *VMHB*, vol. 72, pp. 259-92. See chapter 10.

14. Brown I, pp. 623-31, 692-4, and II, pp. 833-4.

15. Benjamin IV, Harrison in 1726 built the present Georgian Mansion at Berkeley, which over the next hundred years became the meeting place for the leading politicians and military personalities of Virginia, and later of the United States. Every American President from George Washington (1789 and 1793) to James Buchanan (1857) was entertained within its walls. Two of the Harrison family became Presidents, William Henry (1841) and Benjamin (1889-93). In addition, since 1958 Berkeley Plantation has been the venue of the Virginia Thanksgiving Festival, which commemorates the landing of the original Berkeley settlement party in 1619 and their Thanksgiving Service – See 'The Berkeley Thanksgiving', appendix 1.

16. Stith, p. 217, sums up the situation thus, 'So that, from this time, there was no public attempt, nor any school or institution, purposely designed for the education and conversion, before the benefaction of the late Honourable Robert Boyle, Esq; which shall be fully related, in its proper time and place.' Unfortunately Stith failed to relate the story.

17. His son, Maurice, who survived, married Barbara, daughter of Sir Walter Large, and is reputed to be the ancestor of the present Berkeleys in Virginia. See Berkeley MSS, *WMQ*, vol. VI, pp. 155f.

18. F.E. Lutz, *Chesterfield, An Old Virginia County*, Richmond 1954, p. 38.

19. Brown II, p. 470.

20. Smyth I, 3 (37); in Kingsbury III, p. 674.

21. There were Shippyes in our fragmented church registers as early as 1614, and there are Shipways still living here.

22. P.R.O., C.O.1, vol. II, no. 38; in Kingsbury II, pp. 245-6.

23. *Minutes of the Council and General Courts of Colonial Virginia 1622-1623*, edited H.R. McIlwaine, Richmond, 1924, p. 42.

24. The Revd. David Sandys, possibly came over to the colony in 1621 at the time that Mr. George Sandys took up his post as Colonial Treasurer.

25. Smyth I, 3 (31); in Kingsbury III, pp. 396-7.

26. McIlwaine, op.cit., p. 43. In the muster roll taken the same month Milton is registered as of 'Jordans Journey', Charles City County. His holdings – obviously personal and not of the Company – were 4 bushels of corn, a firearm with 2 lbs of powder and 50 of lead, 3 pigs, 2 fowls, and 2 horses. He was now an embryonic planter. In 1977 Mr. Richard Milton, of the American Embassy in Warsaw, wrote saying that his ancestor, the above Berkeley survivor, had been baptized at St. Mary's Church, Cheltenham, in 1594.

27. Thorpe, Tracy and Oldisworth (each designated Esq) had been Councillors of State. All

were now dead. The ranks of the 'Gents' had been decimated. The Revd. Robert Pawlet had 'departed from us'. Blanchard, Came, Keene and Yate had returned to England. Longe and Arthur Kemis had died, and Fereby had possibly been killed. Holmaden had been 'disposed of', but may have returned some time after the massacre. Thus the only remaining 'Gent' was Thomas Kemis, who, naturally, succeeded Thorpe as leader. It is believed that by about 1623 or 4 he too had died.

28. Virginia State Library Publication no. 25., *A Hornbook of Virginia*, revised ed., 1965, p. 63.

28. Virginia State Library Publication no. 25., *A Hornbook of Virginia*, revised ed., 1965, p. 63.

29. Brown II, p. 277.

30. Guild Hall, London, Commissionary of London Wills 1616-17, MS.9172/29, Item 75. See H.C. Porter, *The Inconstant Savage*, Duckworth, London, 1979, p. 407.

31. Letter from Young Robinson to Sir Francis Wyatt. Kingsbury I, pp. 5-6. This point has been emphasized because it has considerable relevance when Thorpe's estate in Virginia is considered.

32. See Edward Waterhouse's – official history of the 'massacre' published about September, 1622; in Kingsbury III, p. 555.

33. Colonial Papers, vol. 4, no. 12. An anstract of this plea may be seen in the McDonald and De Jarrette Papers in Virginia State Library, Richmond, and has been published in *VMHB* vol. 16, pp. 30-1.

34. Letter of Governor of Virginia to John Smyth, 10 January 1620 in which he warned the latter of possible trouble from West. Smyth I, 14, in Kingsbury III, pp. 248-9.

35. Brock, op.cit., p. 20; Campbell, op.cit., pp. 182-3. Sir George Yeardley, also sitting on 7 March was instructed to appoint men to 'prise' Thorpe's goods – *VMHB* vol. 19, pp. 142-4.

36. McIlwaine, op.cit., pp. 17-18.

37. Duty boys = boys sent over in 1619 in the *Duty* to be servants and apprentices. These may well have been amongst those condemned as unfit. They could just as well have been a Henrico responsibility.

38. McIlwaine, op.cit., p. 36.

39. Ibid., p. 47.

40. McIlwaine, ibid., p. 48.
    'A copy of the Lady Dale her letter to Capt. Thorpe
    Cousin Thorpe
        I have received your letter, and do give you thanks for putting me in mind of my

promise, to the performance of which I do willingly Subscribe and would have written to my overseer Henry Watkins to deliver you a young heifer, but that I understand you have her already and I intreat you would be pleased to show this my letter to Henry Watkins for his discharge, Least he should follow my general directions, and so cross me in this that I would by no means fail to perform, this commending my love unto you, And you to the mercy and good protection of the Lord I shall always rest

Your assured Loving Cousin
Elizabeth Dale.

From Thistlewood this vii of September
To my much esteemed Cousin
Mr George Thorpe
in Virginia this to be dlivered.'

41. Ibid.

42. Smyth I, 19; in Kingsbury III, p. 291.

43. Smyth I, 44.

44. Smyth II, vol. 8, MS. no. 84. See appendix 6.

45. Smyth I, 3 (37). Smyth's list of survivors proves this point.

46. Rundlet or runlet – early modern English – 'a little tun or barrel, a unit of capacity, according to statutes of 1439 and 1483, to 18½ gallons, but in modern times usually reckoned at 18 gallons.' *The Century Dictionary*, vol. vi, p. 5273.

47. Rosa Solis – 'A cordial made of spirits and various flavourings, as orange flower and cinnamon and formerly much esteemed.' Ibid., p. 5229.

48. Brown I, p. 1047.

49. Campbell, op.cit., p. 183. 'Pott was found guilty, but, in consideration of his rank and station, judgement was suspended until the king's pleasure should be known.

50. This was his second term of office in addition to a term of office as Deputy Governor, April 1616 – May 1617. See *A Hornbook of Virginia History*, Virginia State Library. Pub. 25, p. 103.

50. This was his second term of office in addition to a term of office as Deputy Governor, April 1616 – May 1617. See *A Hornbook of Virginia History*, Virginia State Library. Pub. 25, p. 103.

51. The Virginia Company had had its Charter withdrawn in May 1624. Perhaps Yeardley had thus been unable to recover his outlay on the Chief's house from official sources, and, as the only alternative, was seeking to recompense the cost out of Thorpe's estate.

52. F.W. Craven, *The Southern Colonies in the Seventeenth Century*, p. 143.

10

George Thorpe – The Verdict of History

In this chapter an attempt will be made to present the judgement on Thorpe pronounced by his contemporaries and later historians. Where possible the opinions of leading members of the Virginia Company on both sides of the Atlantic who knew Thorpe well personally, or who were familiar with his activities both in England and Virginia will be sought. In the following centuries the views expressed will, of necessity, be American, for in England his accomplishments, indeed his very memory, had well-nigh been lost.

First it must be remembered that Thorpe before he even set sail for the New World had made his mark in England. He had been appointed a Gentleman Pensioner, a Gentleman of the King's Privy Chamber, a member of His Majesty's Council for Virginia and a member of Parliament, offices which suggest ability and the confidence of authority both royal and civil. When Thorpe was appointed by the Virginia Company as deputy for the College lands he was described in their Court's records as a very sufficient and able man, a Gentleman of the King's Privy Chamber and one of His Majesty's Council for virginia.[1] At a later Court he was referred to as one 'well known to the Company for his sufficiency.'[2]

On 12 June 1620, John Pory, secretary of the colony, wrote to Sir Edwin Sandys, the Company's Treasurer, and in that letter he reported the recent arrival of Thorpe thus:

> 'The coming hither of that virtuous gentleman Capt Thorpe, was to us in many respects as of an Angel from heaven, neither did I ever see any man's face out of my native country, that did more joy me. He will help to bear our burden, and will be able in many matters soundly to resolve you at home. I pray God send more like unto him.'[3]

It is clear that Thorpe's reputation had preceded him, and that Pory was aware that Thorpe was not a product of the common mould. Pory clearly felt that the new arrival would be able to help considerably, not only in the local administration, but also because probably he was in a position, both socially and technically[4] to represent the interests and problems of the colony to the governing body in London.[5]

The second selected colonial assessment of Thorpe is that of the Governor,

Sir George Yeardley, who clearly knew him well. In a letter amongst the Ferrar Papers, from Yeardley, to Sir Edwin Sandys, Yeardley draws the attention of the Council of the Company to the fact that he would shortly be ending his term as Governor and that a new appointment would be necessary. In that letter, which Dr. Kingsbury believed to be in reality parts of two or even three letters,[6] the Governor, at three different points, strongly commended Thorpe to Sandys and the Council as one fit and fully qualified to succeed him in his commission. He wrote, 'Capt Thorpe who I can never sufficiently commend, nor give you enough thanks for, will be exceedingly strengthened and in all good things forwarded, for Capt Thorpe especially of whom I have had most experience, I find to be a most sufficient gent virtuous and wise, and one upon whose shoulders the frame of this godly building the government of this whole Colony would most fitly sit.'[7] Later he returned to the subject thus:

'I am assured you tender most dearly the welfare of this plantation you would be pleased my time of 3 years being expired in the Government, to commend unto the good regard of the Company this worthy person Capt Thorpe whom I do find to be a man most jealously affected unto the well proceed[ing] of the whole plantation, and being it pleaseth God to give him health and strength having also been well seasoned to the Country assuredly will be the most fit man to be Governor of Virginia unto whom I shall be most willing to surrender my place and Command, and to be as ready and forward to do my best service to the colony in what I may as if I still remained in the Government, neither will it seem harsh to me to be commanded as I myself have done especially by one whom I can obey with such love, and I shall do unto him,'[8]

Yeardley's final commendation in that letter ran:

'I do now therefor beseech you Sir since my service to the Country shall be no less but more, that you would be pleased my time of 3 years being expired to give your furtherance for this gent Capt Thorpe to be chosen and established Governor of Virginia in my stead, wherein I know and am well assured you shall do a most worthy work.'[9]

Yet a fourth commendation of Thorpe is contained in a letter, dated 16 May 1621, from Sir George Yeardley to Sir Edwin Sandys.[10] In this letter Yeardley thanks Sandys and his colleagues for sending him 'These two worthy gents Captain Thorpe and Captain Nuce.' Yeardley then referred to Sandys' 'promise of taking care to provide me such a successor as may equal to these in the rank of his place, I must acknowledge therein your singular love to me, but for my part as formerly I have desired so I wish still that one of these (who either of them will well deserve it) may have the place, being men all ready especially for the one well seasoned to the country.' In his earlier letter to Sandys[11] Yeardley had described Thorpe as 'well seasoned in the colony', so it would appear that Thorpe was still his first choice as his successor. It would seem from the word 'still' that Yeardley had already

heard from Sandys that his nomination of Thorpe was not acceptable to
Sandys and the Council. Despite this, Yeardley continued to press the claims
of his two local men, and especially his well seasoned Thorpe. Obviously
Sandys had not told Yeardley that at the General and Quarterly Court of the
Virginia Company in January, 1621, Sir Francis Wyatt, who had married a
daughter of Sir Samuel Sandys, a brother of Sir Edwin, had been 'with the
whole consent and approbation of the same (save only two whose balls were
found in the negative box) chosen to be the succeeding Governor of Virginia.'[12]

These, indeed, are very strong recommendations by the Governor, but
they probably were put on one side (as I have already suggested) for two
substantial reasons. All previous Presidents of the Council in Virginia or
Governors had had considerable military experience, as had the three principal Deputies, Gates, Dale and Argall, whereas Thorpe, as far as is known,
had had none, save perhaps in the militia in England or the local defence
groups in Virginia. Secondly, Sir Francis Wyatt was married to the niece of
Sir Edwin Sandys, whereas Thorpe had no such close blood relationship with
either of the three past-Treasurers of the Company. A third possible reason is
that Yeardley was temporarily somewhat out of favour with certain members
of the London Council which might not have helped Thorpe's cause.

It is proposed now to postpone the consideration of the Revd. Patrick
Copland's comments on Thorpe, which chronologically should follow at this
point, until two other reflections on his character and his work have been
quoted and examined. By so doing the importance of Copland's contribution
will become the more obvious.

Some weeks after the news of the Indian massacre had arrived in England,
Edward Waterhouse, Secretary of the Virginia Company, presented to that
body his *Declaration of the State of the Colony of Virginia*, to which, he
attached his considerable account of the 'Barbarous Massacre' by the Indians.[13]
Having stated quite fairly that the colonists had been lulled by the long peace,
the financial advantages of trade with the Indians, as well as in some cases by
their hopes for the 'conversion to Christianity' of the natives, into a relaxation
of security measures, Waterhouse described the treacherous conduct of the
Indian King, the co-ordination and suddenness of the assault and the
savagery of the natives. He passed on to the effects, as far as were known,
upon the colony and the settlers. The attention of the Company was then
focused upon the fate of Thorpe before the subject of the massacre was dealt
with in a more general manner. This was followed by an outline of the
important part played by Pace[14] in alerting (and so saving) Jamestown and
the nearby plantations, before presenting seven observations on the affects of
the massacre upon the thinking and actions of the Company and colonists.

Waterhouse in his long laudatory discourse on Thorpe pointed out that he, because he 'did so truly and earnestly affect,' the conversion of the Indians, and was 'so tender over them' had, in common with the majority of the colonists, from the Governor downwards, been completely duped. In that eulogy, which began 'That worthy religious Gentleman, Master George Thorpe Esquire,' Waterhouse narrated in some detail the story – obviously well known – of the house built for the King and the enjoyment which that royal personage derived from it, and also the account of the mastiffs. He added – clearly a judgement made in retrospect, and resulting from Thorpe's burning missionary enthusiasm – that Thorpe 'was not only too kind and beneficial to the common sort, but also to their King.' Waterhouse went on to say of the relationship with the King that Thorpe was 'Thus insinuating himself to this King for his religious purposes, he conferred after with him oft, and intimated to him matters of our Religion; and thus far the Pagan confessed, moved by natural principles, that our God was a good God, and better than theirs.'

Waterhouse was in no doubt as to Thorpe's deep concern for the conversion and civilization of the natives, and (again with hindsight, for he added 'as the sequel showed') was fully convinced that the friendliness of the Indians, King and commoner alike, towards the settlers in general and Thorpe in particular was a dissimulation and a false façade.

Waterhouse concluded this tribute to Thorpe, ending with a full account of his murder, by summarizing his feelings. These, presumably, represented a verdict based upon company records generally, the information gleaned from letters recently received and the statements of returning settlers and company personnel. It runs: 'And thus these miserable wretches, not he, hath lost by it, who to the comfort of us all, hath gained a Crown of endless bliss, and is assuredly become a glorious Martyr, in which thrice-happy and blessed state we leave him.' (p. 553).

In September a second account of the massacre was published. This was the poem by Christopher Brooke to which brief reference has been made in chapter 9. Brooke suffered personal loss as a result of the massacre, for two of the most prominent victims, Captains George Thorpe and Nathaniel Powell, were his friends.

Brooke's poem, 'A Poem on the Late Massacre in Virginia . . .' made particular mention of the principal casualties. [15]

It occupies, as has been said, nineteen pages (of approximately thirty-two lines), of which the first nine pages are of a general nature. On the tenth page begins what might be termed a funeral oration along the lines of that given by Pericles in the fifth century B.C. Brooke opens his panegyric to the dead with eight lines on 'Noble Powle' (Powell), which is followed by a further twelve that are headed 'Simile'. Maycock and John Berkeley come next, and their tribute – which runs together – occupies twenty-six lines. Then follows the eulogy on Thorpe, the last of the slain 'men of note' mentioned by Brooke. This testimonial takes up a full forty lines, and may be viewed not only as an expression of deep personal sorrow at the death of a friend, but also as a clear indication of Thorpe's stature and moral standing in the eyes of a contemporary, and of his devotion to the missionary work of the Church amongst the Indians in Virginia. It must be remembered that missionary enterprise was one of the basic objectives of colonial settlement laid down both in the royal charters and also in the 1618 'Great Charter' of the Company itself.

The Thorpe extracts merit quoting in full.

'Brave Thorpe, thou true deserver of thy Style,
Whose mind with things exorbitant, or vile
Had no affinity; thy worthy deeds
Virginia's hand shall spread like virtual seeds
And from thy dust thy Blade shall rise and flourish,
Which Time shall dew, and Sons of men shall nourish.
Thou that wert used to negotiate
In matters of Religion as of State;
Who didst attempt to make those Indians know
Th'Eternal GOD; their sinewy necks to bow
To his obedience; and on that ground
To make them apt to what thou didst propound
For our Commerce with them; their good, our peace,
And both to help with mutual increase.
What though thou faild'st, and of their seeming shew
Wert credulous (as all of us may know,

On the Massacre

That were our men so multiply'd as sands
And each of them Briarius[16] hundred hands,
They could not loose the hold the Devil hath,
Or bring them to the knowledge of our Faith)
Yet noble Thorpe, be thy attempt renown'd,
Thy virtue memoriz'd, thy volour crown'd
And on thy Tomb obscure thus I engrave
Thy short, and well deserving Epitaph.

HIS EPITAPH

Here lyes inclos'd the Corpse of Him,
Who had for every dying Limb
A living virtue; could extract
From Theory, and put in Act
Wisdom Humane, and Things divine:

And by the level of that Line
Drew all his Life, and squar'd his Deeds;
Who as he sow'd, shall reap those seeds,
To his increase a thousand fold:
Whose noble Name is here enrold
With other Captains of this Land,
Slain by many a bloody hand.
Heroic THORPE sleep in thy urne,
Whilst making Hearts in Incense burn
Of love to thee, and to they Fame,
Thy Valour, Virtue, and thy Name.'

To return to Mr. Copland.

The Virginia Company in England had received during March and April, 1622, encouraging reports from the colony, as may be gleaned from the minutes of the Company's Courts, e.g. 13 March, 'Mr. Deputy acquainted the former court . . . of the safe arrival of eight of their ships in Virginia with all their people and provisions,'[17]. It was therefore decided to express their gratitude to God not only by an acknowledgement in a court, but also by a sermon 'by some learned Minister . . . before a general Assembly of the Company'. The motion was approved, and it was decided to await the expected arrival of other vessels before fixing the date and other details. The news that Mr. Gookin's ship with forty young cattle in good condition had landed safely in the colony[18] also caused great satisfaction. The arrival of the *George* was announced at the court on 27 March. She carried, as usual, letters, some of which were read in court. One of these, from Mr. John Berkeley, contained the cheering news that the iron works 'so long and earnestly desired' was almost at production point.

At the Court on 10 April the earlier motion was re-affirmed and the Revd. Patrick Copland was 'requested' to preach.[19] The service took place at Bow Church on Thursday, 18 April, 'before the Honourable Virginia company' when Copland took as his text Psalm 107VV.22-30[20]. During the sermon Copland spoke thus of Thorpe: 'Do not you know what that religious and judicious overseer of your college lands hath writed unto you from thence "no man", sayeth he, "can justly say that this country is not capable of all those good things that you in Your wisdom, with great charge [cost] have projected, both for the wealth and honour, and also all other good things that the more opulent parts of Christendom do afford, neither are we hopeless that the country may also yield things of better value than any of these".'[21]

Here in that final phrase of this now lost letter can be seen Thorpe's overriding interest in the conversion of the Indians. Wealth, honour and 'all other good things of an opulent community' were desirable and achievable, but there was the potentiality too of things of better value than any of these, namely the salvation of the native soul.

This laudatory reference to Thorpe and the presence of the Honourable Virginia Company are both interesting and significant. The commendation came from one who was closely concerned and connected with the heavily missionary-orientated Henrico project. Copland had, as has been said, been involved in furthering the Company's educational schemes, and as rector-designate of the college would have been working in close association with the Virginia Company authorities in London. Thus he would have been fully aware of the work which Thorpe had been engaged upon. Consequently in a measure (because, as far as is known, Thorpe and Copland never met, though they may have corresponded) the judgement of Copland must also have been the verdict of the Company. This suggestion is supported by the Company's appointment of Thorpe's replacement as Deputy for the College lands. They asked particularly that George Sandys, who was then in Virginia in the post of Treasurer of the colony, and was a brother of Sir Edwin Sandys, should become responsible for the College interests, stating as their reason for this request that 'We esteem the college affairs not only a public but a sacred business.'[22]

Some may claim that the Company's assessment of Thorpe was more clearly given in the official report of the massacre presented by Edward Waterhouse, their secretary, or in that poem of Christopher Brooke, another prominent member of the Company. There is, however, a very subtle and indeed vital difference. The report and the poem were both written soon after the account of the massacre had reached England in the *Seaflower*, and critics could well suggest that emotion may have been partly responsible for the lavishness of the praise poured upon Thorpe in both works. In defence of Thorpe's reputation it must be pointed out to such detractors – if any exist – that it is the comparison of the praise relating to Thorpe, and that given to those other Councillors of State, who also had perished, which bears witness to the former's high qualities.

The real significance of Copland's remarks, however, lies in the fact that they were made in April 1622, nearly three months before the news of the massacre had reached England. That Thorpe was already dead has no relevance, for the fact was not known, and so Copland was speaking of a man who had, and was displaying, a humanitarianism and religious concern for his fellows, white and black, which marked him out as a figure of great distinction and worthy of emulation. Herein, surely, lies the true value of Copland's words.

Here then are the assessments of Thorpe's ability, character and standing by five of his contemporaries. Of these Yeardley knew him both in England and Virginia, as, in all probability, did Pory. Brooke, a fellow M.P. in the 1614 Parliament, and Waterhouse were acquainted with him in the councils of the Company and later through the reports received from Virginia after Thorpe's arrival in the colony. The fifth member whose testimony has been quoted, the Revd. Patrick Copland, may well not have known Thorpe personally, though this is not impossible. However, as one who had been closely associated with fund-raising for the educational projects of the Virginia Company for several years, and as the recently appointed rector-designate of Henrico, Copland must have been made fully aware of Thorpe's work as Deputy of the College lands which were to provide the finance for the maintenance of the buildings and the salaries for the staff of that proposed educational establishment. It is possible, indeed probable, that they had corresponded with each other on matters of mutual concern, while it is clear from comments in his sermon that Copland knew and approved of Thorpe's humanitarian and missionary endeavours.

All these five men were persons of education and standing in the Virginia Company, who themselves were heavily involved – in slightly differing fields it is true – in the general policy of colonization and Anglo-Indian relations. Yeardley and Pory were respectively Governor and Secretary of Virginia, while Waterhouse was Secretary of the Company and Brooke a Barrister spokesman for the Company in Parliament and member of a committee representing the Company to the King in 1620. Copland, as has been said, was a man of education possessing a desire to further the scholastic ideals and policies of the Virginia Company.

There is a sixth contemporary of Thorpe whose comments on the life and character of the latter merit mention, namely Captain John Smith, who was one of the original settlement party at Jamestown in 1607. He was nominated as a member of the President's council soon after the landing, and served as President of Virginia in 1608-9. Furthermore Smith was the author of what has come to be accepted by most critics as the first genuine attempt at a history of the developing colony from 1608 to 1624.

Captain Smith was a man who stood out from amongst his fellows, but his character, perhaps more than that of any other Adventurer of the first two decades of colonization, has been the subject of debate and controversy. He has been termed hero, charlatan, able historian and a purveyor of fanciful tales for self-glorification. His principal denigrator would appear to be Alexander Brown who in the biographical section of his *Genesis of the United States* devotes nine columns to Captain Smith,[23] more than half of which amounts to nothing less than a vitriolic attack. His honour, integrity and ability are questioned in an attempt, it would appear, at a complete defamation of character. Brown, however, had to admit that Smith's *History of Virginia and the Summer Isles'* published in 1624 'was for about 225 years almost the only source of information regarding our beginnings.'[24]

A more balanced judgement on Captain Smith may be found in Stith's history, where mention is made of 'the excellent but confused materials, left us in Captain Smith's History'[25]. All critics freely admit Smith's exaggeration of his own importance in affairs in Virginia and elsewhere, but the majority accept the value of his *History*. This is clearly seen in most nineteeth and twentieth-century authorities. Two examples must suffice. C.D. Warner wrote (1881) of Smith that 'he is the most readable chronicler of his time, the most amusing and as untrustworthy as any . . . He had a habit of accurate observation, as his maps show, and this trait gives his statements and descriptions, when his own reputation is not concerned, a value beyond that of those of most contemporary travellers.'[26] H.M. Jones comments that 'Recent discoveries about Smith's earlier years have not only severely shaken the common charge that he is untrustworthy as the chronicler of his own adventures but have also antiquated most of the earlier biographies.'[27]

In view of these re-appraisals of Smith's position, the inclusion of his remarks on Thorpe and his work appear fully justified.

Smith naturally devoted several pages to the 1622 massacre and the fate of some of the more prominent British Adventurers. He reviewed also certain circumstances connected with the death or survival of ten colonists, stating that 'The letters of Master George Sands, a worthy Gentleman,[28] and many other besides them returned, brought us that unwelcome news.' Thus Smith clearly was basing his narrative upon the statements of many who had survived that holocaust, and had witnessed certain of the events which he was recording. Smith devoted nearly a page to Thorpe's life and work in Virginia and his tragic and untimely end.[29] Smith began his panegyric by saying that 'That worthy religious Gentleman M. George Thorpe' was so concerned about the conversion of the Indians, that he was prepared to punish severely those settlers who treated them badly. He instanced this by stating that Thorpe had ordered that some of the mastiffs belonging to the colonists, which had caused the Indians trouble and fear, should be destroyed or gelded. Smith also mentioned that Thorpe built for the 'Indian King' (Opechancanough) 'a fair house after the English fashion in which he [the King] took such pleasure . . . Thus insinuating himself into the King's favour for his religious purposes [and] conferred oft with him about religion . . .'[30]

In the account of Thorpe's actual death Smith said – and here clearly he was relying upon eyewitnesses' reports – that Thorpe had been warned by his servant 'upon his fatal hour' that the Indians ('those hell-hounds') were threatening the lives of the settlers and that he (Thorpe) should 'look to himself' i.e., flee for safety to one of the houses and defend himself there (as presumably did the servant who survived to tell the story). Instead Thorpe 'void of suspicion' went to meet and reason with the Indians and was murdered.

Smith's statements concerning Thorpe's character, missionary zeal, and his courage too, must be taken seriously and given considerable weight. It must also be remembered that the author was describing a man whom he probably knew personally, and that he was writing two full years after the massacre, by which time the early emotions had died down and those tragic events were being looked at in a more rational manner.

The only firm derogatory comments on Thorpe and his work which appear to have survived, relate to his devotion to the Indian cause, as for example in a letter written a year after the massacre by a disappointed and disgruntleds 'ancient planter.'[31] The author was a William Capps, 'gent', who is mentioned as one of the two burgesses elected to represent Kiccowtan at the General Assembly held at James Town 30 July to 4 August 1619.[32] He also signed a petition (along with four others) to the King protesting against 'the freight and your Majesty's customs and duties' on tobacco, on behalf of themselves ' and the rest of your poor distressed Subjects of the Plantation.'[33] The petition is believed to have been sent in 1622.

On 31 March 1623, Capps wrote from Virginia to John Ferrar[34] complaining bitterly of his treatment and the conduct of three of the leading figures in the colony and also of the Treasurer (President) of the Virginia Company itself, whom he appears to blame for the massacre and his distress. He began his letter thus – 'Complements I must refuse,'. He later continued

'You know I was awarded xxx[Li] and by Your means I was not to have it myself but was first to adventure it with Sir William Naughtworth: He dying in Virginia the Treasurer seizeth of all, & there is an end of that and my 7 years toil . . . Thorpe he hath brought such a misery upon us by letting the Indians have their head and none must control them. The Governor stood at that time for a Cypher whilst they stood ripping open our guts: Captain Newce he cuts our throat on the other side and he lets in the Indians, . . . The Country is poor and the Company is poor and Capps is poor already, . . . You see I never had [a] penny of you for all my pains: . . . My Lord of Southampton did promise me he would see me satisfied but perhaps its forgotten therefore you must bestir your self,'

When considering this letter of complaint and abuse three things must be remembered –

1. The author was a frustrated and embittered seasoned colonist.

2. Thorpe nearly two years earlier had added a postscript to a letter which he and John Pory (Secretary of the colony) (signed only by Thorpe)

had sent to Sir Edwin Sandys, formerly Treasurer of the Company and still one of their most powerful members. In that postscript Thorpe had suggested that because of his own campaign, which he was determined to win, against 'drunkenness & some other sins', he might be 'ill spoken of'.[35]

3.   Thorpe, the Governor and Newse had only been attempting to carry out the pro-Indian policies laid down by the royal charters and the Company's own 'Great Charter' of November 1618. Some colonists felt however that those policies were too liberal. Perhaps others went further and resented legislation which discouraged personally beneficial exploitation of the natives. Consequently this complaint against Thorpe would appear to carry little weight.

Most eighteenth and nineteenth-century historians of the early settlement period in Virginia mentioned incidents in the life of George Thorpe. these references were almost always factual repetitions of a few colourful accounts of events which, while they might capture the popular imagination, e.g., the house built by Thorpe for the Indian King, the treatment of the mastiffs, the drink made from Indian corn, Thorpe's attempt at parleying with the natives during the massacre, did not stress their significance. They appeared to ignore the fact that those actions of Thorpe were symbolic of his natural feelings, and demonstrated his humanitarian outlook and missionary fervour, despite the fact that many of Thorpe's contemporaries had recognized and commented upon those powerful motivations. It was not, however, until the twentieth century that American historians began to re-examine Thorpe's life in the colony, to analyse and discuss his actions and to assess his place and position in early colonial development. Occasionally they also considered Thorpe's contribution towards the building up of an Anglo-Indian relationship such as was envisaged by those who had formulated the idealistic objectives which had been laid down for the settlers under the auspices of the Virginia Company of London. This is particularly true of the post 1939-45 war period. Once again a small number of examples will suffice to demonstrate that these writers were seeking to understand Thorpe, and to stress the fact that here was a man who stood out amongst his fellows, and for whom conscience was a 'remembrancer' and guide.

The first of these twentieth century 'recognitions' to be quoted is in the form of an inscription on a metal object. Nevertheless its significance is considerable, for it represents the consensus of opinion of a group of eminent academics. Henrico University and College, with which Thorpe had been associated[36] was planned as the first educational establishment in British North America.

In 1923 the students, *alumni* friends of the College of William and Mary marked the 230th anniversary of the granting of its royal charter by presenting the College with a silver mace, measuring four feet in height and fabricated by the Gorham Manufacturing Company.[37] An American eagle, representing liberty and freedom of thought, perches proudly at its head. Beneath, in separate zones, are the names of distinguished men who are held in honour and esteem by the College and Colony, i.e.

1.   Chancellors of the College. These include three Archbishops of Canterbury[38] and George Washington.

2.   Six prominent men claiming historical connection with the College. Amongst these are Christopher Wren, Lord Cornwallis and Louis XVI of France.

3.   The Presidents of the early Colonial Council and the later Royal Governors. Two of these forty seven were members of cadet branches of the Lords Berkeley of Berkeley Castle, i.e., Sir William Berkeley of Bruton, Somerset, and Lord Botetourt, the last male Berkeley of the Stoke Gifford branch from which came the Richard Berkeley who had been one of the four original founders of the Berkeley Company.

4.   Forty two eminent men 'before the Revolution,' representing exceptional ability in a variety of activities. The name of Thorpe appears in this list.

Finally in zones (5) and (6) follow the names of thirty outstanding *alumni* of the College and its Presidents.

It is fitting that Thorpe should be thus honoured and it is most pleasing too that his place in early colonial history should have been recognized by so eminent an academic body.

Professor W.F. Craven, in his *History of the Southern Colonies,* while pointing out that Thorpe was one about whom they, the historians, really knew very little, but of whom they wished to learn a great deal more, summed up his character, upon the sparse available information, and compared him with certain better known figures of a slightly later date.

The Professor mentioned Thorpe's connection with the Berkeley Hundred and his office of Deputy of the College lands, pointing out that 'As deputy he was responsible for making good the invested endowment of the college.' He added 'But what is known of him indicated that he did more, that he stands first, in point of time, amongst those spokesmen of humanitarian and religious interests who in the colonies sought to make the record of relations between the English settlers and their Indian neighbours something other than it became. A worthy fore-runner of Father White, John Eliot, and Eleazer Wheelock, he found time to court the friendship of the natives, and especially of Powhatan's successor Opechancanough . . . Upon the colonists,

The Mace of the College of William and Mary (*Courtesy of the Swem Library, College of William and Mary, Williamsburg, Virginia*)

suspicious and contemptuous, he urged fair dealing and co-operation in the training of their children, so much, indeed that he was frequently charged with responsibility for the Indian massacre of 1622.'[40]

When writing of Maryland (p. 192) Craven again linked Thorpe with the above three as follows: 'Father White[41] and his colleagues, seeking out Indian Villages by the riverways, preaching and healing through the day and camping on the river's bank of an evening, present a charming picture that stands with that of Thorpe in Virginia and Eliot in New England[42] to prove that English colonization was not wholly divorced from a Christian and humanitarian concern for the welfare of the natives.'

Craven also referred to the English style house for Opechancanough and the 'satisfactory alcoholic beverage from the Indian corn.'

Professor Robert C. Johnson, in his Introduction to Christopher Brooke's poem on the Indian massacre of 1622, undoubtedly because of the latter's concern about Thorpe and his work, wrote at some length on Thorpe, whom he termed a 'deeply religious person', adding that he was 'vitally interested in the welfare of the Indians, and he soon became the chief English missionary to them.' Johnson ended his considerable section on Thorpe by quoting the declaration of Edward Waterhouse in his official account of the massacre and the settlers' casualties – (Thorpe) 'hath gained a Crown of endless bliss, and is assuredly become a glorious Martyr.'[42]

Amongst the twentieth-century authorities, who recognized in Thorpe a man of more than normal stature, must be included Howard Mumford Jones of Cambridge, Massachusetts. In his *The Literature of Virginia in the Seventeenth Century* – one of the 'Memoirs' of the American Academy of Arts and Sciences – he included George Thorpe amongst the 'literary' men of the exploration and settlement period of Virginian history. He wrote 'During the formative years the proportion of gentlemen with some tincture of letters seems to have been unusually high for a wilderness settlement.'[43] He supported this assertion with twelve names (and six 'educated ministers'). The former included Captain John Smith, William Strachey, John Pory, Ralph Hamor, George Thorpe and Peter Wynne.[44]

Wynne appears to qualify as a literary man on the strength of a long report-letter written from Jamestown (26 September 1608) of which Jones comments that he, Wynne, 'compares Indian dialects with the Welsh language,'[45] and writes an 'easy prose'. With that as a yardstick Thorpe would certainly qualify, for his all too few surviving letters to John Smyth, Sir Edwin Sandys, John Ferrar, Sir George Yeardley etc. are well written, informative and descriptive, yet concise and clear. This may have been one of the fruits of his training at the Middle Temple and his career-life in London which followed, bringing out inherited or latent literary talent. These abilities or characteristics, added to Thorpe's obvious religious and humanitarian fervour and missionary zeal, support the earlier suggestion that, Thorpe may well have been the formulator of, or at least a major contributor to, the instructions to Woodleefe and the rules and regulations of the foundation settlement of the Berkeley Plantation enterprise in 1619.

As a contribution to the 250th Anniversary of the initial landing at Jamestown, the Institute of Early American History and Culture, planned and sponsored a symposium for a series of working conferences to be held from the 7-12 April 1957. Sixteen scholars were invited to take part, nine of whom were required to prepare papers on various aspects of the early settlement period. Those essays were circulated in advance and formed the subjects of the daily discussions. Later they were revised, and in 1972 were published as one volume entitled, *Seventeen-Century America*. One of those essays, 'Politics and Social Structure in Virginia', written by Bernard Bailyn of Harvard, ranked Thorpe highly amongst the early pioneer personalities. He wrote 'For at least a decade and a half after the founding there had been in the Jamestown settlement a small group of leaders drawn from the higher echelons of English society.' He named twelve, George Percy, son of the Earl of Northumberland, four sons of Lord de la Ware, Christopher Davison the Colonial Secretary, John Martin, son of Sir Richard Martin, twice Lord Mayor of London, Sir Francis and Haute Wyatt, grandsons of Sir Thomas Wyatt who led the rebellion against Queen Mary in 1554, George Sandys, son of the Archbishop of York, and George Thorpe, 'a former M.P. and a Gentleman of the Privy Chamber.' Bailyn pointed out that these men, and others then in Virginia, also represented a high level of achievement in the intellectual and literary world, and that of the 20 Councillors in 1621 eight had been educated at Oxford, Cambridge or the Inns of Court, several of whom were poets or writers of merit. The six identified were: Davison 'a poet in a family of poets', Thorpe, 'a student of Indian views on religion and astronomy', Francis Wyatt, the Revd. Alexander Whitaker (son of the Master of St. John's College, Cambridge, and Regius Professor of Divinity), John Pory, a 'protege and disciple of Hakluyt' and George Sandys, 'poet, traveller, and scholar.'

By 1622 Percy, Davison and Pory had left the colony, while Whitaker had been drowned in 1617 and Thorpe had died in the Indian massacre on 22 March 1622, as had five other Councillors of State. Thus it was little wonder that Sandys, the new Colonial Secretary, obviously in deep dejection in 1623, complained of the lack of character and leadership in the council, and opined that some of the councillors were 'no more than Ciphers'. Bailyn, referring to that complaint, pointed out that the whole 'social foundations of political power were being strangely altered.'

Dr. J.F. Fausz in his doctoral dissertation on the Powhatan uprising of 1622[46] wrote 'There was no better symbol for illustrating the Powhatans' cruelty or for generating English reprisals than the so-called martyrdom of Thorpe. He was a perfect late-Jacobean martyr in the Foxe tradition. A conscientious protestant and a tireless laborer for Indian conversion.'[47]

Fausz maintained that Thorpe's death 'had a great impact on contemporary Englishmen', and that his 'influence from the grave was more significant than his deeds in life.' To them he 'symbolized the mission of colonization.'[48] This suggestion is amply illustrated in Brooke's poem and the report of Waterhouse to the Virginia Company, extracts of which have already been quoted. In his epilogue Fausz summed up Thorpe's life and endeavour by saying 'For one fleeting moment under George Thorpe, the Virginia Company's ideological mission came close to fulfilling Hakluyt's idealistic dreams of Indian conversion.'[49] This is indeed a fitting epitaph of a good and faithful servant of God.

It has been clearly stated above that George Thorpe has since the mid-seventeenth century been completely ignored in national, county and local histories in this country, save for seven newspaper articles and two Presidential Addresses of mine between 1969 and 1978.[50] My verdict, for what it is worth after more than ten years of research, is that Thorpe was a man in many ways typical of his period and position, in that he did the things that young men of the country gentry were expected to do, e.g., he obtained royal preferments, became a Member of Parliament, made advantageous marriages, and 'ventured' in the current enterprises in the old and New Worlds, i.e., East India Company, Bermuda and Virginia. Over and above these activities he possessed, in a greater measure than most of his contemporaries, a deep sense of moral responsibility, which mainfested itself and blossomed most clearly on his arrival in Virginia in 1620. There too, judging by his own statements and actions, but much more through the eyes and pens of his contemporaries and later American historians, one sees him not only as a man who gave himself in service to his fellows, not only as an able leader trusted by the highest authorities both in Virginia and London, but above all as one who gave of his best and finally himself in the service of God for the education and salvation of the Indian peoples of the Powhatan nation. I repeat what I wrote as early as 20 May 1972[51] that I consider George Thorpe was the first known missionary martyr of the Church of England in the history of the New World, an assessment that subsequent study has amply confirmed.

In contrast to this incomprehensible neglect by his native land we find that

the country which he helped to found has treated him, as has been demonstrated above, more generously, but even there his greatness is so far only
recognized by the higher echelons in the academic world. Slowly but, I
believe, surely there is spreading a more general appreciation of the real
stature of this Wanswell squire who deserves to take his place alongside
Canon John Trevisa, the fourteenth-century Vicar of Berkeley, and Dr.
Edward Jenner,[52] of vaccination fame, as one of the three greatest known
figures in the history of that ancient borough, and as a person of considerable
interest and importance on both sides of the Atlantic during the opening
phases of colonization in Virginia.

NOTES

1. Kingsbury I, p. 332 (3 April 1620)

2. Ibid., p. 349 (17 May 1620)

3. Ferrar Papers, quoted in Kingsbury III, pp. 300-306.

4. Perhaps because Thorpe had already had investment experience in the Somers Isles, the East India Company, and the Smythe Hundred in Virginia.

5. Ferrar Papers (pencil no. 1019, no date) shows that Thorpe lost little time in 'resolving' (advising or even criticising) certain practices of the London Company. See chapter 7.

6. Kingsbury III, pp. 122-29. That this letter is composite appears probable, but as I have said previously, I am not entirely happy with the division suggested by Dr. Kingsbury.

7. Ibid., p. 123.

8. Ibid., p. 124.

9. Ibid., pp. 124-5.

10. Ferrar Papers; in Kingsbury III, pp. 452-3.

11. Kingsbury, op.cit., pp. 122-9.

12. Kingsbury I, p. 440.

13. Kingsbury III, pp. 541 ff. The list of known printed copies is on p. 541.

14. See above – chapter on the Massacre.

15. Published September (?) 1622. Printed, with Introduction by Professor R.C. Johnson, in VMHB, vol. 72, pp. 259-92.

16. Briareus, a giant of Grecian mythology, fabled to have a hundred hands and fifty heads.

17. Kingsbury I., p. 613.

18. Ibid., p. 618.

19. Ibid., p. 628.

20. 'And let them sacrifice the sacrifice of thanksgiving, and declare his works with rejoicing. They that go down to the sea in ships, that do business in great waters; these see the works of the Lord . . . the stormy wind . . . they reel to and fro . . . and are at their wits end . . .

they cry unto the Lord . . . he bringeth them out of their distress . . . Then were they glad because they be quiet; so he bringeth them unto their desired haven.'

21. The sermon was published, under the title *Virginia God be Thanked*, in London, and 'Printed by JD for William Sheffard and John Bellamie and are to be sold at the two Greyhounds in Corne-hill, near the Royal Exchange. 1622' The above extract is also quoted in *The English Colonization of America during the Seventeenth century*, by E.D. Neill, London 1871, p. 151. Neill, incidentally, states that Thorpe's letter was written from Jamestown on 17 May 1621. I, however, have failed to trace it.
    In the above work Neill refers to Thorpe as 'a gentleman of Stirling character' (p. 123) and 'the refined and educated gentleman' (p. 170)

22. Kingsbury III, p. 671.

23. This entry is extremely long, and is exceeded only by that relating to Sir Thomas Smythe, for many years head of both the Virginia and Somers Isles Companies. Sir Thomas has eleven columns allotted to him, Sir Thomas Dale eight and that outstanding figure, Sir Edwin Sandys, albeit for a shorter period than that of either Smythe or Dale, a mere three.

24. This is hardly true, for there were histories, reputable works, of the early American settlement published between 1624 and 1849, e.g., William Stith's in 1747.

25. Stith, op.cit., p. iii.

26. C.D. Warner, *Captain John Smith (Lives of American Worthies)* New York, 1881, p. 303. Quoted in H.M. Jones, *The Literature of Virginia in the Seventeenth Century*, University Press of Virginia, Charlottesville, 2nd Ed. 1968, p. 38.

27. H.M. Jones, op.cit., p. 36.

28. Smith book IV, pp. 362-3.

29. Ibid, pp. 359-60.

30. It is clear that here Smith closely follows the Statement of Waterhouse.

31. A colonist who had landed before the departure of Sir Thomas Dale in 1616.

33. J. Pory, *Proceedings of the First General Assembly in Virginia*, (Pory was Speaker of the Assembly), ed. W.J. Van Schreeven and G.H. Reese, Jamestown, 1969, p. 1. State Papers Domestic, James I, vol. 1, no. 45. Also in Kingsbury III, pp. 153-77.

34. Kingsbury III, pp. 580-1. State Papers, C.O. 1. vol. II, no. 15.

35. One of H.M.'s Council for Virginia, and Deputy Treasurer, 28 April 1619 – 22 May 1622.

35. Ferrar Papers, in Kingsbury III, p. 447.

36. Chapter 8.

37. *WMQ*, series II, vol. 3, pp. 122-28.

38. Thomas Tenison (1695-1715), William Wake (1715-37) and Thomas Hayter. This third named Archbishop (*WMQ*, series II, vol 1, p. 127) poses a problem, for in the accepted lists of Archbishops of Canterbury, e.g., Crockford, there is no such name. The Crockford list, however, records that a Thomas Hayter was bishop of London in 1761. It would appear that the *WMQ* article merely made an incorrect attribution.

39. See p. 143. The statement 'frequently charged' with responsibility for the massacre might better be expressed 'occasionally charged' but not so by authority.

40. Father Andrew White, a Jesuit priest, who in 1634 migrated to Maryland in the hope of founding a mission.

41. John Eliot, a Cambridge graduate who landed at Boston in 1631 and settled at Roxbury in 1632, and has been called 'The apostle of the Indians' because he largely devoted his life to them.

42. *VMHB*, vol. 72, p. 266.

43. See p. 3.

44. Commissioned Lieutenant Governor of Virginia – see Brown I, pp. 416-7. Probably related to William Wynne, who, as far as I know, was the second person in Britain whose comment (dated 13 July 1622) on the Indian massacre in Virginia has survived. My wife, who bears the name Wynne, is, through her mother, related to that family.

45. See pp. 4-5, quoted from a MS in the Hungtington Library.

46. *Powhatan Uprising of 1622: A Historical Study of Ethnocentrism and Cultural Conflict*, College of William and Mary, 1977.

47. Ibid., p. 432.

48. Ibid., p. 433.

49. Ibid., p. 580.

50. Except for a publication of 1979 which came to hand after this chapter had been written. I am grateful to Dr. H.C. Porter for drawing my attention to his book *The Inconstant Savage: England and the North American Indian, 1500-1660*, Duckworth, London, 1979.

51. Gloucester Journal – established 1771.

52. Since the completion of this study I have discovered that Dr. Jenner's great, great, great, grand-mother was Alice, the sister of Sir William Throckmorton, the co-founder, with Thorpe, Berkeley and Smyth, of the Berkeley Company.

11

The Berkeley Company – The End of an Era

1. A RÉSUMÉ – 1622-30

The post-massacre information of the Berkeley Company and Plantation is sparse. At some date – not known – the surviving Berkeley settlers and their cattle were moved to the Shirley Plantation, presumably on the score of defensibility. That summer a few new colonists for the Berkeley foundation arrived in Virginia, and in August Smyth recorded the names of the Berkeley personnel 'that remaineth' – ten men and perhaps three women. In April, 1623, there is an account of 'a small supply sent over to Virginia . . . in the *Bonny Bess* . . . upon advertizement of our servants great necessity.'[1] These were indeed meagre, i.e., 18½ bushels and 3 lb of 'best old wheat meal', 4 bushels of peas and one bushel and one peck of oatmeal. The total cost for the items was £7. 5s. 10d., and £2. 18s. 11d. for casks for the above, and packing and freight charges etc. In addition a 'copy of the Council's letter from Virginia', of seven pages which was for Mr. Berkeley, via Collingwood, the secretary of the Virginia Company in London, cost 3s. 4d. In July, 1623, Smyth pledged that he would contribute £100 to succour the Berkeley contingent. On 3 January 1625, a deposition recorded that there were sixteen men in the Berkeley party, but no women were mentioned. Nothing further is known until 1631.

2. THE FINAL PHASE – 1631-7

From the period 1631-3 three documents, two letters and an appeal (Smyth I, nos. 40-42), have survived. These throw some light upon the appalling problems which faced both the Berkeley colonists and also the two remaining Gloucestershire founders of the Berkeley Company, i.e., Richard Berkeley and John Smyth. All three documents – which are clear and largely self-explanatory – will be set down *verbatim* and chronologically. They will be introduced and followed by short personal comments and observations.

Finally brief reference will be made to the passing of the Berkeley Plantation into other hands, and the demise of the parent company.

No. 40

This letter is divided into two parts. The first is a list of the cattle belonging to the Berkeley Plantation party. It is stated to be in the hand of Richard Milton, and is a report to the Berkeley Company founders in England on the herd which was in his charge. This is indicated in a note on the back of the letter which reads, 'Richard Milton's own note of the cattle in his custody in Virginia belongong to Mr. John Smyth and others.' Milton is, of course, the Milton who came over amongst Tracy's party in 1620. The second and longer portion is an explanatory cover-note, possibly written by Thomas Combe, who has figured in earlier Smyth of Nibley Papers. The memorandum on the back reads, 'This was brought over by Mr. Ferrar of the Council, and delivered by him here in England to Thomas Combe in Midsummer term 1631.' Mr. William Ferrar was the younger son of Nicholas Ferrar Sr., and brother of John Ferrar who was Deputy Treasurer, i.e., second in command of the Virginia Company from April 1619 – May 1622. John was the Ferrar to whom Thorpe wrote several letters which are preserved amongst the Ferrar Papers in Magdalene College, Cambridge, and which are quoted in chapter 7. William was a Councillor of State in Virginia from 1625-33.

'A note of the Berkeley cattle. The owners of them are Mr. Smith of Nibley near Bristol and Mr. Richard Berkeley of Berkeley 2 miles of [from] Bristol. Item 10 milch cows, 1 heifer, 2 years old, 1 bull, 2 years old, 3, year old cows, female, 2, year old cows, male, 6 sucking cows, female.'

....

'Mr William Ferrar that brought this note from Richard Milton came from Virginia 7 April 1631. A little before his coming away he saith, Sir John Harvey was about to dispose of the aforesaid cattle, having promised to Captain Francis Epps, and Mr. Graine, a minister, some of them.

Mr. Thomas Palmer that came over about the same time confessed to Thomas Combe that he hath one of the young heifers in his custody.

Mr. Ferrar avouched to Thomas Combe that Sir John Harvey would have had all mens' cattle that inhabited not in Virginia to have been challenged as belonging to the King, and that he had moved the Council to that effect, but they would not agree unto it. This Mr. Ferrar protested to be true, but said he was loathe to be questioned about it.

He saith further that these cattle were kept all this time by Milton in Western Shirley Hundred Island, which being the plantation of other men, were a burden unto them, and were complained of[2] to the Governor.

Berkeley Hundred lies about half-way up the river, which runs East and West. It is bounded with the river on the South, and with the Mayne on the North. Captain Pawlet's plantation is on the West of it, and Kemishe's Creek on the East. And none but Savages to the North. At Mr. Ferrar's going back again into Virginia, John Gibbs (that was servant there to Mr. Oldisworth when he died) went over thither with him, by whom Thomas Combe wrote two letters, one to Sir John Harvey, the Governor, and the other to the Council there, both to this effect that the planters of that Hundred were willing that if the said Gibbs and Milton should join together and return again to that plantation, they should then have the cattle delivered to them to [stay?] and to [settle?] them there. And after they had built them a house and made provision to receive others unto them [we would?] then send over more servants, of whom they should have the government.

Another letter was written also to Milton to the same effect, that he might be more willing to join with the said Gibbs, and to draw others also unto them. John Gibbs had instructions at his going away of divers particulars to write back, by a servant of one Mr. Deacon, a [cheese?] monger by Billingsgate, who is gone over, with certain magazine commodities to fetch [tobacco?] for the said Mr. Deacon and Captain Prinne.'

No. 41

This letter is addressed on the back, 'To the worthy his very good friend John Smyth Esqr at his house at North Nibley this to be delivered.' It is also inscribed 'From Thomas Combe June 1632 Virginia.' The text reads:

'Sir

I was in great hope to have seen you here this term, which was the cause I kept these enclosed so long, for I was told that you would have been here the last day of term. But seeing you came not, Mr Street of Sadbury [Sodbury?] being to come down, I take the opportunity to send them to you by him. I told you when you were last here that I had written into Virginia by John Gibbs to the Governor and to the Council there, and likewise to Richard Milton, but I received no other answer than what I send you, but there being other ships to come home, I hope to receive some letter from the Governor. But howsoever, you see by these how our cattle are being disposed of, And the Governor is not so much our friend as he professed he would be, which I pray Mr. Berkeley and you to take notice of and to write to him accordingly.

He makes over our cattle to others rather for their advantage than ours, for Milton would have kept them as he did, and have bred us some increase, I doubt now our increase will be given away in favour to those that keep them. I wrote to Milton by John Gibbs that they should unite themselves together and take our stock and go upon our plantation, but I collect by his answer that he had rather do that by himself than with a partner, and therefore as you may see by his letter he would have us send him over 3 servants for himself and 3 more for us, that he might be sole master of them. What you please to do therein, I shall willingly agree unto, so as we may have a joint stock and proceeding therein. And if John Gibbs were as free as Milton is I think he would be the fitter man, but I think he is in covenant with Mr. Ferrar with whom he went over for a year. But you see he desires to buy both our land and our cattle which shows his intention to be a planter for himself. But considering we have both lands and cattle there and some ground already cleared and that Milton and Gibbs may both be made their guides [guards?], I hold it more wisdom to adventure somewhat now then heretofore, because such servants as we shall now send over shall have wherewithall to keep them, only they must be furnished with apparel and munition and corn for half a year, which would be no great charge for 3 men. But I leave it to Mr. Berkeley and you to advize better thereupon. And whereas there is a challenge made of two of our kine, though it is not unlike to be true that so many of them were borrowed, yet we lost there more goods than they were worth, both by the Governor and the Council; and beside I know not what company they now belong to in Virginia, but when our Charter here was on foot, there was no company then but ours. And for aught I know yet we have the same interest as before. But you better understand this point than myself which I leave to your consideration. I have one letter more from John Gibbs to myself in particular, and by another messenger, but of the same effect as these I send you, and therefore I reserve it. There are other commodities beside tobacco, as pot ashes to make soap, the rarest in the world, and some samples of cedar and black walnut besides beaver and deer skins. And as those that come from thence tell me, they begin to plant vines and make wine in that country, having both bread and beer and butter and cheese as plentifully there for those that are to spend it as we have here, wanting nothing at all but hands to attempt some greater matters. I pray you confer with Mr. Berkeley and some other friends for the reviving of our plantation though we adventure but a small matter, and let it grow till we may have profit from thence to make it greater. I hope to see you here the next term and to understand what Mr. Berkeley and you have resolved upon that we may return answer to those letters accordingly. Till when with my humble service both to him and you I take my leave And rest ever

At your pleasure to be commanded

Thomas Combe.'

From Mr Fowches house in
Chancery Lane this
Whitmonday, 1632.

....

No. 42

'Sir

I have received your kind letter, wherein you express your willingness to join in the adventure I impart to you, and in the proportion as myself do. I have sent you the book by this bearer, where in one of the blanks you may please to subscribe your sum. Mine is already down, but I will not beguile you, it is not all mine own; some friends (2 of them gentlewomen) were willing to go along with me in the adventure, but would not have their names seen in the book. Your son shall be welcome to me; and I shall be glad to take all occasions to acknowledge that love I have ever found from you. I pray God give us good success; with my kind respects I commend you to his gracious keeping.

Your most loving friend

Richard Berkeley'

Rendc. [Rendcomb] August 3, 1633.

A postscript at the side of the page reads:

'If there shall be any of your acquaintances willing to have a part in this great work, you may multiply the favour, if you shall please to let your clerk express the form in the same manner as those already in the book; so, as but 2 in one [two word illeg.] successively following the others there.'

The letter is addressed 'To my worthy and kind friend Mr. John Smyth at Nibley.'

Also written on that side is what clearly is a list of subscribers and the amounts they are prepared to 'Adventure', namely: Bainham Throckmorton (son and heir of Sir William Throckmorton) £60 Edward Stephens £50, Thomas Chester £30, Thomas Veel £25, Richard Berkeley £120, John Smith £100.

In the above three documents certain points require comment.

1.   There is no surviving information, save in a few oblique references in the minutes of the Virginia courts, of Smyth's relations with, or feelings for, the Berkeley Plantation and its people between 1623 and 1631. It would seem from Combe's letters that he now had some vested interest in the Berkeley project, and that the situation of the Berkeley contingent was very bad. The Governor, no more honest than some of his predecessors, was proposing the disposal of the cattle of absentee landlords. The indications are that he had also confiscated part of the Berkeley herd at an earlier date.

2.   It also appears to be suggested that the Berkeley title to the land was being questioned. If this was so, then it could well be that the powerful West family was behind such a move. They owned the plantations of Westover and Shirley which flanked the Berkeley Plantation.

3.   The Admission by Combe that in the past 'so many of them' (i.e., the cattle) had been borrowed, would appear to support my contention that the charges against Thorpe, relating to the 'borrowing' of cattle, for which repayment was being demanded, were highly speculative and probably fraudulent. This is particularly so when it is remembered that Yeardley and West were involved.

4.   Finally Combe's suggested revival of the Berkeley Plantation, for which Berkeley sent out his letter of appeal to friends and relations, appears not to have been received with enthusiasm, as the financial response shows. The writing was clearly on the wall, and an epitaph such as 'Too little was done, and far, far too late,' would have been fully justified.

The end of the Berkeley Company came on 9 February 1637 when a new patent relating to the Berkeley Plantation was issued. It ran:

'To all to whom these presents shall come, I Sir John Harvey Kt. Governor, &c. send &c . . . .

Whereas by Instructions from the King's most Excellent Majesty directed to me and the Council here resident, bearing the date the 22th of May in the twelfth year of his Majesty's Reign, His Majesty was graciously pleased for the better encouragement of all Adventurers and planters to authorize and command us to give and assign to all freemen such portions of land as were theretofore given and granted Unto the planters being freemen of this colony.

Now Know Ye that I the said Sir John Harvey Kt. do by these presents with the consent of the Council of State accordingly give and grant unto William Tucker, Maurice Tompson, George Tompson, William Harris, Thomas Deacon, James Stone, Cornelius Loyd of London, Merchants, and Jerimiah Blackman of London, Mariner, and their Associates and Company, Eight Thousand acres of land, situated, lying and being in the County of Charles City, being a tract of land commonly called by the name of Berkeley Hundred.

Bounding East upon the land of Captain Thomas Pawlet, beginning at a small gut that runneth into the woods at the west end of the clift of Westover, and West upon Kimiges Creek . . .

The said Eight Thousand acres of land being due unto them the said William Tucker and others as aforesaid by Deed of Sale from the Adventurers and Company of Berkeley Hundred Exemplified Under the great seal of England . . .'

EPILOGUE

Looking back at the tragic demise of the Berkeley Company it is clear that the
basic trouble was that after the massacre the Berkeley Plantation had no one
in Virginia who possessed the social standing and strength of character to
fight for their rights, to make decisions and generally to organize and firmly
to take command. This is seen in Combe's complaint about the actions of the
Governor and others, and his request, 'I pray Mr. Berkeley and you to take
notice of, and to write to him [the Governor] accordingly.' Such a remon-
strance from afar could never replace personal representation. Furthermore,
it should be remembered that this cry for help must have come after months,
indeed years, of increasing and obviously insidious despotism by higher
authority. If this problem had been tackled in its infancy, its growth would
probably have been prevented. In addition, there was the time lag of three to
six months between Combe's letter being despatched and a reply being
received; and much could happen in the meanwhile. This lack of authoritative leadership ought to have been obvious to Smyth and Berkeley soon after
the extent of the losses sustained at the plantation, occasioned by the
massacre and natural causes, were known. This must have been patent by
1624 at the latest, as can be judged from the various lists of Berkeley colonists
already considered. Both founders were to blame. The situation for the
Berkeley people in Virginia from about 1625 must have been desperate.
Their key man in Virginia, Thorpe, who had been one of the leading figures
in the colony, was dead. Thomas Kemis, who had succeeded Thorpe in the
governship of the plantation, was also dead. Either Smyth or Berkeley should
have gone over to take charge, or else they should have engaged some one
who had the necessary ability, strength of character and social standing
required to deal with the Governor and the Council. There is little doubt that
had either course been taken the new leader would soon, himself, have been
elected to the Council of State. Thorpe, Oldisworth, Tracy and the Rev.
Robert Pawlet, all of the Berkeley Plantation, had been elected to that august
body almost upon their arrival in the colony. Smyth and Berkeley failed to
take either course, and because of that lack of positive leadership, coupled
with the circumstances in Virginia, Berkeley Plantation withered away. The
effect of energetic local leadership is clearly demonstrated when the later
development of the Berkeley Plantation is examined. The estate was sold to a
London syndicate in February 1637. Some years later it was bought by a
Benjamin Harrison, a man who may not have had an illustrious family
background – although this is debatable, certainly possessed drive and
business acumen. This resulted very rapidly in Berkeley Plantation rising,

phoenix like, from its ashes, and by the first half of the eighteenth century becoming one of the great plantations of Virginia, and the meeting place for the political and social leaders of the colony.[3]

POSTSCRIPT

It is interesting to observe that Combe's remark that Gibbs 'shows his intention to be a planter for himself.', was prophetic. The Virginia patents between 1636 and 1650 confirm that within fifteen years of the sale of the Berkeley Plantation both Gibbs and Milton were planters in their own right, with estates of around one thousand acres each. This, for both men, had been a gradual process, and was, no doubt, the result of hard work coupled with the considerable colonial experience they had gained with the Berkeley Company, and in the case of Gibbs, while also with Mr. Ferrar.

NOTES

1. Smyth III, 3 (38); in Kingsbury, IV, p. 79.

2. The West family once more causing trouble for the Berkeley Company.

3. Appendix 10.

Appendix 1

Thanksgiving Day

What is the genesis of America's national Thanksgiving Day which strives to promote a consciousness of family unity and interdependence, along with an awareness of spiritual responsibility, while endeavouring to surround the whole with an aura of love and festivity? To a considerable extent it appears to follow the lines of the Mothering Sunday reunion of the family (with its violets and simnel cakes), and its corporate worship in the parish or mother church, which was a cherished yearly event in Britain a century and more ago, a day well established in the church calendar. Is there however any indisputable progenitor for Thanksgiving Day to be found in any event, practice or custom of the New World during the seventeenth to nineteenth centuries?

Professor W.F. Craven in his *The Legend of the Founding Fathers*[1] discussed at some length the subject of 'Thanksgiving'. He pertinently remarked (p. 61) that 'Not until the Civil War' would there be a national holiday commemorating an event associated with the original settlement of the country. He pointed out that there were however, even in colonial days, 'certain usages . . . that made an early bid for national acceptance.' He instanced the Continental Congress which, on several critical occasions during the War of Independence decreed that particular days should be set aside for prayer and fasting. They also ordained days of Thanksgiving at least twice, (1) in 1778 for the French alliance, and (2) in 1783 for the victorious conclusion of their struggle for independence. All these, however, related to specific occasions with no instructions on perpetuation.

In a footnote on page 116 Craven referred to attempts being made to set aside annual days of Thanksgiving, citing Sarah Josepha Hale's campaign concerning Harvest Festival, and the decree of the Governor of Virginia in 1855.

The American historian, Dabney, wrote' "The first Thanksgiving held in America" has long been credited to the Pilgrim Fathers. Major histories and encyclopedias unite in declaring that our annual custom of giving Thanks began at Plymouth in 1621, when the pious New England settlers decided to express their gratitude to God for a "fruitful and liberal harvest." This is interesting, but unfortunately it isn't true.'[2]

Of recent years several rivals have come forward supporting Mr. Dabney's contention that the Plymouth gathering was by no means the first Thanksgiving Service in American history; and basically these contestants are correct in pointing out that the Pilgrim Fathers did not inaugurate 'Thanksgiving', nor can they rightly claim – as still they do – that their service was the foundation stone upon which the edifice of Thanksgiving Day has been built up. What then are the details and general backgrounds of the rival Thanksgiving Services?

The Pilgrims' claim, because of the perpetuation of their myth, has every right to be examined first. Their Thanksgiving was what may be termed a normal Harvest Festival, the duration of which was prolonged for three days, possibly even longer. It included prayers and what appears to have been a plenteous and protracted harvest supper, the menu of which included fish (clams and eels), poultry (geese and turkey) and meat (venison) while amongst their beverages mentioned by an unnamed recorder was ' " comfortable warm water which was drank freely." '[3]

Could this have been the origin of the name 'Fire Water' given to the spirits sold to the Indians in later years? Incidentally in 1623 the pilgrims, after a disastrous hailstorm, held a day of prayer. Miraculously the beaten down corn recovered rapidly, and starvation was averted. These two services of the Pilgrim Fathers were spontaneous reactions devised to meet a particular situation, i.e., (1) a bountiful harvest, (2) the prospect of great hunger, and possibly actual starvation such as had faced and killed off many settlers in Virginia in the early days, being avoided.[4] Incidentally Dabney quotes Rear Admiral Samuel Eliot Morison of Harvard, 'the greatest living historian of New England,' as saying that "The Pilgrims never had a regular fall Thanksgiving Day",' thus emphasizing the spontaneity of their early service or services.

Excluding Thanksgiving Services or Laudatory prayers known to have been held by foreign nationals in the New World, e.g., Columbus at Watling Island in 1492, Cartier at the Isle Au Coudres or Menendez's Jesuit mission in 1570 at modern Newport News,[5] there were similar occasions involving British persons or parties, e.g., an English expedition at Baffin Land in 1578, Drake in 1579, during his voyage round the world, landed on Californian soil and held a Thanksgiving Service. Five years later a Captain Barlow – sent to America by Raleigh – held a similar service of Thanksgiving, while the Virginia Company's expeditionary force in 1607 landed at a point on the Chesapeake, which they named Cape Henry after the heir to the British throne, and, having erected a cross, knelt and thanked God for their safe crossing of the Atlantic. It would indeed, be surprising, bearing in mind the part which religion played in men's lives during the late sixteenth and seventeenth centuries, were not numerous such spontaneous prayers and thanksgivings held when crews, having spent many weeks crossing the wide and weatherwise unpredictable Atlantic cooped up in ships as small as twenty tons, landed safely in the New World. Religion and relief would demand such an expression of gratitude.

America's national Thanksgiving Day is an offically legislated and recognised festival dating, it is generally accepted, from President Abraham Lincoln's Thanksgiving Proclamation, and scheduled as an annual event in their calendar. The annual American Thanksgiving is then an event which was established by an official decree, set down in writing at the command of the highest authorities recognized by the people for whom the legislation was formulated, i.e., the President of the United States of America. Furthermore the principle of perpetuation was specified. Of the several claimants for the distinction of being the Thanksgiving which approximated most nearly to the annual American celebration, it would appear that the one ordered by the sponsors of the Berkeley Company in 1619 merits careful consideration, for the peculiarities marking out the Berkeley claim are clear-cut.

In 1619 the Berkeley Company was formed and sponsored by four Gloucestershire gentlemen by whom a grant of land in Virginia had been negotiated with the Virginia Company of London, of whom the sponsors were members, and its principal agent in the colony, the Governor, Sir George Yeardley. A few days before the Berkeley party sailed from the Hungrode, near Bristol, (16 September) its appointed leader Captain Woodleefe, received the following orders:

'Ordinances, directions and Instructions to Captain John Woodleefe for the government of our men and servants in the Town and hundred of Bearkley in Virginia given by us Sir William Throkmorton knight and baronet Richard Berkeley esq; George Thorpe esq; and John Smyth gent whereunto our commission of the date hereof made . . the fourth day of September 1619 Anno xvij. Jac. regis Angliae etc.'

The first of the ten orders which followed reads:

'Impr we ordain that the day of our ship's arrival at the place assigned for plantation in the land of Virginia shall be yearly and perpetually kept holy as a day of thanksgiving to Almighty God.'[6]

Objections are sometimes raised that there is no documentary proof that the instructions were carried out. The order was given, as were the other nine, and it must be assumed, unless there is clear evidence to the contrary, that this first order was obeyed. The onus lies upon the rivals to produce

Mrs. Mary Smyth, wife of John Smyth of Nibley, and their son John. Artist unknown (*Courtesy of Mrs. Jean Apperly*)

Artist's impression of the First Official Thanksgiving (*Courtesy of Mr. Malcolm Jamieson*)

His Excellency Mills E. Godwin, Jr., Governor of Virginia 1966–70 and 1974–8, greets the author at the Capitol, Richmond, Virginia, November 1974 *(Courtesy of the Governor and Mr. Steve Ring, the photographer)*

Virginia Thanksgiving Festival at Berkeley Plantation, November 1974. The Governor's Guard of Honour heads the procession *(Courtesy of Mr. and Mrs. David Reins)*

documentation showing that the direction was ignored.

Two points must be remembered:

1.   The *Margaret*, which had brought the Berkeley Company to their grant, sailed for England early in the new year. Her Captain would undoubtedly have carried back letters to the sponsors giving news of the voyage out (over and above the diary kept by Yate on Thorpe's instructions[7]) and of events between 4 December – the date of their arrival in the colony on the James river – and the day the *Margaret* sailed for England. In those letters, both official (including of necessity a report from Captain Woodleefe to the four sponsors) and personal ones to families of the adventurers, it would have been reasonable to expect mention of life at their settlement, including religious observances such as were outlined in the orders of 4 September. If the Thanksgiving Service set out in those orders had not been carried out Woodleefe would, of obligation, have had to state the reasons why his instructions had not been followed. No such letters are known to have survived. The only real record is a brief report, dated 14 December 1619 at Charles City and signed by the Governor of Virginia, Sir George Yeardley, and the Secretary of his Council, John Pory, to the Virginia Company in London, that the *Margaret* had arrived at James City [Town] on 4 December and that the thirty five settlers, whose names are given, were 'all in safety and p[er]fect health.'[8]

2.   Thorpe came over to Virginia in May 1620 to supervise the 10,000 acre estate set aside for the maintenance and endowment of the embryonic Henrico College. Later, on the deposition of Woodleefe, he became Governor of the Berkeley settlement. With his strong religious leanings, and bearing in mind the fact that he was one of the principals who had laid down the instructions for holding the Thanksgiving service and its annual observation, it is inconceivable that he would not have ensured its observation early in December of 1620 and 1621, during which time he was actually in Virginia carrying out his twofold office. During the period May 1620 to 22 March 1622 it would be natural to suppose that he must have sent several reports both to the Virginia Company and also to Smyth or Berkeley his co-sponsors in England. In addition there must have been letters to his wife and family and also to friends.

The only letters or reports – as against covenants and agreements – written by Thorpe which are known to have survived are:

(i)   To Smyth, 19 December 1620, reporting on morale and the corn drink.[9] In it he mentions a letter to his wife. It would have been in that letter, so close to the anniversary of the landing, that a reference to the Thanksgiving would have been expected.

(ii) To Mr. Felgate, 24 March 1621 asking him to care for some freight.[10]

(iii-v) To Sir Edwin Sandys, Secretary of the Virginia Company in London, 9, 15 and 16 May; 27 June 1621 – the first two were written in conjunction with John Pory, Secretary of the Council of State in Virginia.

(vi-vii) To John Ferrar, a member of the Virginia Council.[11] The second of those letters was written on an unknown date in 1621, but probably prior to 15 May. The second is firmly dated 15 May.

It must be remembered that *The Smyth of Nibley Papers* passed through many hands before being presented to the New York Public Library, many of the records of the Virginia Company in London have been lost,[12] and the Berkeley Plantation suffered heavily as a result of the massacre on 22 March 1622. Thorpe was killed that day – as were ten others – and all his records and those of the town and hundred appear to have been lost,[13] apart from those in the Smyth of Nibley collections in the New York Public Library, and in the County Library in Gloucester, England, and in the Ferrar Papers in Cambridge. Thus it is understandable that so little material has survived, which might be termed documentary evidence proving that the Thanksgiving did or did not take place. One is left therefore with only two known facts. Firstly, the orders for the observance were issued by the sponsors (4 September 1619), two of whom, Thorpe and Smyth were known to be deeply religious men. Secondly, Thorpe himself was in Virginia on the first and second anniversary of the initial landing. Thus the assumption must be that the Thanksgiving Service was held in 1619, 1620 and 1621, and that thus it was the first *Official* Thanksgiving Service in American History.

In view of the conditions prevailing in Virginia, and especially at the Berkeley Plantation after the massacre and the several changes of ownership of the estate in the next seventy five years, it must be assumed that the practice ceased after 1621, only to be revived in 1951, through the agencies of Mr. M. Jamieson and Professor Tyler, and later of the Virginia Thanksgiving Festival Incorporated.[14]

Before this subject is concluded two other official Virginia Thanksgivings must be mentioned, both of which, like their predecessor at Berkeley Plantation, appear to have had very short lives, despite specific legislation passed by the highest authority in the colony. The first of these two was decreed as a result of the massacre which undoubtedly ultimately 'killed off' the Berkeley Thanksgiving.

On 4 March 1623 the Governor of Virginia, Sir Francis Wyatt, issued an order, with the advice of the Council of State, that the 22 March, 'both this present year and for ever hereafter', should be set aside, in memory of their preservation in the recent massacre, as an 'holy day, spending the same in prayer and thanksgiving to God, and other holy exercise;'[15] The order ended with the enjoiner that 'The like *(mutatis mutandis)* [be communicated] to the Commander of each Plantation.'

A year later this declaration was reiterated and approved, as will be seen in Heming's Statutes at Large, where on page 121 begin the 'Laws and Orders concluded by the General Assembly [of Virginia], March the 5th, 1624.'[16] The first three 'Acts' dealt with religious practices to be observed in the colony, i.e., (1) the place of worship, (2) penalties for avoidable absence from divine worship, (3) there must be uniformity 'as near as maybe to the canons in England' in local churches. The fourth legislated for a new and special Holyday, and it was explicit as to observance and dating, ran thus: that 'the 22nd of March be yearly solemnized as holyday, and all other holydays (except when they fall two together) betwixt the feast of the annunciation of the Blessed Virgin and St. Michael the archangel, then only the first to be observed by reason of our necessities.'[17]

Hening in a footnote on Act 4 explained that 'This was in commenoration of the escape of the colony from entire extirpation by the fatal massacre of the Indians on the 22 March 1622. See Burk's *Hist Virg vol. 1*, p. 240.'

This service, unlike that which follows, has not, as far as I am aware, been referred to by any historians.

The final service to be considered was decided upon and legislated for in 1644-5 while Sir William Berkeley, the Governor of Virginia since 1641, was in England. During his absence Richard Kempe, a member of the Council of Virginia, became acting Governor. Dr. R.A. Brock, on page 23 of volume I of his *Virginia and Virginians* wrote that 'It is notable that during his [Kempe's] incumbency the first fast and thanksgiving days in the colony of which any record is preserved were ordered.' He then continued, quoting Hening's Statutes I, pp. 289, 290 'At James City the 17th of February, 1645' it was (Act 1) 'enacted by the Governor, Council and Burgesses of this present Grand Assembly for God's glory and the public benefit of the colony to the end that God might avert his heavy judgements that are now upon us, that the last Wednesday in every month be set apart for a day of Fast and humiliation, and that it be wholly dedicated to prayers and preaching;' also (Act 4) 'that the eighteenth day of April be yearly celebrated by thanks-givings for our deliverance from the hands of the Salvages.'[18]

From this it is clear that the Fast Days and the Thanksgivings were occasioned by separate events. The former were to be undertaken in humility and penitence for previous misdeeds; while the Thanksgiving Day to be held each year was intended to remind the colonists of the deliverance of much of the colony during the second great Indian rising and massacre in 1644, when, as in 1622, several hundred settlers were killed.

These services, like the Berkeley Thanksgiving of 1619, were officially laid down and legislated for, and it was decreed should be celebrated annually. As with the Berkeley service, it seems probable that their yearly observance was short lived. The orders for the holding of the Berkeley Thanksiving however, were drawn up and issued in September 1619, a fact of which Brock obviously was unaware, while he appeared equally ignorant of the 1623 official order, or he would not have claimed that the one of which he was writing was 'the first fast and thanksgiving days in the colony of which any record is preserved.' The reason for this ignorance of the Berkeley service is clear and understandable, for it will be recalled that the Smyth of Nibley Manuscripts relating to the Berkeley Company and Virginia, amongst which the 1619 order is numbered, had remained in the ownership of the Smyth family,[19] latterly through the female line in Condover Hall, Shropshire, until late in the nineteenth century when they were sold, and subsequently offered for sale by the well known dealer Bernard Quaritch at £150. They were bought by a Mr. Alexander Maitland who presented them to the New York Public Library. Many of these documents (including the Thanksgiving instruction) were transcribed and published in the *NYPLB* in 1898. Brock's failure to trace the 1623 order, however, is strange.

Thus these three seventeenth century Thanksgiving Services were 'official' in the fullest sense of the term, taking precedence over the occasional spontaneous Thanksgivings such as that of the Pilgrim Fathers in 1621; and of the three statutory ones the Berkeley Thanksgiving Service, is, as far as known records demonstrate, the first *official* Thanksgiving service in American history.

ADDENDUM

President James Carter began his 1978 Thanksgiving Day Proclamation, 'Since 1621 the people of this country have gathered each year to celebrate with a feast their good fortune in their continued ability to provide for families and friends.' This Proclamation was read on the BBC network by his Excellency the Honourable Kingman Brewster, the American Ambassador. Letters of protest were sent to the Ambassador by Mr. John Cope, M.P. for South Gloucestershire, and myself. In his reply the Ambassador commented 'Old myths die hard, especially when galvanized by inheritance.' No reply was received to my letter to President Carter.

NOTES

1. New York University Press, 1956.

2. Virginius Dabney, 'That Mythical "First Thanksgiving".' *The Saturday Evening Post*, 29 November 1958, p. 38 ffs.

3. Dabney, ibid., p. 110. See also Edward Winslow's letter to a friend published in *The Relation or Journal of the beginnings of the English Plantations in Plimouth in New England*, London, 1622.

4. Especially 1609/10 – known as the 'starving years.'

5. See above. S.M. Bemiss, *Ancient Adventurers*.

6. Smyth I, 3 (6); in Kingsbury III, pp. 207-10.

7. Smyth I, 13; in Kingsbury III, pp. 109-14.

8. Smyth I, 3 (18); in Kingsbury III, p. 230.

9. Smyth I, no. 33.

10. ibid., 35.

11. Ferrar Papers nos. 1019 and 1022 See chapter 7 above.

12. Kingsbury, I, pp. 107-18.

13. Attention must be drawn to an 'iron-bound trunk' belonging to Thorpe which survived the massacre. It contained 'wrightings and papers not to be prised.' See appendix 2.

14. Dowdey, op.cit., Gethyn-Jones, *BGAS*, vol. 94, pp. 5-17; appendix 10.

15. Kingsbury IV, p. 40.

16. 1809 Edition printed in Richmond, Virginia.

17. ibid., p. 123.

18. Henings Statutes at Large – The Laws of Virginia, p. 290.

19. Smyth III, vol. I, pp. v and vi.

Appendix 2

The Inventory – An Iron-bound Trunk

Smyth I, 43, an inventory of Thorpe's effects, has already been considered in chapter 9. However, a curious entry demands comment.

Towards the end of this long inventory comes a group of eight entries which are termed 'Other goods not valued nor prised'. The second of these seemingly valueless items is 'an iron bound trunk full of writings and papers not to be prised'. What were those papers? If they were, as well they may have been, nothing more than Thorpe's private correspondence and similar items, then to the 'prisers' they would have been, as catalogued, of no value. Yet these supposedly valueless papers were stored, not in a waste-paper receptacle, a loose wooden box perhaps, not even in a normal trunk, but in an iron bound trunk. This surely means a wooden 'cabin' type trunk reinforced with iron bands and corner-pieces? This is strange. It must be remembered, however, that Thorpe was employed in various capacities in the colony, Governor of the Berkeley Plantation, manager of the Henrico College estate, Councillor of State, and at the same time he was involved in Indian affairs and legal matters, and, perhaps, for a time he may have been Secretary of the Colony. A man with such diverse interests and obligations, some of which, as seen by his letters to Sir Edwin Sandys and John Ferrar, were of a highly confidential nature, would need to keep his accounts and files where they would be safe from physical destruction and undesirable human scrutiny. Might it not be that the iron bound trunk was George Thorpe's office safe? This is a distinct possibility. If this was so, why should the papers be termed of no value? The destruction of such papers, following upon the chaos of the massacre, and especially if litigation of ownership and similar matters were pending, might well be advantageous to some survivors. Records of agreements, debts, exchanges, loans and payments may well have been in that office safe, if safe it was, and its destruction might have been of advantage to some officials in the colony.

It could have been that suggestions were made to the assessors that the papers were of no value and so could, legitimately, be burned. In either case, private correspondence or official records, their destruction represents a major loss for later historians.

Appendix 3

Was George Thorpe Ordained?

In 1914, when describing the Indian massacre of 1622, Professor T.F. Wertenbaker wrote, 'One of the first to fall was the Reverend George Thorpe, a member of the Virginia Council and a man of prominence in England.'[1] A review published in that same year pointed out that Thorpe was not a clergyman.[2] The Gloucester diocesan ordination, licencing and induction registers and Hockaday's *Abstracts*[3] do not mention Thorpe as a clergyman. The surviving records of the Virginia Company of London refer to him as Mr., Master, Captain or Esquire, while John Smyth, a lawyer and one meticulous in his nomenclature, and other members of the Berkeley Company, address him in similar terms. Finally no Bishop visited Virginia between 1620 and 1622. Thus the principal bodies of evidence maintain Thorpe's lay status, and suggest that the Professor was misled by the frequent contemporary references to Thorpe as a Godly or religious man.

NOTES

1. *Virginia Under the Stuarts*, Princeton, 1914 – reprinted 1959, p. 50.

2. *VMHB*, vol. 22 (1914), p. 221.

3. The Hockaday *Abstracts* and *Collections* form the finest compilation of parochial and personal events in Gloucestershire. The Abstracts alone fill 453 volumes of manuscript and typescript material. This mammoth undertaking was begun in 1908 and only ended with the death of Mr. F.S. Hockaday in 1924. The *Abstracts* are now deposited in the Gloucester County Library.

Appendix 4

Abstract of the Will of Nicholas Thorpe
(Select Will 29 in Berkeley Castle – Jeayes, p. 259)

Will of Nicholas Thorpe, 24 Feb. 1600, of Wanswell in parish of Berkeley, esquire.

Bequeaths soul in to hands of 'the Lord who have redeemed me and my body to the Earth whence it came in full assurance that it shallbe raised again and made like to the glorious body of my Saviour and Redeemer Christ Jesus by the Force of his power whereby he is able to subdue all things to himself'

Wife Anne to have house room in his dwelling for life

To son Nicholas £300

To wife Anne (on condition that she claim no dower and that she release all title in lands and tenements) all goods and plate which she brought on marriage

To son George (on conditions that he pay wife Anne an annuity of £30 and that he shall make an estate to wife Anne and sons William and John of Great Read Croft, Little Redd Croft and Redd Croft Meadow for 70 years at 4 s. rent p.a., that he pay to sons William and John £200 each and to son-in-law Richard Lawrence £100, subject to Richard and heirs bringing no suit against George, and all conditions to be followed by wife Anne 'and her Son Lawrence' or all dispositions to wife Anne, sons William and John and son-in-law Richard to be void.

To Anne Collson dr. of Richard and Margaret Collson 4 marks p.a.

To Margaret Collson after decease of Richard tenement in Berkeley, orchard, garden and meadow held by Richard at rent already reserved for his heirs

To son George and his heirs lawfully begotten all lands and tenements and in default of such issue to son Nicholas and his heirs lawfully begotten, and likewise remainer to sons William or John or 'to the right heires of the said Nicholas'

To poor of Berkeley, Saniger, Halmer and Wanswell £3

Residue of estate to son George, sole executor

Overseers of will, Sir Hen. Winston kt., and Joseph Baineham, esq.

To Anne Frier, daughter of John Frier, one cow

To Mary Frier, daughter of said John Frier, one cow

Witnesses to this postscriptum (i.e. the Frier bequests) Jane Knight, John Richemond, Mathew Smith, John Clutterbooke, William Flower, John Richemond.

Proved: Prerogative Court of Canterbury, 5 June 1600.

Appendix 5

Abstract of the Inquisition Post Mortem of George Thorpe

(P.R.O. C 142/ 395/ 107.) The calendar of those who died intestate indicates that Thorpe is believed to have made no will)

Inquisition taken at Gloucester Castle, 9 Jan 20 Jas. I (1623), after the death of George Thorpe esq. late of Wanswell in Gloucestershire, by the oath of Fabian Clutterbooke, Giles Gardiner, James Sanford, Christopher Windowe, Thomas Payne, Richard Elland, Edward Beard, William Bullocke, Wm. Buckle, John Foster, Henry Beard, Wm. Partridge, John Rogers, John Beard. (Jurors)[1].

Who say on their oath that the said George Thorpe before his death was seized in his demesne in fee of the site of the mansion or capital messuage and demesne lands of the manor of Wanswell in Berkeley called Wanswell Court and in all lands, tenements (etc.) pertaining thereto, and a close of pasture called Leywall Gaston (20 acres), a close of pasture with a meadow adjacent called Gosty Leaze (15 a.), and closes of pasture called Cutcrofte (18 a.), Prestfield (6 a.), Tyntockes Leaze (4 a.), Burye Crofte (8 a.), and Bushey Leaze (4 a.), all in the parish of Berkeley.

And that long before his death, to wit on 20 Feb. 8 Jas. I (1611), it was agreed by a certain indenture bearing that date between George Thorpe on the one part, and John Bennett of the City of London, kt. and Thomas Bennett, Citizen and Merchant of London, on the other part, as follows:

Whereas it is intended and agreed that a marriage shall by the Grace of God be shortly had and solemnized between the said George Thorpe and Margaret Harris, daughter of David Harris late of the City of Bristol, gentleman, deceased and of Ann his wife, which Ann is sister to the said Sir John Bennett and to Thomas Bennett.

Now this indenture farther witnesseth that in consideration of the said marriage and for some preferment and stay of living and part of a jointure to be had and assured to the said Margaret for her maintenance in time to come (in case she shall survive the said George Thorpe), and for the settling and establishing of the said site, capital messuage, lands (*etc.*) to and in the use of the body of the said Margaret lawfully to be begotten for such estates and in such manner as hereafter in and by these presents is limited and declared. And for and upon sundry other good lawful and valuable causes and reasonable considerations to him the said George Thorpe given before then sealing hereof him the said George Thorpe hereunto especially moving, he the said George Thorpe for himself his heirs, executors, administrators and assignes and for every of them doth covenant, and grant to and with the said Sir John Bennett and Thomas Bennett and either of them, their and either of their heirs (*etc.*) by these presents That he the said George Thorpe and his heirs (etc.)

That is to say to and for the only use and benefit of the said Margaret and her assignes during the term of her natural life, and after her decease to and for (as before) the said George Thorpe and the heirs of the body of the said George and Margaret (*etc.*)

And the Jurors say that after the making of the aforesaid indenture to wit on 21 Feb. 8 Jas. I (1611), the said George Thorpe took to wife the said Margaret Harris at the church of St. Pancras, London. And they say further that George Thorpe was at the time of his death seized in all rents and services of the said manor. And that William Thorpe is his first-born son and heir, and at the time of his death was below the age of 21 years, to wit 10 years old on the 2nd September last before the date of this Inquisition, and that the said Margaret is surviving at Wanswell, And that the Manor of Wanswell appurtenences is held of George Lord Berkeley as of his manor of Berkeley and is worth £6:13:4 per annum; and that George Thorpe had no other manors or lands in Gloucestershire.

NOTES

1. Probably most were drawn from the Hundred of Berkeley, some perhaps from Berkeley itself.

Appendix 6

Letter of Margaret Thorpe to John Smyth –
30 June 1622

Sir now in my distress I have sought for friends but can find few only one here hath promised me of late to help me in this case with the loan of some money for my need to redeem Slimbridges as I thank you very kindly you did offer it to me at my being in London that I should have it for money which it was agreed on between you and Mr. Thorpe so I hope you will continue your love to me in it and let me have it according to your bargain with Mr. Thorpe. pray Sir deny me not this request but let me have it with your good will and I will be thankful to you I hope to hear from Mr. Thorpe concerning it ere long for I wrote to him you offered it me I desired your help concerning an extent went out of woodes croft the last year and you promised me you would take some course with Mr. Bird concerning it if I might be so bold as to desire it I will be thankful to you for it that it may not come out any more for my means is short this year by reason of another charge out of it this year also this ceasing to trouble you any more at this time with my love and [courtesy?] to you and Mrs Smith

       I rest your assured

                    loving friend

                    Margaret Thorpe

Wanswell this
30 June.

The letter is addressed:

  'To the Worshipful
  and my loving friend
  Mr. John Smith gent
  this with speed'

and endorsed on back (by Smyth):

  'Mrs Thorpe from
  Wanswell about
  Slimbr[idge] 1622
  June'

(The spelling has been modernized. There is no punctuation.)

Appendix 7

Abstract of the Will of Margaret Thorpe, Widow of George Thorpe Esq.

(Select Will 35 in Berkeley Castle – Jeayes, p. 260.)

The will is dated 29 June 1629, and is unsigned and unsealed.

She commends her soul to God and commits her body to the earth to be buried in the seat wherein she usually sat in the church of Berkeley.

To son William, if he marry to the approval of the overseers, the marriage portion and the wardship granted to the testator by King James I; if not, it will be divided between son John and daughter Margaret. William will also receive a silver bowl.

To son John a meadow called Woodcroft in Thornbury, and also his mother's land at Possett in Somerset held by Alderman John Gunning of Bristol, and his son John Gunning, who will convey the land to John Thorpe, John will also receive a wedding ring 'wherein are fourteen diamonds' and a silver bowl.

To daughter Margaret £300, and all my wearing apparel; my cabinet; the rest of my plate, jewels and rings etc.

To 'Mr. Dr. Chetwyne' (Edward Chetwynd D.D., vicar of Berkeley 1627-39, when he died, and the Dean of Bristol) 20ˢ – 'I do desire him to preach at my funeral'.

A Mr. Yeomans, a preacher at Bristol, and a Mr. Marshall of Berkeley, each to receive 10ˢ, a sum also bequeathed to Margaret Gonne, daughter of William Gonne, Clerk. Three pounds were left for the poor of Berkeley. Son John was the residuary legatee and executor, but the administration during his minority would be in the hands of William Edwards of Thornbury. A number of overseers and witnesses are mentioned, but have no relevance for this study.

The will was proved in February 1630. John came of age in September 1637 and established his position in the following April.

Appendix 8

Depositions relating to the death of William Tracy in 1621

(Copy in the Smyth of Nibley Papers in Gloucester City Library. Vol. 5, page 65 – both sides.)

Deposition 1.

Deposed in the court of common pleas 17 November 19 Jacobi 1621 in Mr. Waller's office John Mennye of Sandwich in the county of Kent Gent aged 23 years or thereabouts maketh oath that in June last past he this deponent was in the house late of Mr. William Tracy in the Town called Barkly in the Hundred of Shurly in the land of Virginia at which time the widow of the said Mrs. Tracy did keep her chamber as a mourner, and also deposeth that he was much conversant in the company of his son with whom he did lodge together as bedfellows for divers nights namely a fortnight or thereabouts by all which mean and divers others he is in his conscience assuredly persuaded that the said Mr. William Tracy is dead.

Deposition 2.

John Huddleston of Ratcliffe in the county of Middlesex Gent Master of the good ship called the *Bona Nova* of London maketh oath that he was in the land of Virginia in the month of April last and for the space of three months or thereabouts before that time and that he came in that said month of April to the house where late was Mr. William Tracy in the town of Barkly where he did see and speak with Mistress Tracy and also with Captain Powell who had married the daughter of the said Mr. Tracy both which and also the daughter and servant of the said Mr. Tracy were then mourners for the death of the said Mr. Tracy who was buried the day before this deponent coming thither as they affirmed And this deponent continuing there until towards the end of May last Did then hear and fully understand by divers assured means that the said Mr. Tracy there died in the said month of April last.

Deposition 3.

William Jackson of Ratcliffe aforesaid mariner and master gunner of the said ship called *Bona nova* deposeth that in the month of January last he this deponent did see the said Mr. Tracy within the land of Virginia And that he this deponent was in the said land when it was generally and credibly reported that the said Mr. Tracy was buried whereof he both then was and now is fully assured And that he did speak with very many persons who reported unto him the death of the said Mr. Tracy in the said country.

(Sheet 2)
Deposition 4.

John Ward of Ratcliffe aforesaid mariner deposeth that he continued in the land of Virginia from January until May last And that in April last he was in the Town of Barkly where Mr. Tracy dwelt and died (as it then was said) And that he was in the house of Captain Powell there who married the daughter of the said Mr. Tracy by whom as also by the son and daughter of the said Mr. Tracy and by many other credible persons there he did fully hear and understand of the death of the said Mr. Tracy whereof he is in conscience most assured.

Deposition 5.

George Hooper of Ratcliffe aforesaid mariner deposeth that he was in the land of Virginia in the month of January last And did there see the said Mr. Tracy at his first arrival there And that he this deponent was in the Town called James City where as he did credibly hear of the death of the said Mr. Tracy whose death was there in divers places of the said land much lamented And that he is in his conscience most assured of the death of the said Mr. Tracy which happened in April last.

Deposition 6. *(This is in a different hand).*

There were also other depositions afterwards taken, as Mr. Thomas Tracy and George Keen, and which likewise remain with the secondary in Mr. Waller's office, the prynotary, which prove Mr. Tracy's death before the verdict was given against him upon the court at former assises at glouc.

(Thomas Tracy and George Keen were, undoubtedly, William Tracy's son and George Keen, Gent, who landed in Virginia 29th January, 1621, and of whom Smyth recorded against both names in Smyth I, 3 (31), 'returned for England')

Appendix 9

Members of the Known Contingents of the Berkeley Company

Name and Condition	Indenture period	Acres allotted	Other details, mainly Smyth's comments

1. *Sent out in April 1619 by Captain Woodleefe* – A Recce party perhaps? Willm Mettrickes, Willm Moores, Robert Taylor, John Brunnet – all dead. Smyth I, 3 (9), Sept. 1619.

2. *Captain Woodleefe's main party* – Smyth I, 3 (9), September 1619 and Smyth I, 3 (10) September 15, 1619.

Name and Condition	Indenture period	Acres allotted	Other details
Ferdinando Yate, gent (Log book keeper)	3 yrs	50 acres	Brother of Gyles Yate, joint Lord of the Manor of Uley with Sir Richard Berkeley. 'returned 20 March, 1620'
John Blanchard, gent	3 yrs	50 acres	
Richard Godfry, joiner (Wanswell?)	3 yrs	0 acres	drowned
Rowland Paynter (servant to John Cook of Stoke Bishop)	3 yrs	50 acres	dead
Thomas Coopy, carpenter & smith fowler and turner N. Nibley)	3 yrs	30 acres	dead
Henry Peerse, gent	4 yrs	25 acres	dead
John Cole	7 yrs	40 acres	dead
Humfrey Osborne	3 yrs	30 acres	dead
Stephen Torfet	4 yrs	25 acres	dead
Humphry Plant, sawier & carpenter	3 yrs	30 acres	dead
Thomas Davis, cooper & shingler	3 years	30 acres	dead

Xristopher Nelme, shoe-maker (N. Nibley)	3 yrs	20 acres	dead
Richard Sherife the elder, carpenter	3 yrs	30 acres	went with Mr. Thorpe (dead)
Richard Sherife the younger, cooper	3 yrs	30 acres	'dead' but crossed out
William Clement, cook and gardener	6 yrs	20 acres	
Thomas Peirse 'for hops & wode'	7 yrs	30 acres	dead
Xristopher Bourton, taylor	4 yrs	30 years	
Thomas Molton, cook & gardener	4/5 yrs	25 acres	
James Cley, joiner	3 yrs	0 acres	dead
Charles Coyfe, gunmaker & smith, and for fish pitch & tarre	3 yrs	40 acres	dead
Edward Paynter	7 yrs	30 acres	slain
Walter Hampton	3 yrs	30 acres	dead
Samuel Coopy	3 yrs	15 acres	dead
William Cole	7 yrs	30 acres	dead
William Parker	6 yrs	30 acres	dead
John Hurd	5 yrs	30 acres	dead
William Patche	6 yrs	30 acres	dead
Thomas Patche	6 yrs	30 acres	dead
Thomas Sandford	6 yrs	30 acres	dead
William Stone	6 yrs	30 acres	q of him
John Taylor, als Stokeley	6 yrs	25 acres	dead
John Jones, gardener & smith	8 yrs	30 acres	dead
Thomas Denton	8 yrs	20 acres	dead
Thomas Thorpe	7 yrs	30 acres	slain

In Smyth I, 3 (10), Toby Felgate, gent, pilot of the *Margaret*, and John Singer, surgeon, 'who went not', are included.

3. *Those who sailed with George Thorpe on the* London Merchant, *27 March 1620*

Richard Sherife the elder, Thomas Carter, Henry Towensend, Richard and Charles Partridge, '3 of whom Mr. Thorpe chose for our servants.' Smyth I, 3 (19).

4. *Those who sailed on the* Supply *under William Tracy in September 1620* Smyth I, 3 (30) and 3 (31).

William Tracy Esq. (Councillor of State in Virginia)			dead 8 April 1621
Mary Tracy his wife			dead
Thomas Tracy their son			returned for England
Joyce Tracy their daughter			married to
Capt Nath: Powell (Councillor of State in Virginia) both slain			
Arnold Oldisworth Esq (Councillor of State in Virginia)			dead
Robert Pawlet, Divine us (Councillor of State in Virginia			departed from
Thomas Kemis, gent	3 yrs	50 acres	Died *after* the massacre
Arthur Kemis	4 yrs	50 acres	dead
Robert Longe, gent	3 yrs	50 acres	dead
Richard Holland	?	?	dead
John Holmeden, gent	3 yrs	50 acres	disposed of by Mr. Tracy
Richard Fereby, gent	?	?	slain
Thomas Shepy, gent	?	?	
George Keene, gent	3 yrs	50 acres	returned for England
Nicholas Came, gent	3 yrs	50 acres	returned in
June 1621 with the same ship			
Francis (sic) Grevill			married to Mr de la war
Joan Green			went not
Elizabeth Webbe			married to. . .
Isabell Gifford			married to
Adam Reymer at sea departed to Mrs Joyce Powell			
Giles Carter	3 yrs	50 acres	dead in England

George Hale, drummer			
John Bayly			dead
Thomas Baugh			
Gabriell Holland			'dead'
John Page			went not, but stayed in Ireland
Francis (sic) his wife			
William Piffe			stayed in Ireland
John Linsey			stayed in Ireland
Giles Brodway			slain
Richard Dutton			dead
Richard Milton			became a

'planter' after the sale of Berkeley Plantation

William Finch	3 yrs	50 acres	dead
Elizabeth his wife	3 yrs	50 acres	remarried to...

(called Margaret in disembarkation list)

Francis their daughter (In the list of the Mayor of Bristol Francis is described as their son. In the disembarkation litst the designation is 'daughter', and in Smyth's master list 'sonne' is crossed out and 'daughter' substituted)

John Gibbs   (became servant to Mr. Oldisworth) became a 'planter after the sale of Berkeley Plantation

Robert Baker

John Howlet the elder	3 yrs	50 acres	
John Howlet his son			both slain in

massacre at Iron foundry run by Captain John Berkeley. Berkeley was also killed

Roger Linsey			stayed in Ireland
Walter Prosser			dead
William Howlet son of above			survived
James Jelfe			dead
Richard Rowles)			
Jane his wife)			all slain
Benedict Rowles)			
Alexander Brodway			
Joan Coopy			dead
Anthony Coopy her son			dead
Elizabeth her daughter			

An Alice Heskyns is mentioned in Smyth's list. He clearly does not know her, for he notes, 'who is this Alice?'

5. The following appear on the certificate of the Mayor of Bristol as having embarked upon the *Supply*, but find no place on Smyth's above list. Giles Wilkins, William Peirs the elder, Richard Peirs, Richard Hopkins, Richard Smyth, Joan his wife and their sons Anthony and William, and Robert Bysaker and Faith his wife. The reason for certain of these absentees e.g., the Smyths and Bysaker, is recorded in the text. Smyth I, 3 (30), 18 September 1620.

6. The disembarkation certificate of the Governor of Virginia contains the names of Alice Heskins, Giles Wilkins, a Philip Vrange and a Frances wife of Benedict Rowles, (Smyth I, 34, 29 January 1621). The remaining 46 are all on Smyth's master list, (Smyth I, 3 (31) dated 3 September 1620).

7. The following are recorded in the official (Waterhouse) casualty lists of the Virginia Company of London as having been killed in the Indian massacre (22 March 1622) 'At Berkeley Hundred some five miles from Charles City':
    'Capt George Thorpe Esq. one of his Majesty's Pensioners, John Rowles, Richard Rowles, his wife and child, Giles Wilkins, Giles Bradway, Richard Fereby, Thomas Thorpe, Robert Jordan, Edward Painter.' (See Kingsbury III, p. 567.)
    The list of those killed 'At Captain Berkeley's Plantation seated at Falling Creek some 66 miles from James City . . .', 27 in all, include John Berkeley Esq and John Howlet and his son John who went out with Tracy's party in Sept; 1620. (See Kingsbury III, p. 565). Howlet was, no doubt, the furness builder lent by Thorpe to Berkeley to assist in the building of the Iron Foundry.

8. Smyth I, 3 (36), (In Kingsbury III, pp. 618-9), is an account of the outlay incurred when the Company sent out four servants for the plantation in the *Furtherance* in May, 1622; before, of course, the news of the massacre had reached England. They were George Pelton, Richard Willis, Clement Melton and Richard Buttry, a tailor. They embarked at Gravesend, and the bill for their equipment and stores came to £40-10-5. The list shows, again, the care taken by the company in apparelling their people:- suits of hose and cassocks, waistcoats, stockings, garters, shirts, shoes, sea rug, chest, diet, fees for a surgeon 'to look into' them etc. A Mr. Allin, who was conducting them to

Gravesend, was to finance their 'one night's supp and breakfast before they should be taken in a shipboard.' The four were even provided with money (over and above their wages) 'to serve them at the Ile of Wight . . . [and] . . . in Virginia at their arrival while they should stay in James City.'

9. On 1 August 1622, Smyth compiled 'A List of Servants remaining to us in Virginia'. Understandably, because the first news of the massacre had only arrived in England in early July, this list is not complete, as will be seen from the extract of the minutes which follows. Thomas Kemis,[1] governor (He had obviously taken over the command on the death of Thorpe), Thomas Baugh, Richard Milton, John Gibbs, Thomas Shipway (Sheepy?), Alexander Bradway, William Clement, Richard Sherife, Thomas Molton, George Hale (drummer), Frances the daughter of William Finch and Elizabeth his wife, 'with mother of new married to . . .', Elizabeth Webb 'married to . . .', Elizabeth Coopy daughter of Thomas. Smyth added the four[2] who had been sent over on the *Furtherance* 'in June' (Sic), and also John Burdely, 'who bore his own charge. And went in August 1622 in the *Margaret and John* Mr. Langly Mr q: of Peter Dun.' (Smyth I, 3 (37).)

10. The minutes of the Council and General Court of Colonial Virginia for 3 January 1625 contain the last known attested list of Berkeley Plantation personnel – all male.
    Sergeant Gabriel Holland (who appears to be the leader), Richard Firmely (Ferely?), William Clement, Richard Sherife, Thomas Moulton, Edward Purquite, John Taylor, Charles Partridge, Mr. Hamden (Holmeden, Gent?) Theophilus Bearstone, Thomas Peck, William Gillman, – Prisman, – Bullman, Nicholas Pierse and – Croser. Were the names of females deliberately omitted, or had all left the plantation by that date? I feel that the policy of omission is the more probable solution. It is interesting to note that a Gabriel Holland was reported dead in Smyth's list, yet one of a similar name leads the Berkeley list of 3 January 1625, and was a burgess for the College lands (of which Thorpe had been Governor) in the Virginia Assembly of 1623/4. See H.R. McIlwaine, Ed. p. 42.

NOTES

1. Against whose name, in Smyth's master copy, is written the word 'dead'.

2. In this list Willis has 'dead' entered against his name.

Appendix 10

The Berkeley Company – A Postscript

Although the life of the Berkeley Company ended in 1637, its foundation, the principal object of the Company's formation, lived on, and has preserved defiantly the town, family and company name of Berkeley in Virginia through the vicissitudes of more than two and a half centuries. Furthermore, it is today a viable plantation and, at the same time, has become one of the most visited historic houses along the Tidewater. Thus, it is appropriate that a brief history of the plantation from 1637 to the present day should be included in the appendices. This is being done that present and future generations will appreciate that men and women from the Berkeley Vale, the Cotswold Edge and the Hayles area were amongst that intrepid band of pioneers who by their 'blood, toil, tears and sweat'[1] helped to lay the foundations from which has sprung the great American nation. This relies heavily upon the latter part of my presidential address delivered at the Wheatstone Hall, Gloucester, on 22 March 1975 – the 353rd anniversary of the Indian massacre, to the Bristol and Gloucestershire Archaeological Society. Much of the Harrison saga – and they were *Seigniors* of Berkeley Plantation for more than one hundred and fifty years – is based upon C.D. Dowdey's *The Great Plantation*, a work of considerable readability and interest.

The Benjamin Harrison who had signed a copy of the inventory of George Thorpe's effects on 10 April 1634, whatever his origins or connections, prospered, and was elected to the House of Burgesses in 1641 – the year Sir William Berkeley of Bruton was appointed governor of Virginia. In the following year Benjamin bought 500 acres of land, and two years later his son, Benjamin II, was born.

Benjamin II increased the family's holdings and enhanced its social standing, becoming sheriff of the county, a member of the House of Burgesses and finally, at fifty-three, a member of the council. In 1691 he bought the Berkeley Hundred, which had suffered many vicissitudes since 1637. This estate he handed over to his son, Benjamin III (born in 1673), who with two of his sisters married into the principal colonial families, thus setting the seal on the family fortunes. One of those sisters, Sarah, caused a sensation at her wedding by interrupting the priest (who was asking her to make the declaration of obedience) with the comment 'No obey', repeating the statement a second time – and she won her point!

Benjamin III died in 1710 (two years before his father) leaving his wife to cope with the young children and the plantation – and how well the dual task was performed. Benjamin IV married Anne Carter, a daughter of his father's great friend, and reputedly the richest man in Virginia, hence his nickname 'King Carter' – he owned 330,000 acres and over 1,000 slaves. It was Benjamin IV who, in 1726, built the Georgian mansion house at Berkeley which over the next hundred years became the meeting place for the leading politicians and military personalities of Virginia, and later, of the United States – every American president from George Washington (1789 and 1793) to James Buchanan (1857) was entertained within its walls.

Benjamin V, Colonel Harrison, a close friend of George Washington, was a member of the Continental Congress, a signatory of the Declaration of Independence (4 July 1776), and an active but moderate revolutionary, who played, with Washington, an important part in the dark, difficult and dangerous days between the Declaration of Independence and the peace treaty of 1783. He was three times governor of Virginia. This tragic conflict, the product of British arrogance and avarice and colonial youthful impetuosity and intolerance, brought calamity to Berkeley. General Arnold, traitor to his fellow Americans, led his English troops on Berkeley, and, in spite against Colonel Harrison, deliberately removed and burnt all family portraits handing within the house.

The Colonel's younger son, William Henry, gained a high reputation as a frontiersman, both as a statesman and Indian fighter, earning the nickname of 'Old Tippecanoe'. In 1841 he was elected president of the United States. His brother, Benjamin VI, who had inherited the plantation, lacked initiative, ambition and ability. In 1799, aged forty-four, he died an utter failure, and the sun had begun to set on the Berkeley fortunes. Benjamin VII was but twelve when his father died. He inherited debt and decay and, unfortunately, he had neither the energy nor the shrewdness of the first five Benjamins. He died in 1842, and soon afterwards the Bank of the United States foreclosed on his son, Benjamin VIII, and Berkeley was bought by his distant kinsman, Hill Carter.

The estate was worked by a succession of planters until the fratricidal war between the northern and southern states broke out. During that war Berkeley Plantation, known temporarily as Harrison's landing, served for a time as GHQ for General McClellan, and it was while stationed at Berkeley, in the summer of 1862, that General Butterfield composed Taps, the U.S. army call comparable to our Last Post. A hundred thousand troops, some put the figure at 140,000, descended upon the plantation, reducing, within hours, the fields and gardens to a muddy paste, and the mansion house used as a temporary hospital, to a shambles, to which the owners did not return. In 1888 a grandson of Colonel Harrison – yet another Benjamin, became president of the United States. He too, in his youth, had stayed at the ancestral home, Berkeley. Towards the end of the nineteenth century, the plantation was again occupied for marginal farming, but it appeared that, metaphorically, the words *sic transit gloria mundi* were written large upon its walls.

In 1905, however, a New York Scotsman, Mr. John Jamieson, bought the wrecked manor house and 1,400 acres of the plantation. His son, Malcolm, with the vision and energy of the original colonists or the earlier Harrisons, some years later began the task of reclamation and restoration. The result is remarkable, for Berkeley, phoenix-like, has risen from the ashes of the dead, and is once more a working plantation, possessing the gracious dignity of the Age of Elegance, which it shares with the thousands of visitors who come annually to see for themselves some little of their country's past refinement and gentility.

No account of Berkeley Plantation is complete today without some reference to a movement which began in 1931. During that year Mr. Jamieson heard from Dr. Tyler, President of the College of William and Mary, Williamsburg, of the Smyth papers in New York, and of the instructions given to the first Berkeley party in 1619 relating to the holding of a Thanksgiving Service upon the landing at their grant, and its annual observance in perpetuity. Both Mr. Jamieson and Dr. Tyler realized the implication. It had been generally accepted for many years that the first Thanksgiving Service upon the landing at their grant, and its annual observance in perpetuity. Both Mr. Jamieson and Dr. Tyler realized the implication. It had been generally accepted for many years that the first Thanksgiving Service in American history had been that held by the Pilgrim Fathers in Massachusetts in 1621. Smyth's original papers now proved conclusively that the Berkeley Thanksgiving Service in Virginia antedated that in Massachusetts by nearly two years. Patriotism welled up within them. This fact – important to them – MUST be made known, and if possible, accepted nationally. The movement grew, and by the 1950's was state-wide.

The Virginia Thanksgiving Festival Inc. was established in 1958, as a 'non-profit making organisation composed of business, religious and civic leaders in Virginia. Its purpose was to gain appropriate recognition for Virginia's

Berkeley Plantation Mansion, built 1726. The home of Mr. Malcolm Jamieson.

An historic meeting – Berkeley Castle, 19 May 1975. Mr. John Berkeley of Berkeley Castle welcomes Mr. and Mrs. Malcolm Jamieson of Berkeley Plantation, Virginia, U.S.A. (*Courtesy of the* Gazette)

documented claim to the first official Thanksgiving in America – held at Berkeley Hundred, now Berkeley Plantation, in December 1619.' In 1961 a delegation from Virginia, headed by State Senator John Wicker, Jr., challenged the Governor of Massachusetts on the subject.

In 1962 the President of America, John F. Kennedy – himself a Massachusetts man – in his presidential address credited the Pilgrim Fathers with America's first Thanksgiving Service. This drew an immediate protest from Mr. Wicker in the form of the following telegram.

WESTERN UNION TELEGRAM

Honourable John F. Kennedy
President of the United States of America
Washington D.C.

Your Presidential Proclamation erroneously credits Massachusetts Pilgrims with America's first Thanksgiving observance. As we demonstrated a year ago to the Governor of Massachusetts by original historical records of the Congressional Library, America's first Thanksgiving was actually celebrated in Virginia in 1619 more than a year before the Pilgrims ever landed, and nearly two years before the Massachusetts Thanksgiving. Virginia's claim was officially recognized by President Abraham Lincoln nearly a century ago and further substantiated by Historian Dabney's comprehensive article in the November 29, 1958 Saturday Evening Post. As a matter of fairness, please issue an appropriate correction.

John H. Wicker
Honorary Chairman
Richmond Thanksgiving Festival.

The President's reply a few weeks later was magnanimous:

THE WHITE HOUSE – WASHINGTON

Dear Mr. Wicker,

The President has asked me to reply to your telegram about the Thanksgiving Proclamation statement. You are quite right; and I can only plead an unconquerable New England bias on the part of the White House Staff.

We are all grateful to you for reminding us of the Berkeley Hundred Thanksgiving; and I can assure you that the error will not be repeated in the future.

Arthur Schlesinger, jr.
Special Assistant to the President.

The President, in his address on 23 November 1963, made full amends by saying 'Over three centuries ago, our forefathers in Virginia and in Massachusetts, far from home in a lonely wilderness, set aside a time of Thanksgiving . . .', thus giving pride of place to the Berkeley Service in Virginia.

We in the west of England, and especially those in Glouestershire and Avon, can feel a sense of pride that men from our area formulated the original instructions and took part in that service. To me it was a never-to-be-forgotten experience to stand on that historic Berkeley site in Virginia and to give what they termed 'the keynote address' during the service when in November 1974 we commemorated the 355th anniversary of that first official Thanksgiving Service in American History.

FINALE

The history of the Berkeley Plantation cannot be complete without the amazing fairy-story-like account of a young drummer boy's dream and ambition, which years later resulted in his acquisition of that estate. This is told by his son, Mr. Malcolm Jamieson, in 'Macs' own words, and with his permission.

'During the American Civil War (1861-65), John Jamieson and his older brother Walter, were standing on a street corner one night watching troops being marched off to war. One of the draftee's wife and children were running behind them crying. Her husband, a Scot, was the person who had found a home for the Jamieson family when they arrived there from Scotland. My Father's older brother, Walter, felt sorry for this family and volunteered to take the man's place, since he had located a home for them. At that time, a draftee could have his place taken by a volunteer, or pay someone to go for him. After some time in the Service, Walter Jamieson was encamped at Berkeley Plantation. As they were there for two months, and things were very quiet, he sent for my Father and had him appointed a drummer boy in General McClellan's army of the Potomac. The amazing part of this story is that 50 years later, of the 140,000 soldiers encamped at Berkeley, the drummer boy ended up owning the Plantation. Incidentally, when he was about 35 years old, he built the base on which stands the Statue of Liberty given to the United States July 4, 1884, by France.'

NOTES

1. Mr. Winston Churchill on 13 May 1940. This was his first speech to the House of Commons after assuming the office of Prime Minister, following Germany's invasion of Norway and Denmark on 9 April, and that of the Low Countries on 10 May.

Appendix 11
Genealogical Tables

(Based largely on Smyth III, i.e., his Lives of the Berkeleys and The Hundred of Berkeley)

Sir Richard Berkeley of Stoke Gifford married twice

(1) Elizabeth d. of Wm Read, of Mitton nr. Tewkesbury

(2) Eleanor wd. of Robert Roe (no issue)

Henry m. Mirriell d. of Thomas Throckmorton of C. Warwick

Elizabeth m. Sir Tho. Throckmorton of Tortworth

Mary m. Sir John Hungerford of Down Ampney

Katharine m. Sir Rowland Lee of Long-barrow (Glos)

(1) Anne
(2) Dorothy both S.P.

Richard m. Mary d. of Robert Roe and sis. of Sir Tho. Roe

Elizabeth

Margaret

Six sons and six daughters

Sir Thomas Throckmorton of Tortworth (above) m. Elizabeth Berkeley (above)

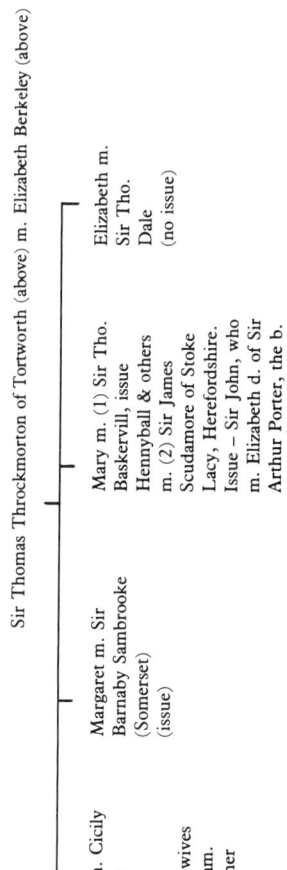

Sir *William* m. Cicily d. of Thomas Bainham of Clearwell m. two other wives Heir – Bainham. Had many other children

Margaret m. Sir Barnaby Sambrooke (Somerset) (issue)

Mary m. (1) Sir Tho. Baskervill, issue Hennyball & others m. (2) Sir James Scudamore of Stoke Lacy, Herefordshire. Issue – Sir John, who m. Elizabeth d. of Sir Arthur Porter, the b. in law of *George Thorpe*

Elizabeth m. Sir Tho. Dale (no issue)

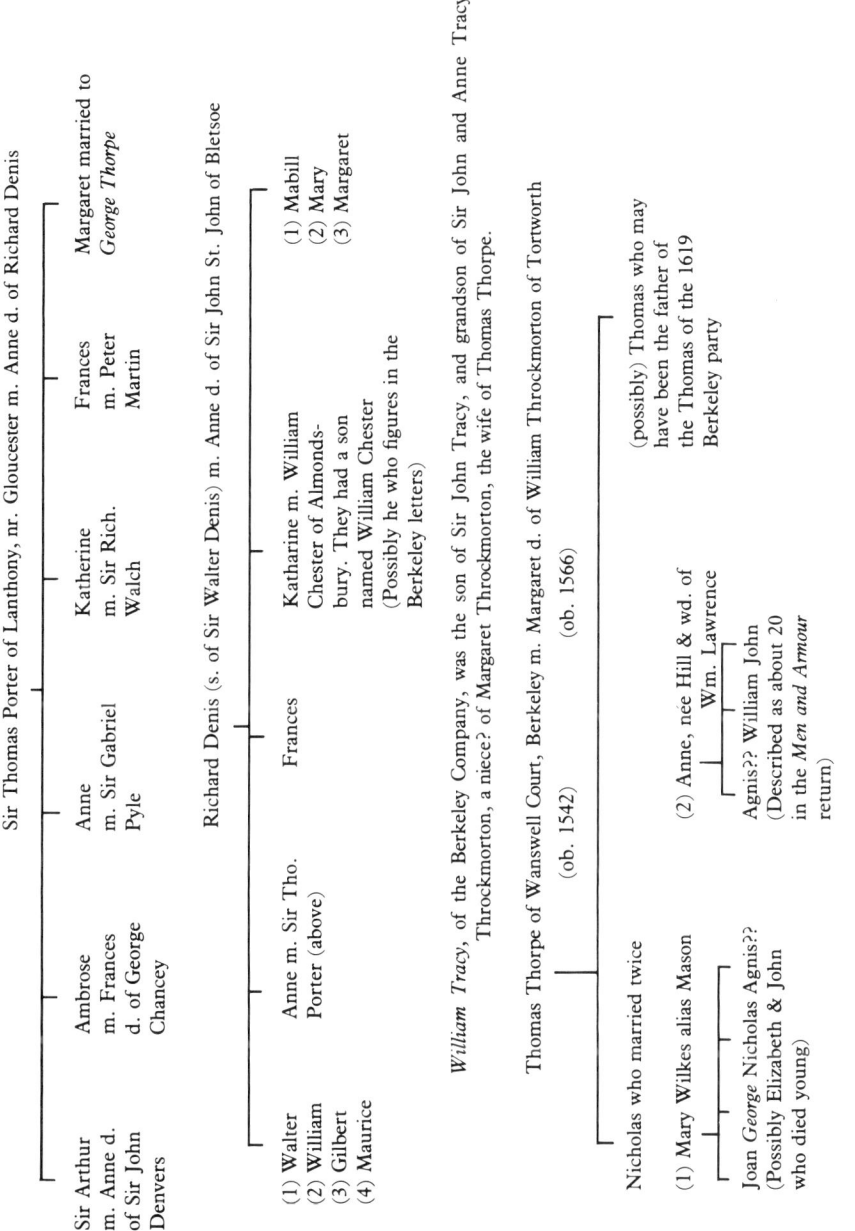

Sir Thomas Porter of Lanthony, nr. Gloucester m. Anne d. of Richard Denis

| Sir Arthur m. Anne d. of Sir John Denvers | Ambrose m. Frances d. of George Chancey | Anne m. Sir Gabriel Pyle | Katherine m. Sir Rich. Walch | Frances m. Peter Martin | Margaret married to *George Thorpe* |

Richard Denis (s. of Sir Walter Denis) m. Anne d. of Sir John St. John of Bletsoe

Anne m. Sir Tho. Porter (above)   Frances   Katharine m. William Chester of Almondsbury. They had a son named William Chester (Possibly he who figures in the Berkeley letters)

(1) Mabill
(2) Mary
(3) Margaret

(1) Walter
(2) William
(3) Gilbert
(4) Maurice

William Tracy, of the Berkeley Company, was the son of Sir John Tracy, and grandson of Sir John and Anne Tracy, nee Throckmorton, a niece? of Margaret Throckmorton, the wife of Thomas Thorpe.

Thomas Thorpe of Wanswell Court, Berkeley m. Margaret d. of William Throckmorton of Tortworth

(ob. 1542)　　　(ob. 1566)

Nicholas who married twice

(1) Mary Wilkes alias Mason

(2) Anne, nee Hill & wd. of Wm. Lawrence

Joan *George* Nicholas Agnis?? (Possibly Elizabeth & John who died young)

Agnis?? William John (Described as about 20 in the *Men and Armour* return)

(possibly) Thomas who may have been the father of the Thomas of the 1619 Berkeley party

The above *George Thorpe* married twice

(1) Margaret Porter d. of Sir Thomas Porter and sis. of Sir Arthur Porter (above) (no issue)
(2) Margaret Harris d. of David Harris of Bristol

| William (below) (1612) | Margaret (1614) | John (1615) Entered Lincoln College, Oxford in March 1637, became a doctor | Richard (1616) | George Born and buried (1620) |

William m. (1612)

(1) Ursula d. of *John Smyth* of N. Nibley (in 1637)

George (born 1640) who entered Trinity College, Oxford, 1660
Anne (born 1645) who died in 1666.
John, born 1642.
Sarah, born 1651.

(2) Bridget Oldisworth of Bradley (Wotton) (married her in 1659)

The Berkeley Company connection within a circle of blood relations is further emphasized when it is noted that:

(1) Tacy, sister of Thomas Porter (above) m. Edward Oldisworth, and their son Arnold sailed with *William Tracy*, and died at Berkeley Plantation.

(2) Bridget, another sister of Thomas Porter, m. Christopher Bainham of Clearwell, an uncle, it is believed, of *Sir William Throckmorton's* first wife.

Italics indicate a partner in the Berkeley Company.

A Brief Bibliography

1. MANUSCRIPT

Smyth of Nibley Papers   New York Public Library
Smyth of Nibley Papers   Gloucester City Library
Ferrar Papers   British Library
Wyatt Papers   Magdalene College Library, Cambridge

Manchester Papers   Public Record Office
Thorpe (I.P.M.)   Public Record Office
Wynne Papers no. 1027   National Library of Wales

Many of the above have been published, in full or part, in Dr. S. Kingsbury's *Records of the Virginia Company of London* (1906-35, vols. I-IV). Abstracts of some are contained in many works, e.g., Alexander Brown, D.E. Neill and Conway Robinson, below.

Thorpe wills   Berkeley Castle muniments room
Berkeley Parish Registers   Berkeley Church
Coaley Parish Registers   County Records Office, Gloucester
North Nibley Parish Registers   County Records Office, Gloucester
(The Bishop's Transcripts for the above are all in the C.R.O.)
St. Martin-in-the-Fields Parish   Westminster Public Library
    Register
St. Pancras, Soper Lane, Parish   Guild Hall Library, London
    Register
MS. E. 327   Kenneth Spencer Research Library
(Transcript made by Dr. Maija J. Cole of Yale Center for Parliamentary History)

The following were seen in America:

Thomas Jefferson Papers – Misc. Bound vols. nos. 17 and 20 – Virginia Company of London Records, 1619-24, and Misc. Records 1606-26. Both on microfilm – reels nos. 64 and 65 in the Library of Congress.

The following Abstracts were examined in the Virginia State Library, Richmond, (All had been abstracted from original papers in the Public Record Office, London)

D.C. DeJarnette	Abstracted from the original papers in the P.R.O. London Documents nos. 5250-5338
A.W. McDonald	Documents nos. 5395-5528
W.N. Sainsbury	Documents I-535, 3047-3786
F.A. Winder	Documents nos. 5109-5161

Court of Chancery Records in the Public Record Office.

2. PRINTED MATERIAL

(i) Primary source material

Bemiss, Samuel M., ed. *The Three Charters of the Virginia Company of London and Seven Related Documents.* Jamestown 350th Anniversary Historical Booklet no. 4 (Williamsburg, 1957). These important booklets here-after cited, Jamestown no. . . .

Beverley, Robert, *The History and Present State of Virginia.* ed. Louise B. Wright, (Reprinted, University of North Carolina Press, 1947).

Brooke, Christopher, 'A Poem on the Late Massacre in Virginia.' (London, 1622), ed. Robert C. Johnson, *VMHB* Vol. 72, pp. 259-292.

Brown Alexander, *The Genesis of the United States.* (Reprinted, New York, 1964).

Brown Alexander, *The First Republic of America.* (Reprinted, New York, 1969).

Force, Peter, ed. *Tracts and other Papers Relating to . . . Colonies in North America . . . to the year 1776.* (Washington D.C., 1836-46). 4 vols.

Hamor, Ralph, *A True Discourse of the Present State of Virginia.* ed. A.L. Rouse, (Richmond, 1957).

Hening, H.H., ed. *Statutes at Large . . . All the Laws of Virginia from . . . 1619.* (Richmond, 1809-13), 13 vols.

Journal of the House of Commons for 1614.

Kingsbury, Susan M., ed. *Records of the Virginia Company of London.* (Washington D.C., 1906-35), 4 vols.

Middle Temple, *Register of Admission to the Honourable Society of the Middle Temple*. (Temple Bar, 1949). (The Registers of the other Inns of Court are also of importance)

McIlwaine, H.R., ed. *Minutes of the Council and General Courts of Colonial Virginia, 1622-1632 and 1670-1676*. (Richmond, 1924).

Pory, John, *Proceedings of the General Assembly of Virginia, July 30 to August 4, 1619*. eds. W.J. Van Schreeven and G.H. Reese, (Jamestown, 1969).

Purchas, Samuel, *Purchas His Pilgrimes*. (Reprinted, Glasgow, 1905-7). 20 vols.

Robinson, Conway, ed. *Abstracts of the Records of the Virginia Company of London, 1619-1624*. edited in 1856 (?) by R.A. Brock. Re-edited by Robinson in 1888, and published by the Virginia Historical Society. Has extensive Introduction.

Smyth, John, *The Lives of the Berkeleys* and *The Hundred of Berkeley*. ed. Sir John Maclean, and published by the *BGAS*, 1883-5, 3 vols.

Smyth, John, *The Names and Surnames of All the Able and Sufficient Men in body fit for his Majesty's Service in the Wars within the County of Gloucester . . 1608*. Editor not stated. Published by Henry Sotheran, London, 1902.

Smyth, John, *Smyth of Nibley Papers*. (Gloucester Collection). Local History Sources No. I. (Gloucester County Library Service, 1978).

Waterhouse, Edward, *A Declaration of the State of the Colony and Affaires in Virginia. With a Relation of the Barbarous Massacre . . . 22 March last*. (London, 1622). Reproduced in full in Kingsbury III.

(ii)   Secondary source material

Bailyn, Bernard, 'Politics and Social Structure in Virginia'. *Seventeenth Century America: Essays in Colonial History*. ed. J.M. Smith, (New York, 1972).

Brock, R.A., *Virginia and Virginians*, vol. I, (Richmond, 1888. Reprinted, Spartenburg, S.C., 1973).

Campbell, Charles, *History of the Colony and Ancient Dominion of Virginia*. (Reprinted, Spartenburg, S.C., 1965).

Cooke, James H., 'Wanswell Court and its Occupants for Seven Centuries.' *BGAS*, vol. 6, pp. 310-23.

Craven Wesley, F., *Southern Colonies in the Seventeenth Century*. (Richmond, 1954).

Craven, Wesley, F., *The Virginia Company of London, 1606-1624*. Jamestown no. 5.

Dabney, Virginius, 'That Mythical First Thanksgiving', *The Saturday Evening Post*, 29th November, 1958.

Dowdey, C.D., *The Great Plantation*. (Charles City, 1957).

Fausz, J. Frederick, *Settlement on the James River Basin*. M.A., Thesis, College of William and Mary, Williamsburg, 1971.

Fausz J. Frederick, *Powhatan Uprising of 1622: A Historical Study of Ethnocentrism and Cultural Conflict*. Ph.D., Dissertation, College of William and Mary, Williamsburg, 1977.

Fausz, J. Frederick, 'George Thorpe, Nemattanew, and the Powhatan Uprising of 1622.' *Virginia Cavalcade*, Winter Issue, 1979, pp. 111-117.

A Hornbrook of Virginia History. Virginia State Library Publication no. 25 (Richmond, 1965).

Jones, H.M., *The Literature of Virginia in the Seventeeth Century*. (Charlottesville, 1968). 2nd ed.

Marshall, John, *Agricultural History of Gloucestershire*. (1796), reprinted, Gloucester, 1979.

Neill, Edward D., *History of the Virginia Company of London, With Letters . . . Never Before Printed*. (Reprinted, New York, 1968).

Neill, Edward, D., *The English Colonization of America during the Seventeenth Century*. (London, 1871).

Rutman, D.B., *A Militant New World, 1607-1640*. Ph.D., Dissertation of the University of Virginia, 1959.

Sams, S., *The Conquest of Virginia, The Third Attempt, 1610-1624*. (New York, 1939).

Smith, J. Morton, *Seventeenth-Century America: Essays in Colonial History*. (A nine essay symposium . . . held by the Institute of Early American History and Culture in 1957). (New York, 1972).

Stith, William, *The History of the First Discovery and Settlement of Virginia*. (1747, reprinted, Spartanburg, S.C., 1965).

Tann, Jennifer, *Gloucestershire Woollen Mills*. (Newton Abbot, 1967).

Thirsk, Joan, 'Projects for Gentlemen, Jobs for the Poor: Mutual Aid in the Vale of Tewkesbury, 1600-1630.' *Essays in Bristol and Gloucestershire History*. Centenary Volume of the *BGAS*, 1976, eds. P. Magrath and J. Cannon, pp. 147-169.

Wasburn, Wilcomb E., 'A Moral History of Indian-White Relations: Needs and Opportunities for Study.', *Ethno-history*, 4, 1957, pp. 47-61.

White, John, *The Planters Plea*. (London, 1620, reprinted, Rockport, Mass. 1930).

Index

1. The index has of necessity been selective.
2. Grouping of subjects has, occasionally, been employed, e.g., Berkeley Company Personnel. However, the families of the five sponsors of the company have been indexed separately and headed by the respective sponsor.
3. The spelling of names in the index will, in most cases, follow the modern form, but in the text, occasionally the contemporary spelling has been retained.
4. The brief genealogical tables (appendix eleven) have not been indexed.